Canadian Short Stories

Canadian Short Stories

Selected by
Robert Weaver

Toronto
Oxford University Press

This selection of Canadian Short Stories
was first published in the World's Classics in 1960.
Reprinted as an Oxford in Canada Paperback in 1966.

12 13 14 15 — 0987

Selection and Introduction
© *Oxford University Press 1960*

ISBN 0-19-540131-x

Printed in Canada by
HIGNELL PRINTING LIMITED

CONTENTS

CONTENTS

CONTENTS

INTRODUCTION

THERE have been so few collections of Canadian short stories that there is no tradition which an editor is required either to follow or to explain away. But perhaps for that reason I should begin this introduction by mentioning some of my prejudices. This book is designed to give a very general impression of the development of the short story in Canada, but I have omitted a number of writers who were represented in earlier anthologies, and I decided that there was not much point in venturing very far back into Canadian writing of the nineteenth century in a search for the short story. I have tried to avoid including fiction for historical or sociological reasons that I do not much admire on literary grounds. Most of the stories were published after 1920 and many of them in the years following the Second World War. I suppose this shows plainly enough that I believe few short stories of much literary consequence were published in Canada before the First World War. Some writers I would have liked to include have been left out because the size of any book must be limited, and there are some good writers of fiction who do not appear here because they are novelists and have not experimented with the short story.

I should also explain why there are three stories in the book in translation. They are being published in translation instead of the original French because the World's Classics is a series of books in English. But there are only three stories, and this of course does not begin to acknowledge the significance in this country of the language and literature of French

Canada. This book is, however, the first comprehensive anthology of Canadian stories to make any attempt to include fiction from both cultures. There have been good reasons for restricting Canadian anthologies to writing in one language, and there is no sense pretending that even today there is a consistent or vital connexion between the literatures of French and English Canada. But in the past few years some short stories from French Canada (and a good deal of poetry) have been published or broadcast in translation, and it seemed worth recognizing this important, if hesitant, meeting of the two cultures by reprinting three of those stories here.

I am writing this introduction just thirty years after Raymond Knister, who appears in this book as a writer of short stories, edited an earlier anthology which was also called *Canadian Short Stories*. For that book Knister wrote a sensitive, moderately optimistic, but often wistful essay on the state of the short story in Canada. He admitted that the novel and the short story had been slow to flourish in this country, but he believed that in the 1920's the situation was at last beginning to change. Knister and his friend Morley Callaghan had published their early stories in the 'little magazines' in Paris and the American mid-West—*The Exile, transition, This Quarter, The Midland*—and that must have seemed a good omen for what was then (and is still to a large extent) a provincial literary society. Knister died a few years later, but Morley Callaghan continued to publish in the best literary magazines abroad, and his stories appeared year after year in annual collections of the best short fiction published in North America. It is because he has been for more than thirty years Canada's most distinguished novelist and short-story writer that Morley Callaghan is the only author represented in this book by two stories.

Knister and Callaghan published abroad in the 1920's because there were almost no outlets in Canada for serious and experimental short fiction. This fugitive existence of the short story has continued until today in this country. Many writers publish two or three or even a half dozen good stories, but only a handful have managed to create any substantial body of work in this field. Some of the younger Canadian writers must still find their first publication abroad. There are no stories in this book that first appeared in the mass-circulation magazines or national weekly newspapers in this country, and in recent years most of those periodicals have abandoned the short story almost entirely. (The one exception is a monthly magazine for women readers, *Chatelaine*, and it is unfortunate that that magazine is not represented in this book.) There are few short-story writers in Canada these days and even fewer markets, and which is cause and which effect it is difficult to say.

Since 1920 the serious Canadian short-story writer has found his most sympathetic medium of publication in a few small literary periodicals—*The Canadian Forum, Preview, First Statement, Northern Review, Here and Now, The Tamarack Review*—and in one university journal, *Queen's Quarterly*. The Canadian Broadcasting Corporation has also been providing the short-story writer with a form of publication through readings broadcast over its radio network, and since I have been a short-story editor with the C.B.C. for ten years I hope that I have not included too many stories from that source in this book.

But there have also been markets abroad. It may be ironical that a Canadian short-story writer, through publication in such American magazines as *Harper's*, *The Atlantic Monthly*, *The New Yorker*, and *Esquire*, will be able to reach a substantial audience in his own country for which there is no comparable Canadian publication. It is an unhealthy situation, and Canada needs a greater variety of magazines—which are unlikely to appear because the Canadian reader has such a wealth of American periodicals easily available to him. But this situation is not quite as unfortunate as it may sometimes appear to be. The years since the Second World War have been a time of vigorous literary internationalism, and the Canadian writer, with no problem of language to overcome, is in an increasingly enviable position to exploit the literary market-places in London and New York (and in Paris, if he writes in French). Those same years since the Second World War have also been a time of cultural nationalism in Canada (much of it centred in our universities), and the Canadian writer who publishes abroad for practical reasons may incidentally do something to diffuse and contain that cultural nationalism. Writers in small countries inevitably search for readers abroad, and the situation of the writer in Canada today is neither unique nor especially discouraging.

I have made no attempt in this book to include stories representative of all the regions of Canada, although regionalism has still an emphatic influence on our literature. But this aspect of our writing is accidentally reflected in this anthology. There is a story from the Maritimes by Thomas Raddall; Ethel Wilson and Malcolm Lowry writing from the West Coast; and stories set in the Prairies by Frederick

Philip Grove, Sinclair Ross, and W. O. Mitchell. There are three stories from French Canada by writers whose language is French; and other stories, like those by Joyce Marshall and Irving Layton, in which the reader will be aware that this is a country with two languages and traditions. The rural areas of Ontario are a source for Stephen Leacock, later for Raymond Knister, and still later for such young writers as James Reaney, Douglas Spettigue, and Alice Munro. Only a few Canadian writers, notably Morley Callaghan, Hugh Garner, and Mordecai Richler, have consistently used urban situations and backgrounds in most of their short fiction. Some readers outside Canada (and possibly some in this country as well) may be struck by the sense of loneliness and melancholy that pervades so many of the stories in this book. This is a quality to be found in much of the more serious fiction published in this country. But we have some humour too. What we do not have is much of that sophistication and intellectual intensity that distinguishes a good deal of the contemporary fiction appearing in the older literary societies abroad. It seems that the Canadian writer still feels able to indulge a certain *naïveté*, and I suspect that some of the virtues and limitations of that outlook are pretty clearly reflected in this book.

ROBERT WEAVER

Toronto, Ontario
November, 1958

The Privilege of the Limits

E. W. THOMSON (1849-1924)

'YES, indeed, my grandfather wass once in jail,' said old Mrs. McTavish, of the county of Glengarry, in Ontario, Canada; 'but that wass for debt, and he wass a ferry honest man whateffer, and he would not broke his promise—no, not for all the money in Canada. If you will listen to me, I will tell chust exactly the true story about that debt, to show you what an honest man my grandfather wass.

'One time Tougal Stewart, him that wass the poy's grandfather that keeps the same store in Cornwall to this day, sold a plough to my grandfather, and my grandfather said he would pay half the plough in October, and the other half whateffer time he felt able to pay the money. Yes, indeed, that was the very promise my grandfather gave.

'So he was at Tougal Stewart's store on the first of October early in the morning before the shutters wass taken off, and he paid half chust exactly to keep his word. Then the crop wass ferry bad next year, and the year after that one of his horses was killed by lightning, and the next year his brother, that wass not rich and had a big family, died, and do you think wass my grandfather to let the family be disgraced without a big funeral? No, indeed. So my grandfather paid for the funeral, and there wass at it plenty of meat and drink for everybody, as wass the right Hielan' custom those days; and after the funeral my grandfather did not feel chust exactly

able to pay the other half for the plough that year
either.

'So, then, Tougal Stewart met my grandfather in
Cornwall next day after the funeral, and asked him
if he had some money to spare.

'"Wass you in need of help, Mr. Stewart?" says my
grandfather, kindly. "For if it's in any want you are,
Tougal," says my grandfather, "I will sell the coat off
my back, if there is no other way to lend you a loan";
for that wass always the way of my grandfather with
all his friends, and a bigger-hearted man there never
wass in all Glengarry, or in Stormont, or in Dundas,
moreofer.

'"In want!" says Tougal—"in want, Mr. McTavish!"
says he, very high. "Would you wish to insult a
gentleman, and him of the name of Stewart, that's
the name of princes of the world?" he said, so he did.

'Seeing Tougal had his temper up, my grandfather
spoke softly, being a quiet, peaceable man, and in
wonder what he had said to offend Tougal.

'"Mr. Stewart," says my grandfather, "it wass not
in my mind to anger you whateffer. Only I thought,
from your asking me if I had some money, that you
might be looking fir a wee bit of a loan, as many a
gentleman has to do at times, and no shame to him
at all," said my grandfather.

'"A loan?" says Tougal, sneering. "A loan, is it?
Where's your memory, Mr. McTavish! Are you not
owing me half the price of the plough you've had
these three years?"

'"And wass you asking me for money for the other
half of the plough?" says my grandfather, very
astonished.

'"Just that," says Tougal.

'"Have you no shame or honour in you?" says my

2

grandfather, firing up. "How could I feel able to pay that now, and me chust yesterday been giving my poor brother a funeral fit for the McTavishes' own grandnephew, that wass as good chentleman's plood as any Stewart in Glengarry. You saw the expense I wass at, for there you wass, and I thank you for the politeness of coming, Mr. Stewart," says my grandfather, ending mild, for the anger would never stay in him more than a minute, so kind was the nature he had.

'"If you can spend money on a funeral like that, you can pay me for my plough," says Stewart; for with buying and selling he wass become a poor creature, and the heart of a Hielan' man wass half gone out of him, for all he wass so proud of his name of monarchs and kings.

'My grandfather had a mind to strike him down on the spot, so he often said; but he thought of the time when he hit Hamish Cochrane in anger, and he minded the penances the priest put on him for breaking the silly man's jaw with that blow, so he smothered the heat that wass in him, and turned away in scorn. With that Tougal went to court, and sued my grandfather, puir mean creature.

'You might think that Judge Jones—him that wass judge in Cornwall before Judge Jarvis that's dead—would do justice. But no, he made it the law that my grandfather must pay at once, though Tougal Stewart could not deny what the bargain wass.

'"Your Honour," says my grandfather, "I said I'd pay when I felt able. And do I feel able now? No, I do not," says he. "It's a disgrace to Tougal Stewart to ask me, and himself telling you what the bargain wass,' said my grandfather. But Judge Jones said that he must pay, for all that he did not feel able.

3

'"I will nefer pay one copper till I feel able," says my grandfather; "but I'll keep my Hielan' promise to my dying day, as I always done," says he.

'And with that the old judge laughed, and said he would have to give judgement. And so he did; and after that Tougal Stewart got out an execution. But not the worth of a handful of oatmeal could the bailiff lay hands on, because my grandfather had chust exactly taken the precaution to give a bill of sale on his gear to his neighbour, Alexander Frazer, that could be trusted to do what was right after the law play was over.

'The whole settlement had great contempt for Tougal Stewart's conduct; but he wass a headstrong body, and once he begun to do wrong against my grandfather, he held on, for all that his trade fell away; and finally he had my grandfather arrested for debt, though you'll understand, sir, that he was owing Stewart nothing that he ought to pay when he didn't feel able.

'In those times prisoners for debt wass taken to jail in Cornwall, and if they had friends to give bail that they would not go beyond the posts that wass around the sixteen acres nearest the jail walls, the prisoners could go where they liked on that ground. This was called "the privilege of the limits". The limits, you'll understand, was marked by cedar posts painted white about the size of hitching-posts.

'The whole settlement wass ready to go bail for my grandfather if he wanted it, and for the health of him he needed to be in the open air, and so he gave Tuncan Macdonnell of the Greenfields, and Aeneas Macdonald of the Sandfields, for his bail, and he promised, on his Hielan' word of honour, not to go beyond the posts. With that he went where he pleased, only taking care that he never put even the toe of his foot beyond a post, for all that some prisoners of the limits would chump ofer them and back again, or maybe swing round them, holding by their hands.

'Efery day the neighbours would go into Cornwall to give my grandfather the good word, and they would offer to pay Tougal Stewart for the other half of the plough, only that vexed my grandfather, for he wass too proud to borrow, and, of course, every day he felt less and less able to pay on account of him having to hire a man to be doing the spring ploughing and seeding and making the kale-yard.

'All this time, you'll mind, Tougal Stewart had to pay five shillings a week for my grandfather's keep, the law being so that if the debtor swore he had not five pounds' worth of property to his name, then the creditor had to pay the five shillings, and, of course, my grandfather had nothing to his name after he gave the bill of sale to Alexander Frazer. A great diversion it was to my grandfather to be reckoning up that if he lived as long as his father, that wass hale and strong at ninety-six, Tougal would need to pay five or six hundred pounds for him, and there was only two pounds ten shillings to be paid on the plough.

'So it was like that all summer, my grandfather keeping heartsome, with the neighbours coming in so steady to bring him the news of the settlement. There he would sit, just inside one of the posts, for to pass his jokes, and tell what he wished the family to be doing next. This way it might have kept going on for forty years, only it came about that my grand-father's youngest child—him that was my father— fell sick, and seemed like to die.

'Well, when my grandfather heard that bad news, he wass in a terrible way, to be sure, for he would be longing to hold the child in his arms, so that his heart was sore and like to break. Eat he could not, sleep he could not: all night he would be groaning, and all day he would be walking around by the posts, wishing that he had not passed his Hielan' word of honour not to go beyond a post; for he thought how he could have broken out like a chentleman, and gone to see his sick child, if he had stayed inside the jail wall. So it went on three days and three nights pefore the wise thought came into my grandfather's head to show him how he need not go beyond the posts to see his little sick boy. With that he went straight to one of the white cedar posts, and pulled it up out of the hole, and started for home, taking great care to carry it in his hands pefore him, so he would not be beyond it one bit.

'My grandfather wass not half a mile out of Cornwall, which was only a little place in those days, when two of the turnkeys came after him.

'"Stop, Mr. McTavish," says the turnkeys.

'"What for would I stop?" says my grandfather.

'"You have broke your bail," says they.

'"It's a lie for you," says my grandfather, for his temper flared up for anybody to say he would broke his bail. "Am I beyond the post?" says my grandfather.

'With that they run in on him, only that he knocked the two of them over with the post, and went on rejoicing, like an honest man should, at keeping his word and overcoming them that would slander his good name. The only thing besides thoughts of the child that troubled him was questioning whether he had been strictly right in turning round for to use the post to defend himself in such a way that it was nearer the jail than he wass. But he remembered how the jailer never complained of prisoners of the limits chumping ofer the posts, if so they chumped back again in a moment, the trouble went out of his mind.

'Pretty soon after that he met Tuncan Macdonnell of Greenfields, coming into Cornwall with the wagon.

'"And how is this Glengatchie?" says Tuncan. "For you were never the man to broke your bail."

'Glengatchie, you'll understand, sir, is the name of my grandfather's farm.

'"Never fear, Greenfields," says my grandfather, "for I'm not beyond the post."

'So Greenfields looked at the post, and he looked at my grandfather, and he scratched his head a wee, and he seen it was so; and then he fell into a great admiration entirely.

'"Get in with me, Glengatchie—it's proud I'll be to carry you home"; and he turned the team around. My grandfather did so, taking great care to keep the post in front of him all the time; and that way he reached home. Out comes my grandmother running to embrace him; but she had to throw her arms around the post and my grandfather's neck at the same time, he was that strict to be within his promise. Pefore going ben the house, he went to the back end of the kale-yard which was farthest from the jail, and there he stuck the post; and then he went back to see his sick child, while all the neighbours that came round was glad to see what a wise thought the saints had put into his mind to save his bail and his promise.

'So there he stayed a week till my father got well. Of course the constables came after my grandfather,

7

but the settlement would not let the creatures come within a mile of Glengatchie. You might think, sir, that my grandfather would have stayed with his wife and weans, seeing the post was all the time in the kale-yard, and him careful not to go beyond it; but he was putting the settlement to a great deal of trouble day and night to keep the constables off, and he was fearful that they might take the post away, if ever they got to Glengatchie, and give him the name of false, which no McTavish ever had. So Tuncan Greenfields and Aeneas Sandfield drove my grandfather back to the jail, him with the post behind him in the wagon, so as he would be between it and the jail. Of course Tougal Stewart tried his best to have the bail declared forfeited; but old Judge Jones only laughed, and said my grandfather was a Hielan' gentleman, with a very nice sense of honour, and that was chust exactly the truth.

'How did my grandfather get free in the end? Oh, then, that was because of Tougal Stewart being careless—him that thought he knew so much of the law. The law was, you will mind, that Tougal had to pay five shillings a week for keeping my grandfather in the limits. The money was to be paid efery Monday, and it was to be paid in lawful money of Canada, too. Well, would you belief that Tougal paid in four shillings in silver one Monday, and one shilling in coppers, for he took up the collection in church the day pefore, and it wass not till Tougal had gone away that the jailer saw that one of the coppers was a Brock copper—a medal, you will understand, made at General Brock's death, and not lawful money of Canada at all. With that the jailer came out to my grandfather.

'"Mr. McTavish," says he, taking off his hat, "you

8

are a free man, and I'm glad of it." Then he told him what Tougal had done.

'"I hope you will not have any hard feelings toward me, Mr. McTavish," said the jailer; and a decent man he wass, for all that there wass not a drop of Hielan' blood in him. "I hope you will not think hard of me for not being hospitable to you, sir," he says; "but it's against the rules and regulations for the jailer to be offering the best he can command to the prisoners. Now that you are free, Mr. McTavish," says the jailer, "I would be a proud man if Mr. McTavish of Glengatchie would do me the honour of taking supper with me this night. I will be asking your leave to invite some of the gentlemen of the place, if you will say the word, Mr. McTavish," says he.

'Well, my grandfather could never bear malice, the kind man he wass, and he seen how bad the jailer felt, so he consented, and a great company came in, to be sure, to celebrate the occasion.

'Did my grandfather pay the balance on the plough? What for should you suspicion, sir, that my grandfather would refuse his honest debt? Of course he paid for the plough, for the crop was good that fall.

'"I would be paying you the other half of the plough now, Mr. Stewart," says my grandfather, comin' in when the store was full.

'"Hoich, but you are the honest McTavish," says Tougal, sneering.

'But my grandfather made no answer to the creature, for he thought it would be unkind to mention how Tougal had paid out six pounds four shillings and eleven pence to keep him in on account of a debt of two pound five that never was due till it was paid.'

Strayed

SIR CHARLES G. D. ROBERTS (1860–1943)

IN the Cabineau Camp, of unlucky reputation, there was a young ox of splendid build, but of a wild and restless nature.

He was one of a yoke, of part Devon blood, large, dark red, all muscle and nerve, and with wide magnificent horns. His yoke-fellow was a docile steady worker, the pride of his owner's heart; but he himself seemed never to have been more than half broken in. The woods appeared to draw him by some spell. He wanted to get back to the pastures where he had roamed untrammelled of old with his fellowsteers. The remembrance was in his heart of the dewy mornings when the herd used to feed together on the sweet grassy hillocks, and of the cloversmelling heats of June when they would gather hockdeep in the pools under the green willow-shadows. He hated the yoke, he hated the winter; and he imagined that in the wild pastures he remembered it would be forever summer. If only he could get back to those pastures!

One day there came the longed-for opportunity; and he seized it. He was standing unyoked beside his mate, and none of the teamsters were near. His head went up in the air, and with a snort of triumph he dashed away through the forest.

For a little while there was a vain pursuit. At last the lumbermen gave it up. 'Let him be!' said his owner, 'an' I rayther guess he'll turn up agin when he gits peckish. He kaint browse on spruce buds an' lung-wort.'

Plunging on with long gallop through the snow he was soon miles from camp. Growing weary he slackened his pace. He came down to a walk. As the lonely red of the winter sunset began to stream through the openings of the forest, flushing the snows of the tiny glades and swales, he grew hungry, and began to swallow unsatisfying mouthfuls of the long moss which roughened the tree-trunks. Ere the moon got up he had filled himself with this fodder, and then he lay down in a little thicket for the night.

But some miles back from his retreat a bear had chanced upon his footprints. A strayed steer! That would be an easy prey. The bear started straightway in pursuit. The moon was high in heaven when the crouched ox heard his pursuer's approach. He had no idea what was coming, but he rose to his feet and waited.

The bear plunged boldly into the thicket, never dreaming of resistance. With a muffled roar the ox charged upon him and bore him to the ground. Then he wheeled, and charged again, and the astonished bear was beaten at once. Gored by those keen horns he had no stomach for further encounter, and would fain have made his escape; but as he retreated the ox charged him again, dashing him against a huge trunk. The bear dragged himself up with difficulty, beyond his opponent's reach; and the ox turned scornfully back to his lair.

At the first yellow of dawn the restless creature was again upon the march. He pulled more mosses by the way, but he disliked them the more intensely now because he thought he must be nearing his ancient pastures with their tender grass and their streams. The snow was deeper about him, and his hatred of the winter grew apace. He came out upon a hill-side, partly open, whence the pine had years before been stripped, and where now grew young birches thick together. Here he browsed on the aromatic twigs, but for him it was harsh fare.

As his hunger increased he thought a little longingly of the camp he had deserted, but he dreamed not of turning back. He would keep on till he reached his pastures, and the glad herd of his comrades licking salt out of the trough beside the accustomed pool. He had some blind instinct as to his direction, and kept his course to the south very strictly, the desire in his heart continually leading him aright.

That afternoon he was attacked by a panther, which dropped out of a tree and tore his throat. He dashed under a low branch and scraped his assailant off, then, wheeling about savagely, put the brute to flight with his first mad charge. The panther sprang back into his tree, and the ox continued his quest.

Soon his steps grew weaker, for the panther's cruel claws had gone deep into his neck, and his path was marked with blood. Yet the dream in his great wild eyes was not dimmed as his strength ebbed away. His weakness he never noticed or heeded. The desire that was urging him absorbed all other thoughts— even, almost, his sense of hunger. This, however, it was easy for him to assuage, after a fashion, for the long, grey, unnourishing mosses were abundant.

By and by his path led him into the bed of a stream, whose waters could be heard faintly tinkling on thin pebbles beneath their coverlet of ice and snow. His slow steps conducted him far along this open course. Soon after he had disappeared, around a curve in the distance there came the panther, following stealthily upon his crimsoned trail. The crafty beast was waiting until the bleeding and the hunger should do its work, and the object of its inexorable pursuit should have no more heart left for resistance.

This was late in the afternoon. The ox was now possessed with his desire, and would not lie down for any rest. All night long, through the gleaming silver of the open spaces, through the weird and checkered gloom of the deep forest, heedless even of his hunger, or perhaps driven the more by it as he thought of the wild clover bunches and tender timothy awaiting him, the solitary ox strove on. And all night, lagging far behind in his unabating caution, the panther followed him.

At sunrise the worn and stumbling animal came out upon the borders of the great lake, stretching its leagues of unshadowed snow away to the south before him. There was his path, and without hesitation he followed it. The wide and frost-bound water here and there had been swept clear of its snows by the wind, but for the most part its covering lay unruffled; and the pale dove-colours, and saffrons, and rose-lilacs of the dawn were sweetly reflected on its surface.

The doomed ox was now journeying very slowly, and with the greatest labour. He staggered at every step, and his beautiful head drooped almost to the snow. When he had got a great way out upon the lake, at the forest's edge appeared the pursuing panther, emerging cautiously from the coverts. The round tawny face and malignant green eyes were raised to peer out across the expanse. The labouring progress of the ox was promptly marked. Dropping its nose again to the ensanguined snow, the beast resumed his pursuit, first at a slow trot, and then at a long, elastic gallop. By this time the ox's quest was nearly done. He plunged forward upon his knees, rose again with difficulty, stood still, and looked around him. His eyes were clouding over, but he saw, dimly, the tawny brute that was now hard upon his steps. Back came a flash of the old courage, and he turned, horns lowered, to face the attack. With the last of his strength he charged, and the panther paused irresolutely; but the wanderer's knees gave way beneath his own impetus, and his horns ploughed the snow. With a deep bellowing groan he rolled over on his side, and the longing, and the dream of the pleasant pastures, faded from his eyes. With a great spring the panther was upon him, and the eager teeth were at his throat—but he knew nought of it. No wild beast, but his own desire, had conquered him.

When the panther had slaked his thirst for blood, he raised his head, and stood with his fore-paws resting on the dead ox's side, and gazed all about him.

To one watching from the lake shore, had there been anyone to watch in that solitude, the wild beast and his prey would have seemed but a speck of black on the gleaming waste. At the same hour, league upon league back in the depth of the ancient forest, a lonely ox was lowing in his stanchions, restless, refusing to eat, grieving for the absence of his yoke-fellow.

Paul Farlotte

DUNCAN CAMPBELL SCOTT (1862–1947)

NEAR the outskirts of Viger, to the west, far away
from the Blanche, but having a country outlook of
their own, and a glimpse of a shadowy range of hills,
stood two houses which would have attracted attention by their contrast, if for no other reason. One
was a low cottage, surrounded by a garden, and
covered with roses, which formed jalousies for the
encircling veranda. The garden was laid out with the
care and completeness that told of a master hand.
The cottage itself had the air of having been secured
from the inroads of time as thoroughly as paint and
a nail in the right place at the right time could effect
that end. The other was a large gaunt-looking house,
narrow and high, with many windows, some of which
were boarded up, as if there was no further use for
the chambers into which they had once admitted
light. Standing on a rough piece of ground it seemed
given over to the rudeness of decay. It appeared to
have been the intention of its builder to veneer it
with brick; but it stood there a wooden shell, dis-
coloured by the weather, disjointed by the frost, and
with the wind fluttering the rags of tar-paper which
had been intended as a protection against the cold,
but which now hung in patches and ribbons. But
despite this dilapidation it had a sort of martial air
about it, and seemed to watch over its embowered
companion, warding off tempests and gradually
falling to pieces on guard, like a faithful soldier who

suffers at his post. In the road, just between the two, stood a beautiful Lombardy poplar. Its shadow fell upon the little cottage in the morning, and travelled across the garden, and in the evening touched the corner of the tall house, and faded out with the sun, only to float there again in the moonlight, or to commence the journey next morning with the dawn. This shadow seemed, with its constant movement, to figure the connexion that existed between the two houses.

The garden of the cottage was a marvel; there the finest roses in the parish grew, roses which people came miles to see, and parterres of old-fashioned flowers, the seed of which came from France, and which in consequence seemed to blow with a rarer colour and more delicate perfume. This garden was a striking contrast to the stony ground about the neighbouring house, where only the commonest weeds grew unregarded; but its master had been born a gardener, just as another man is born a musician or a poet. There was a superstition in the village that all he had to do was to put anything, even a dry stick, into the ground, and it would grow. He was the village schoolmaster, and Madame Laroque would remark spitefully enough that if Monsieur Paul Farlotte had been as successful in planting knowledge in the heads of his scholars as he was in planting roses in his garden Viger would have been celebrated the world over. But he was born a gardener, not a teacher; and he made the best of the fate which compelled him to depend for his living on something he disliked. He looked almost as dry as one of his own hyacinth bulbs; but like it he had life at his heart. He was a very small man, and frail, and looked older than he was. It was strange, but you rarely seemed to see his face; for he was bent with weeding and digging, and it seemed an effort for him to raise his head and look at you with the full glance of his eye. But when he did, you saw the eye was honest and full of light. He was not careful of his personal appearance, clinging to his old garments with a fondness which often laid him open to ridicule, which he was willing to bear for the sake of the comfort of an old pair of shoes, or a hat which had accommodated itself to the irregularities of his head. On the street he wore a curious skirt-coat that semed to be made of some indestructible material, for he had worn it for years, and might be buried in it. It received an extra brush for Sundays and holidays, and always looked as good as new. He made a quaint picture, as he came down the road from the school. He had a hesitating walk, and constantly stopped and looked behind him; for he always fancied he heard a voice calling him by his name. He would be working in his flower-beds when he would hear it over his shoulder, 'Paul'; or when he went to draw water from his well, 'Paul'; or when he was reading by his fire, someone calling him softly, 'Paul, Paul'; or in the dead of night, when nothing moved in his cottage he would hear it out of the dark, 'Paul'. So it came to be a sort of companionship for him, this haunting voice; and sometimes one could have seen him in his garden stretch out his hand and smile, as if he were welcoming an invisible guest. Sometimes the guest was not invisible, but took body and shape, and was a real presence; and often Paul was greeted with visions of things that had been, or that would be, and saw figures where, for other eyes, hung only the impalpable air.

He had one other passion besides his garden, and

that was Montaigne. He delved in one in the summer, in the other in the winter. With his feet on his stove he would become so absorbed with his author that he would burn his slippers and come to himself disturbed by the smell of the singed leather. He had only one great ambition, that was to return to France to see his mother before she died; and he had for years been trying to save enough money to take the journey. People who did not know him called him stingy, and said the saving for his journey was only a pretext to cover his miserly habits. It was strange, he had been saving for years, and yet he had not saved enough. Whenever anyone would ask him, 'Well, Monsieur Farlotte, when do you go to France?' he would answer, 'Next year—next year.' So when he announced one spring that he was actually going, and when people saw that he was not making his garden with his accustomed care, it became the talk of the village: 'Monsieur Farlotte is going to France'; 'Monsieur Farlotte has saved enough money, true, true, he is going to France.'

His proposed visit gave no one so much pleasure as it gave his neighbours in the gaunt, unkempt house which seemed to watch over his own; and no one would have imagined what a joy it was to Marie St. Denis, the tall girl who was mother to her orphan brothers and sisters, to hear Monsieur Farlotte say, 'When I am in France'; for she knew what none of the villagers knew, that, if it had not been for her and her troubles, Monsieur Farlotte would have seen France many years before. How often she would recall the time when her father, who was in the employ of the great match factory near Viger, used to drive about collecting the little paper matchboxes which were made by hundreds of women in the village and the country around; how he had conceived the idea of making a machine in which a strip of paper would go in at one end, and the completed match-boxes would fall out at the other; how he had given up his situation and devoted his whole time and energy to the invention of this machine; how he had failed time and again, but continued with a perseverance which at last became a frantic passion; and how, to keep the family together, her mother, herself, and the children joined that army of workers which was making the match-boxes by hand. She would think of what would have happened to them then if Monsieur Farlotte had not been there with his help, or what would have happened when her mother died, worn out, and her father, overcome with disappointment, gave up his life and his task together, in despair. But whenever she would try to speak of these things Monsieur Farlotte would prevent her with a gesture, 'Well, but what would you have me do—besides, I will go some day—now who knows, next year, perhaps.' So here was the 'next year', which she had so longed to see, and Monsieur Farlotte was giving her a daily lecture on how to treat the tulips after they had done flowering, preluding everything he had to say with, 'When I am in France', for his heart was already there.

He had two places to visit, one was his old home, the other was the birthplace of his beloved Montaigne. He had often described to Marie the little cottage where he was born, with the vine arbours and the long garden walks, the lilac-bushes, with their cool dark-green leaves, the white eaves where the swallows nested, and the poplar, sentinel over all. 'You see,' he would say, 'I have tried to make this little place like it; and my memory may have played me a trick, but I often fancy myself at home. That poplar and this long walk and the vines on the arbour—sometimes when I see the tulips by the border I fancy it is all in France.'

Marie was going over his scant wardrobe, mending with her skilful fingers, putting a stitch in the trusty old coat, and securing its buttons. She was anxious that Monsieur Farlotte should get a new suit before he went on his journey; but he would not hear of it. 'Not a bit of it,' he would say, 'if I made my appearance in a new suit, they would think I had been making money; and when they would find out that I had not enough to buy cabbage for the soup there would be a disappointment.' She could not get him to write that he was coming. 'No, no,' he would say, 'if I do that they will expect me.' 'Well, and why not—why not?' 'Well, they would think about it—in ten days Paul comes home, then in five days Paul comes home, and then when I came they would set the dogs on me. No, I will just walk in—so—and when they are staring at my old coat I will just sit down in a corner, and my old mother will commence to cry. Oh, I have it all arranged.'

So Marie let him have his own way; but she was fixed on having her way in some things. To save Monsieur Farlotte the heavier work, and allow him to keep his strength for the journey, she would make her brother Guy do the spading in the garden, much to his disgust, and that of Monsieur Farlotte, who would stand by and interfere, taking the spade into his own hands with infinite satisfaction. 'See,' he would say, 'go deeper and turn it over so.' And when Guy would dig in his own clumsy way, he would go off in despair, with the words, 'God help us, nothing will grow there.'

When Monsieur Farlotte insisted on taking his clothes in an old box covered with raw-hide, with his initials in brass tacks on the cover, Marie would not consent to it, and made Guy carry off the box without his knowledge and hide it. She had a good tin trunk which had belonged to her mother, which she knew where to find in the attic, and which would contain everything Monsieur Farlotte had to carry. Poor Marie never went into this attic without a shudder, for occupying most of the space was her father's work bench, and that complicated wheel, the model of his invention, which he had tried so hard to perfect, and which stood there like a monument of his failure. She had made Guy promise never to move it, fearing lest he might be tempted to finish what his father had begun—a fear that was almost an apprehension, so like him was he growing. He was tall and large-boned, with a dark restless eye, set under an overhanging forehead. He had long arms, out of proportion to his height, and he hung his head when he walked. His likeness to his father made him seem a man before his time. He felt himself a man; for he had a good position in the match factory, and was like a father to his little brothers and sisters.

Although the model had always had a strange fascination for him, the lad had kept his promise to his sister, and had never touched the mechanism which had literally taken his father's life. Often when he went into the attic he would stand and gaze at the model and wonder why it had not succeeded, and recall his father bending over his work, with his compass and pencil. But he had a dread of it, too, and sometimes would hurry away, afraid lest its fascination would conquer him.

Monsieur Farlotte was to leave as soon as his school closed, but weeks before that he had everything ready, and could enjoy his roses in peace. After school hours he would walk in his garden, to and fro, to and fro, with his hands behind his back, and his eyes upon the ground, meditating; and once in a while he would pause and smile, or look over his shoulder when the haunting voice would call his name. His scholars had commenced to view him with additional interest, now that he was going to take such a prodigious journey; and two or three of them could always be seen peering through the palings, watching him as he walked up and down the path; and Marie would watch him, too, and wonder what he would say when he found that his trunk had disappeared. He missed it fully a month before he could expect to start; but he had resolved to pack that very evening.

'But there is plenty of time,' remonstrated Marie.

'That's always the way,' he answered. 'Would you expect me to leave everything until the last moment?'

'But, Monsieur Farlotte, in ten minutes everything goes into the trunk.'

'So, and in the same ten minutes something is left out of the trunk, and I am in France, and my shoes are in Viger, that will be the end of it.'

So, to pacify him, she had to ask Guy to bring down the trunk from the attic. It was not yet dark there; the sunset threw a great colour into the room, touching all the familiar objects with transfiguring light, and giving the shadows a rich depth. Guy saw the model glowing like some magic golden wheel, the metal points upon it gleaming like jewels in the light. As he passed he touched it, and with a musical click something dropped from it. He picked it up:

it was one of the little paper match-boxes, but the defect that he remembered to have heard talked of was there. He held it in his hand and examined it; then he pulled it apart and spread it out. 'Ah,' he said to himself, 'the fault was in the cutting.' Then he turned the wheel, and one by one the imperfect boxes dropped out, until the strip of paper was exhausted. 'But why,'—the question rose in his mind —'why could not that little difficulty be overcome?'

He took the trunk down to Marie, who at last persuaded Monsieur Farlotte to let her pack his clothes in it. He did so with a protestation, 'Well, I know how it will be with a fine box like that, some fellow will whip it off when I am looking the other way, and that will be the end of it.'

As soon as he could do so without attracting Marie's attention Guy returned to the attic with a lamp. When Marie had finished packing Monsieur Farlotte's wardrobe, she went home to put her children to bed; but when she saw that light in the attic window she nearly fainted from apprehension. When she pushed open the door of that room which she had entered so often with the scant meals she used to bring her father, she saw Guy bending over the model, examining every part of it. 'Guy,' she said, trying to command her voice, 'you have broken your promise.' He looked up quickly. 'Marie, I am going to find it out—I can understand it—there is just one thing, if I can get that we will make a fortune out of it.'

'Guy, don't delude yourself; those were father's words, and day after day I brought him his meals here, when he was too busy even to come downstairs; but nothing came of it, and while he was trying to make a machine for the boxes, we were making them with our fingers. O Guy,' she cried, with her voice rising into a sob, 'remember those days, remember what Monsieur Farlotte did for us, and what he would have to do again if you lost your place!'

'That's all nonsense, Marie. Two weeks will do it, and after that I could send Monsieur Farlotte home with a pocket full of gold.'

'Guy, you are making a terrible mistake. That wheel was our curse, and it will follow us if you don't leave it alone. And think of Monsieur Farlotte; if he finds out what you are working at he will not go to France—I know him; he will believe it his duty to stay here and help us, as he did when father was alive. Guy, Guy, listen to me!'

But Guy was bending over the model, absorbed in its labyrinths. In vain did Marie argue with him, try to persuade him, and threaten him; she attempted to lock the attic door and keep him out, but he twisted the lock off, and after that the door was always open. Then she resolved to break the wheel into a thousand pieces; but when she went upstairs, when Guy was away, she could not strike it with the axe she held. It seemed like a human thing that cried out with a hundred tongues against the murder she would do; and she could only sink down sobbing, and pray. Then failing everything else she simulated an interest in the thing, and tried to lead Guy to work at it moderately, and not to give up his whole time to it.

But he seemed to take up his father's passion where he had laid it down. Marie could do nothing with him; and the younger children, at first hanging around the attic door, as if he were their father come back again, gradually ventured into the room, and whispered together as they watched their rapt and unobservant brother working at his task. Marie's one thought was to devise a means of keeping the fact from Monsieur Farlotte; and she told him blankly that Guy had been sent away on business, and would not be back for six weeks. She hoped that by that time Monsieur Farlotte would be safely started on his journey. But night after night he saw a light in the attic window. In the past years it had been constant there, and he could only connect it with one cause. But he could get no answer from Marie when he asked her the reason; and the next night the distracted girl draped the window so that no ray of light could find its way out into the night. But Monsieur Farlotte was not satisfied; and a few evenings afterwards, as it was growing dusk, he went quietly into the house, and upstairs into the attic. There he saw Guy stretched along the work bench, his head in his hands, using the last light to ponder over a sketch he was making, and beside him, figured very clearly in the thick gold air of the sunset, the form of his father, bending over him, with the old eager, haggard look in his eyes. Monsieur Farlotte watched the two figures for a moment as they glowed in their rich atmosphere; then the apparition turned his head slowly, and warned him away with a motion of his hand.

All night long Monsieur Farlotte walked in his garden, patient and undisturbed, fixing his duty so that nothing could root it out. He found the comfort that comes to those who give up some exceeding deep desire of the heart, and when next morning the market-gardener from St. Valérie, driving by as the matin bell was clanging from St. Joseph's, and seeing the old teacher as if he were taking an early look at his growing roses, asked him, 'Well, Monsieur Farlotte, when do you go to France?' he was able to answer cheerfully, 'Next year—next year.'

Marie could not unfix his determination. 'No,' he said, 'they do not expect me. No one will be disappointed. I am too old to travel. I might be lost in the sea. Until Guy makes his invention we must not be apart.'

At first the villagers thought that he was only joking, and that they would some morning wake up and find him gone; but when the holidays came, and when enough time had elapsed for him to make his journey twice over they began to think he was in earnest. When they knew that Guy St. Denis was chained to his father's invention, and when they saw that Marie and the children hàd commenced to make match-boxes again, they shook their heads. Some of them at least seemed to understand why Monsieur Farlotte had not gone to France.

But he never repined. He took up his garden again, was as contented as ever, and comforted himself with the wisdom of Montaigne. The people dropped the old question, 'When are you going to France?' Only his companion voice called him more loudly, and more often he saw figures in the air that no one else could see.

Early one morning, as he was working in his garden around a growing pear-tree, he fell into a sort of stupor, and sinking down quietly on his knees he leaned against the slender stem for support. He saw a garden much like his own, flooded with the clear sunlight, in the shade of an arbour an old woman in a white cap was leaning back in a wheeled chair, her eyes were closed, she seemed asleep. A young woman was seated beside her holding her hand. Suddenly the old woman smiled, a childish smile, as if she were well pleased. 'Paul,' she murmured, 'Paul, Paul.' A moment later her companion started up with a cry; but she did not move, she was silent and tranquil. Then the young woman fell on her knees and wept, hiding her face. But the aged face was inexpressibly calm in the shadow, with the smile lingering upon it, fixed by the deeper sleep into which she had fallen.

Gradually the vision faded away, and Paul Farlotte found himself leaning against his pear-tree, which was almost too young as yet to support his weight. The bell was ringing from St. Joseph's, and had shaken the swallows from their nests in the steeple into the clear air. He heard their cries as they flew into his garden, and he heard the voices of his neighbour children as they played around the house.

Later in the day he told Marie that his mother had died that morning, and she wondered how he knew.

The Marine Excursion of the Knights of Pythias

STEPHEN LEACOCK (1869–1944)

HALF-PAST six on a July morning! The *Mariposa Belle* is at the wharf, decked in flags, with steam up ready to start.

Excursion day!

Half-past six on a July morning, and Lake Wissanotti lying in the sun as calm as glass. The opal colours of the morning light are shot from the surface of the water.

Out on the lake the last thin threads of the mist are clearing away like flecks of cotton wool.

The long call of the loon echoes over the lake. The air is cool and fresh. There is in it all the new life of the land of the silent pine and the moving waters. Lake Wissanotti in the morning sunlight! Don't talk to me of the Italian lakes, or the Tyrol or the Swiss Alps. Take them away. Move them somewhere else. I don't want them.

Excursion Day, at half-past six of a summer morning! With the boat all decked in flags and all the people in Mariposa on the wharf, and the band in peaked caps with big cornets tied to their bodies ready to play at any minute! I say! Don't tell me about the Carnival of Venice and the Delhi Durbar. Don't! I wouldn't look at them. I'd shut my eyes! For light and colour give me every time an excursion out of Mariposa down the lake to the Indian's Island out of sight in the morning mist. Talk of your Papal Zouaves and your Buckingham Palace Guard! I want to see the Mariposa band in uniform and the Mariposa Knights of Pythias with their aprons and their insignia and their picnic baskets and their five-cent cigars!

Half-past six in the morning, and all the crowd on the wharf and the boat due to leave in half an hour. Notice it!—in half an hour. Already she's whistled twice (at six, and at six fifteen), and at any minute now, Christie Johnson will step into the pilot house and pull the string for the warning whistle that the boat will leave in half an hour. So keep ready. Don't think of running back to Smith's Hotel for the sandwiches. Don't be fool enough to try to go up to the Greek Store, next to Netley's, and buy fruit. You'll be left behind for sure if you do. Never mind the sandwiches and the fruit! Anyway, here comes Mr. Smith himself with a huge basket of provender that would feed a factory. There must be sandwiches in that. I think I can hear them clinking. And behind Mr. Smith is the German waiter from the caff with another basket—indubitably lager beer; and behind him, the bartender of the hotel, carrying nothing, as far as one can see. But of course if you know Mariposa you will understand that why he looks so nonchalant and empty-handed is because he has two bottles of rye whisky under his linen duster. You know, I think, the peculiar walk of a man with two bottles of whisky in the inside pockets of a linen coat. In Mariposa, you see, to bring beer to an excursion is quite in keeping with public opinion. But, whisky—well, one has to be a little careful.

Do I say that Mr. Smith is here? Why, everybody's here. There's Hussell the editor of the *Newspacket*, wearing a blue ribbon on his coat, for the Mariposa Knights of Pythias are, by their constitution, dedicated to temperance; and there's Henry Mullins, the manager of the Exchange Bank, also a Knight of Pythias, with a small flask of Pogram's Special in his hip pocket as a sort of amendment to the constitution. And there's Dean Drone, the Chaplain of the Order, with a fishing-rod (you never saw such green bass as lie among the rocks at Indian's Island), and with a trolling line in case of maskinonge, and a landing-net in case of pickerel, and with his eldest daughter, Lilian Drone, in case of young men. There never was such a fisherman as the Rev. Rupert Drone.

* * * * *

Perhaps I ought to explain that when I speak of the excursion as being of the Knights of Pythias, the thing must not be understood in any narrow sense. In Mariposa practically everybody belongs to the Knights of Pythias just as they do to everything else. That's the great thing about the town and that's what makes it so different from the city. Everybody is in everything.

You should see them on the seventeenth of March, for example, when everybody wears a green ribbon and they're all laughing and glad—you know what the Celtic nature is—and talking about Home Rule.

On St. Andrew's Day every man in town wears a thistle and shakes hands with everybody else, and you see the fine old Scotch honesty beaming out of their eyes.

And on St. George's Day!—well, there's no heartiness like the good old English spirit, after all; why shouldn't a man feel glad that he's an Englishman?

Then on the Fourth of July there are stars and stripes flying over half the stores in town, and suddenly all the men are seen to smoke cigars, and to know all about Roosevelt and Bryan and the Philippine Islands. Then you learn for the first time that Jeff Thorpe's people came from Massachusetts and that his uncle fought at Bunker Hill (it must have been Bunker Hill—anyway Jefferson will swear it was in Dakota all right enough); and you find that George Duff has a married sister in Rochester and that her husband is all right; in fact, George was down there as recently as eight years ago. Oh, it's the most American town imaginable is Mariposa—on the fourth of July.

But wait, just wait, if you feel anxious about the solidity of the British connexion, till the twelfth of the month, when everybody is wearing an orange streamer in his coat and the Orangemen (every man in town) walk in the big procession. Allegiance! Well, perhaps you remember the address they gave to the Prince of Wales on the platform of the Mariposa station as he went through on his tour to the west. I think that pretty well settled that question.

So you will easily understand that of course everybody belongs to the Knights of Pythias and the Masons and Oddfellows, just as they all belong to the Snow Shoe Club and the Girls' Friendly Society.

And meanwhile the whistle of the steamer has blown again for a quarter to seven—loud and long this time, for any one not here now is late for certain, unless he should happen to come down in the last fifteen minutes.

What a crowd upon the wharf and how they pile onto the steamer! It's a wonder that the boat can hold them all. But that's just the marvellous thing about the *Mariposa Belle*.

I don't know—I have never known—where the steamers like the *Mariposa Belle* come from. Whether they are built by Harland and Wolff of Belfast, or whether, on the other hand, they are not built by Harland and Wolff of Belfast, is more than one would like to say offhand.

The *Mariposa Belle* always seems to me to have some of those strange properties that distinguish Mariposa itself. I mean, her size seems to vary so. If you see her there in the winter, frozen in the ice beside the wharf with a snowdrift against the windows of the pilot house, she looks a pathetic little thing the size of a butternut. But in the summer time, especially after you've been in Mariposa for a month or two, and have paddled alongside of her in a canoe, she gets larger and taller, and with a great sweep of black sides, till you see no difference between the *Mariposa Belle* and the *Lusitania*. Each one is a big steamer and that's all you can say.

Nor do her measurements help you much. She draws about eighteen inches forward, and more than that—at least half an inch more, astern, and when she's loaded down with an excursion crowd she draws a good two inches more. And above the water —why, look at all the decks on her! There's the deck you walk onto, from the wharf, all shut in, with windows along it, and the after cabin with the long table, and above that the deck with all the chairs piled upon it, and the deck in front where the band stand round in a circle, and the pilot house is higher than that, and above the pilot house is the board with the gold name and the flag pole and the steel ropes and the flags; and fixed in somewhere on the different levels is the lunch counter where they sell the sandwiches, and the engine room, and down below the deck level, beneath the water line, is the place where the crew sleep. What with steps and stairs and passages and piles of cordwood for the engine—oh, no, I guess Harland and Wolff didn't build her. They couldn't have.

Yet even with a huge boat like the *Mariposa Belle*, it would be impossible for her to carry all of the crowd that you see in the boat and on the wharf. In reality, the crowd is made up of two classes—all of the people in Mariposa who are going on the excursion and all those who are not. Some come for the one reason and some for the other.

The two tellers of the Exchange Bank are both there standing side by side. But one of them—the one with the cameo pin and the long face like a horse—is going, and the other—with the other cameo pin and the face like another horse—is not. In the same way, Hussell of the *Newspacket* is going, but his brother, beside him, isn't. Lilian Drone is going, but her sister can't; and so on all through the crowd.

* * * * *

And to think that things should look like that on the morning of a steamboat accident.

How strange life is!

To think of all these people so eager and anxious to catch the steamer, and some of them running to catch it, and so fearful that they might miss it—the morning of a steamboat accident. And the captain blowing his whistle, and warning them so severely that he would leave them behind—leave them out of the accident! And everybody crowding so eagerly to be in the accident.

Perhaps life is like that all through.

Strangest of all to think, in a case like this, of the people who were left behind, or in some way or other prevented from going, and always afterwards told of how they had escaped being on board the *Mariposa Belle* that day!

Some of the instances were certainly extraordinary.

Nivens, the lawyer, escaped from being there merely by the fact that he was away in the city.

Towers, the tailor, only escaped owing to the fact that, not intending to go on the excursion he had stayed in bed till eight o'clock and so had not gone. He narrated afterwards that waking up that morning at half-past five, he had thought of the excursion and for some unaccountable reason had felt glad that he was not going.

* * * * *

The case of Yodel, the auctioneer, was even more inscrutable. He had been to the Oddfellows' excursion on the train the week before and to the Conservative picnic the week before that, and had decided not to go on this trip. In fact, he had not the least intention of going. He narrated afterwards how the night before someone had stopped him on the corner of Nippewa and Tecumseh Streets (he indicated the very spot) and asked: 'Are you going to take in the excursion tomorrow?' and he had said, just as simply as he was talking when narrating it: 'No.' And ten minutes after that, at the corner of Dalhousie and Brock Streets (he offered to lead a party of verification to the precise place) somebody else had stopped him and asked: 'Well, are you going on the steamer trip tomorrow?' Again he had answered: 'No', apparently almost in the same tone as before.

He said afterwards that when he heard the rumour of the accident it seemed like the finger of Providence, and he fell on his knees in thankfulness.

There was the similar case of Morison (I mean the one in Glover's hardware store that married one of the Thompsons). He said afterwards that he had read so much in the papers about accidents lately—mining accidents, and aeroplanes and gasoline—that he had grown nervous. The night before his wife had asked him at supper: 'Are you going on the excursion?' He had answered: 'No, I don't think I feel like it,' and had added: 'Perhaps your mother might like to go.' And the next evening just at dusk, when the news ran through the town, he said the first thought that flashed through his head was: 'Mrs. Thompson's on that boat.'

He told this right as I say it—without the least doubt or confusion. He never for a moment imagined she was on the *Lusitania* or the *Olympic* or any other boat. He knew she was on this one. He said you could have knocked him down where he stood. But no one had. Not even when he got half-way down—on his knees, and it would have been easier still to knock him down or kick him. People do miss a lot of chances.

Still, as I say, neither Yodel nor Morison nor any-one thought about there being an accident until just after sundown when they—

Well, have you ever heard the long booming whistle of a steamboat two miles out on the lake in the dusk, and while you listen and count and won-der, seen the crimson rockets going up against the sky and then heard the fire bell ringing right there beside you in the town, and seen the people running to the town wharf?

That's what the people of Mariposa saw and felt that summer evening as they watched the Mackinaw lifeboat go plunging out into the lake with seven sweeps to a side and the foam clear to the gunwale with the lifting stroke of fourteen men!

But, dear me, I am afraid that this is no way to tell a story. I suppose the true art would have been to have said nothing about the accident till it hap-pened. But when you write about Mariposa, or hear of it, if you know the place, it's all so vivid and real that a thing like the contrast between the excursion crowd in the morning and the scene at night leaps into your mind and you must think of it.

*　　*　　*　　*　　*

But never mind about the accident—let us turn back again to the morning.

The boat was due to leave at seven. There was no doubt about the hour—not only seven, but seven sharp. The notice in the *Newspacket* said: 'The boat will leave sharp at seven'; and the advertising posters on the telegraph poles on Missinaba Street that began, 'Ho, for Indian's Island!' ended up with the words: 'Boat leaves at seven sharp.' There was a big notice on the wharf that said: 'Boat leaves sharp on time.'

So at seven, right on the hour, the whistle blew loud and long, and then at seven-fifteen three short peremptory blasts, and at seven-thirty one quick angry call—just one—and very soon after that they cast off the last of the ropes and the *Mariposa Belle* sailed off in her cloud of flags, and the band of the Knights of Pythias, timing it to a nicety, broke into the 'Maple Leaf for Ever!'

I suppose that all excursions when they start are much the same. Anyway, on the *Mariposa Belle* everybody went running up and down all over the boat with deck chairs and camp stools and baskets, and found places, splendid places to sit, and then got scared that there might be better ones and chased off again. People hunted for places out of the sun and when they got them swore that they weren't going to freeze to please anybody; and the people in the sun said that they hadn't paid fifty cents to get roasted. Others said that they hadn't paid fifty cents to get covered with cinders, and there were still others who hadn't paid fifty cents to get shaken to death with the propeller.

Still, it was all right presently. The people seemed to get sorted out into the places on the boat where they belonged. The women, the older ones, all gravitated into the cabin on the lower deck and by getting round the table with needlework, and with all the windows shut, they soon had it, as they said themselves, just like being at home.

All the young boys and the toughs and the men in the band got down on the lower deck forward, where the boat was dirtiest and where the anchor was and the coils of rope.

And upstairs on the after deck there were Lilian Drone and Miss Lawson, the high-school teacher, with a book of German poetry—Gothey I think it was—and the bank teller and the younger men.

In the centre, standing beside the rail, were Dean Drone and Dr. Gallagher, looking through binocular glasses at the shore.

Up in front on the little deck forward of the pilot house was a group of the older men, Mullins and Duff and Mr. Smith in a deck chair, and beside him Mr. Golgotha Gingham, the undertaker of Mariposa, on a stool. It was part of Mr. Gingham's principles to take in an outing of this sort, a business matter, more or less—for you never know what may happen at these water parties. At any rate, he was there in a neat suit of black, not, of course, his heavier or professional suit, but a soft clinging effect as of burnt paper that combined gaiety and decorum to a nicety.

*   *   *   *   *

'Yes,' said Mr. Gingham, waving his black glove in a general way towards the shore, 'I know the lake well, very well. I've been pretty much all over it in my time.'

'Canoeing?' asked somebody.

'No,' said Mr. Gingham, 'not in a canoe.' There seemed a peculiar and quiet meaning in his tone.

'Sailing, I suppose,' said somebody else.

'No,' said Mr. Gingham. 'I don't understand it.'

'I never knowed that you went onto the water at all, Gol,' said Mr. Smith, breaking in.

'Ah, not now,' explained Mr. Gingham; 'it was years ago, the first summer I came to Mariposa. I was on the water practically all day. Nothing like it to give a man an appetite and keep him in shape.'

'Was you camping?' asked Mr. Smith.

'We camped at night,' assented the undertaker, 'but we put in practically the whole day on the water. You see we were after a party that had come up here from the city on his vacation and gone out in a sailing canoe. We were dragging. We were up every morning at sunrise, lit a fire on the beach and cooked breakfast, and then we'd light our pipes and be off with the net for a whole day. It's a great life,' concluded Mr. Gingham wistfully.

'Did you get him?' asked two or three together.

There was a pause before Mr. Gingham answered.

'We did,' he said—'down in the reeds past Horse-shoe Point. But it was no use. He turned blue on me right away.'

After which Mr. Gingham fell into such a deep reverie that the boat had steamed another half-mile down the lake before anybody broke the silence again.

Talk of this sort—and after all what more suitable for a day on the water?—beguiled the way.

*　　*　　*　　*　　*

Down the lake, mile by mile over the calm water, steamed the *Mariposa Belle*. They passed Poplar

Point where the high sand-banks are with all the swallows' nests in them, and Dean Drone and Dr. Gallagher looked at them alternately through the binocular glasses, and it was wonderful how plainly one could see the swallows and the banks and the shrubs—just as plainly as with the naked eye.

And a little farther down they passed the Shingle Beach, and Dr. Gallagher, who knew Canadian history, said to Dean Drone that it was strange to think that Champlain had landed there with his French explorers three hundred years ago; and Dean Drone, who didn't know Canadian history, said it was stranger still to think that the hand of the Almighty had piled up the hills and rocks long before that; and Dr. Gallagher said it was wonderful how the French had found their way through such a pathless wilderness; and Dean Drone said that it was wonderful also to think that the Almighty had placed even the smallest shrub in its appointed place. Dr. Gallagher said it filled him with admiration. Dean Drone said it filled him with awe. Dr. Gallagher said he'd been full of it ever since he was a boy; and Dean Drone said so had he.

Then a little farther, as the *Mariposa Belle* steamed on down the lake, they passed the Old Indian Portage where the great grey rocks are; and Dr. Gallagher drew Dean Drone's attention to the place where the narrow canoe track wound up from the shore to the woods, and Dean Drone said he could see it perfectly well without the glasses.

Dr. Gallagher said that it was just here that a party of five hundred French had made their way with all their baggage and accoutrements across the rocks of the divide and down to the Great Bay. And Dean Drone said that it reminded him of Xenophon leading his ten thousand Greeks over the hill passes of Armenia down to the sea. Dr. Gallagher said that he had often wished he could have seen and spoken to Champlain, and Dean Drone said how much he regretted to have never known Xenophon.

And then after that they fell to talking of relics and traces of the past, and Dr. Gallagher said that if Dean Drone would come round to his house some night he would show him some Indian arrow heads that he had dug up in his garden. And Dean Drone said that if Dr. Gallagher would come round to the rectory any afternoon he would show him a map of Xerxes' invasion of Greece. Only he must come some time between the Infant Class and the Mothers' Auxiliary.

So presently they both knew that they were blocked out of one another's houses for some time to come, and Dr. Gallagher walked forward and told Mr. Smith, who had never studied Greek, about Champlain crossing the rock divide.

Mr. Smith turned his head and looked at the divide for half a second and then said he had crossed a worse one up north back of the Wahnipitae and that the flies were Hades—and then went on playing freezeout poker with the two juniors in Duff's bank.

So Dr. Gallagher realized that that's always the way when you try to tell people things, and that as far as gratitude and appreciation goes one might as well never read books or travel anywhere or do anything.

In fact, it was at this very moment that he made up his mind to give the arrows to the Mariposa Mechanics' Institute—they afterwards became, as you know, the Gallagher Collection. But, for the time being, the doctor was sick of them and wandered off round the boat and watched Henry Mullins showing George Duff how to make a John Collins without lemons, and finally went and sat down among the Mariposa band and wished that he hadn't come.

So the boat steamed on and the sun rose higher and higher, and the freshness of the morning changed into the full glare of noon, and they went on to where the lake began to narrow in at its foot, just where the Indian's Island is—all grass and trees and with a log wharf running into the water. Below it the Lower Ossawippi runs out of the lake, and quite near are the rapids, and you can see down among the trees the red brick of the power house and hear the roar of the leaping water.

The Indian's Island itself is all covered with trees and tangled vines, and the water about it is so still that it's all reflected double and looks the same either way up. Then when the steamer's whistle blows as it comes into the wharf, you hear it echo among the trees of the island, and reverberate back from the shores of the lake.

The scene is all so quiet and still and unbroken, that Miss Cleghorn—the sallow girl in the telephone exchange, that I spoke of—said she'd like to be buried there. But all the people were so busy getting their baskets and gathering up their things that no one had time to attend to it.

I mustn't even try to describe the landing and the boat crunching against the wooden wharf and all the people running to the same side of the deck and Christie Johnson calling out to the crowd to keep to the starboard and nobody being able to find it. Everyone who has been on a Mariposa excursion knows all about that.

Nor can I describe the day itself and the picnic

under the trees. There were speeches afterwards, and Judge Pepperleigh gave such offence by bringing in Conservative politics that a man called Patriotus Canadiensis wrote and asked for some of the invaluable space of the *Mariposa Times-Herald* and exposed it.

I should say that there were races too, on the grass on the open side of the island, graded mostly according to ages—races for boys under thirteen and girls over nineteen and all that sort of thing. Sports are generally conducted on that plan in Mariposa. It is realized that a woman of sixty has an unfair advantage over a mere child.

Dean Drone managed the races and decided the ages and gave out the prizes; the Wesleyan minister helped, and he and the young student, who was relieving in the Presbyterian Church, held the string at the winning point.

They had to get mostly clergymen for the races because all the men had wandered off, somehow, to where they were drinking lager beer out of two kegs stuck on pine logs among the trees.

But if you've ever been on a Mariposa excursion you know all about these details anyway.

So the day wore on and presently the sun came through the trees on a slant and the steamer whistle blew with a great puff of white steam and all the people came straggling down to the wharf and pretty soon the *Mariposa Belle* had floated out onto the lake again and headed for the town, twenty miles away.

*   *   *   *   *

I suppose you have often noticed the contrast there is between an excursion on its way out in the morning and what it looks like on the way home.

In the morning everybody is so restless and animated and moves to and fro all over the boat and asks questions. But coming home, as the afternoon gets later and later and the sun sinks beyond the hills, all the people seem to get so still and quiet and drowsy.

So it was with the people on the *Mariposa Belle*. They sat there on the benches and the deck chairs in little clusters, and listened to the regular beat of the propeller and almost dozed off asleep as they sat. Then when the sun set and the dusk drew on, it grew almost dark on the deck and so still that you could hardly tell there was anyone on board.

And if you had looked at the steamer from the shore or from one of the islands, you'd have seen the row of lights from the cabin windows shining on the water and the red glare of the burning hemlock from the funnel, and you'd have heard the soft thud of the propeller miles away over the lake.

Now and then, too, you could have heard them singing on the steamer—the voices of the girls and the men blended into unison by the distance, rising and falling in long-drawn melody: 'O—Can-a-da— O—Can-a-da.'

You may talk as you will about the intoning choirs of your European cathedrals, but the sound of 'O Can-a-da', borne across the waters of a silent lake at evening is good enough for those of us who know Mariposa.

I think that it was just as they were singing like this: 'O—Can-a-da', that word went round that the boat was sinking.

If you have ever been in any sudden emergency on the water, you will understand the strange psychology of it—the way in which what is happening seems to become known all in a moment without a word being said. The news is transmitted from one to the other by some mysterious process.

At any rate, on the *Mariposa Belle* first one and then the other heard that the steamer was sinking. As far as I could ever learn the first of it was that George Duff, the bank manager, came very quietly to Dr. Gallagher and asked him if he thought that the boat was sinking. The doctor said no, that he had thought so earlier in the day but that he didn't now think that she was.

After that Duff, according to his own account, had said to Macartney, the lawyer, that the boat was sinking, and Macartney said that he doubted it very much.

Then somebody came to Judge Pepperleigh and woke him up and said that there was six inches of water in the steamer and that she was sinking. And Pepperleigh said it was perfect scandal and passed the news on to his wife and she said that they had no business to allow it and that if the steamer sank that was the last excursion she'd go on.

So the news went all round the boat and everywhere the people gathered in groups and talked about it in the angry and excited way that people have when a steamer is sinking on one of the lakes like Lake Wissanotti.

Dean Drone, of course, and some others were quieter about it, and said that one must make allowances and that naturally there were two sides to everything. But most of them wouldn't listen to reason at all. I think, perhaps, that some of them were frightened. You see the last time but one that the steamer had sunk, there had been a man drowned and it made them nervous.

What? Hadn't I explained about the depth of Lake Wissanotti? I had taken it for granted that you knew; and in any case parts of it are deep enough, though I don't suppose in this stretch of it from the big reed beds up to within a mile of the town wharf, you could find six feet of water in it if you tried. Oh, pshaw! I was not talking about a steamer sinking in the ocean and carrying down its screaming crowds of people into the hideous depths of green water. Oh, dear me, no! That kind of thing never happens on Lake Wissanotti.

But what does happen is that the *Mariposa Belle* sinks every now and then, and sticks there on the bottom till they get things straightened up.

On the lakes round Mariposa, if a person arrives late anywhere and explains that the steamer sank everybody understands the situation.

You see when Harland and Wolff built the *Mariposa Belle*, they left some cracks in between the timbers that you fill up with cotton waste every Sunday. If this is not attended to, the boat sinks. In fact, it is part of the law of the province that all the steamers like the *Mariposa Belle* must be properly corked—I think that is the word—every season. There are inspectors who visit all the hotels in the province to see that it is done.

So you can imagine now that I've explained it a little straighter, the indignation of the people when they knew that the boat had come uncorked and that they might be stuck out there on a shoal or a mud-bank half the night.

I don't say either that there wasn't any danger; anyway, it doesn't feel very safe when you realize that the boat is settling down with every hundred yards that she goes, and you look over the side and see only the black water in the gathering night.

Safe! I'm not sure now that I come to think of it that it isn't worse than sinking in the Atlantic. After all, in the Atlantic there is wireless telegraphy, and a lot of trained sailors and stewards. But out on Lake Wissanotti—far out, so that you can only just see the lights of the town away off to the south— when the propeller comes to a stop—and you can hear the hiss of steam as they start to rake out the engine fires to prevent an explosion—and when you turn from the red glare that comes from the furnace doors as they open them, to the black dark that is gathering over the lake—and there's a night wind beginning to run among the rushes—and you see the men going forward to the roof of the pilot house to send up the rockets to rouse the town—safe? Safe yourself, if you like; as for me, let me once get back into Mariposa again, under the night shadow of the maple trees, and this shall be the last, last time I'll go on Lake Wissanotti.

Safe! Oh, yes! Isn't it strange how safe other people's adventures seem after they happen. But you'd have been scared, too, if you'd been there just before the steamer sank, and seen them bringing up all the women onto the top deck.

I don't see how some of the people took it so calmly; how Mr. Smith, for instance, could have gone on smoking and telling how he'd had a steamer 'sink on him' on Lake Nipissing and a still bigger one, a side-wheeler, sink on him in Lake Abbitibbi.

Then, quite suddenly, with a quiver, down she went. You could feel the boat sink, sink—down, down—would it never get to the bottom? The water came flush up to the lower deck, and then—thank heaven—the sinking stopped and there was the *Mariposa Belle* safe and tight on a reed bank.

Really, it made one positively laugh! It seemed so queer and, anyway, if a man has a sort of natural courage, danger makes him laugh. Danger? pshaw! fiddlesticks! everybody scouted the idea. Why, it is just the little things like this that give zest to a day on the water.

Within half a minute they were all running round looking for sandwiches and cracking jokes and talking of making coffee over the remains of the engine fires.

*   *   *   *   *

I don't need to tell at length how it all happened after that.

I suppose the people on the *Mariposa Belle* would have had to settle down there all night or till help came from the town, but some of the men who had gone forward and were peering out into the dark said that it couldn't be more than a mile across the water to Miller's Point. You could almost see it over there to the left—some of them, I think, said 'off on the port bow', because you know when you get mixed up in these marine disasters, you soon catch the atmosphere of the thing.

So pretty soon they had the davits swung out over the side and were lowering the old lifeboat from the top deck into the water.

There were men leaning out over the rail of the *Mariposa Belle* with lanterns that threw the light as they let her down, and the glare fell on the water and the reeds. But when they got the boat lowered, it looked such a frail, clumsy thing as one saw it from the rail above, that the cry was raised: 'Women and children first!' For what was the sense, if it should turn out that the boat wouldn't even hold women and children, of trying to jam a lot of heavy men into it?

So they put in mostly women and children and the boat pushed out into the darkness so freighted down it would hardly float.

In the bow of it was the Presbyterian student who was relieving the minister, and he called out that they were in the hands of Providence. But he was crouched and ready to spring out of them at the first moment.

So the boat went and was lost in the darkness except for the lantern in the bow that you could see bobbing on the water. Then presently it came back and they sent another load, till pretty soon the decks began to thin out and everybody got impatient to be gone.

It was about the time that the third boatload put off that Mr. Smith took a bet with Mullins for twenty-five dollars, that he'd be home in Mariposa before the people in the boats had walked round the shore.

No one knew just what he meant, but pretty soon they saw Mr. Smith disappear down below into the lowest part of the steamer with a mallet in one hand and a big bundle of marline in the other.

They might have wondered more about it, but it was just at this time that they heard the shouts from the rescue boat—the big Mackinaw lifeboat—that had put out from the town with fourteen men at the sweeps when they saw the first rockets go up.

I suppose there is always something inspiring about a rescue at sea, or on the water.

After all, the bravery of the lifeboat man is the true bravery—expended to save life, not to destroy it.

Certainly they told for months after of how the rescue boat came out to the *Mariposa Belle*.

I suppose that when they put her in the water the lifeboat touched it for the first time since the old Macdonald Government placed her on Lake Wissanotti.

Anyway, the water poured in at every seam. But not for a moment—even with two miles of water between them and the steamer—did the rowers pause for that.

By the time they were halfway there the water was almost up to the thwarts, but they drove her on. Panting and exhausted (for mind you, if you haven't been in a fool boat like that for years, rowing takes it out of you), the rowers stuck to their task. They threw the ballast over and chucked into the water the heavy cork jackets and lifebelts that encumbered their movements. There was no thought of turning back. They were nearer to the steamer than the shore.

'Hang to it, boys,' called the crowd from the steamer's deck, and hang they did.

They were almost exhausted when they got them; men leaning from the steamer threw them ropes and one by one every man was hauled aboard just as the lifeboat sank under their feet.

Saved! by heaven, saved by one of the smartest pieces of rescue work ever seen on the lake.

There's no use describing it; you need to see rescue work of this kind by lifeboats to understand it.

Nor were the lifeboat crew the only ones that distinguished themselves.

Boat after boat and canoe after canoe had put out from Mariposa to the help of the steamer. They got them all.

Pupkin, the other bank teller, with a face like a horse, who hadn't gone on the excursion—as soon as he knew that the boat was signalling for help and that Miss Lawson was sending up rockets—rushed for a row boat, grabbed an oar (two would have hampered him), and paddled madly out into the lake. He struck right out into the dark with the crazy skiff almost sinking beneath his feet. But they got him. They rescued him. They watched him, almost dead with exhaustion, make his way to the steamer, where he was hauled up with ropes. Saved! Saved!

*   *   *   *   *

They might have gone on that way half the night, picking up the rescuers, only, at the very moment when the tenth load of people left for the shore— just as suddenly and saucily as you please, up came the *Mariposa Belle* from the mud bottom and floated.

FLOATED?

Why, of course she did. If you take a hundred and fifty people off a steamer that has sunk, and if you get a man as shrewd as Mr. Smith to plug the timber seams with mallet and marline, and if you turn ten bandsmen of the Mariposa band onto your hand pump on the bow of the lower decks—float? why, what else can she do?

Then, if you stuff in hemlock into the embers of the fire that you were raking out, till it hums and crackles under the boiler, it won't be long before you hear the propeller thud—thudding at the stern again, and before the long roar of the steam whistle echoes over to the town.

And so the *Mariposa Belle*, with all steam up

again and with the long train of sparks careering from the funnel, is heading for the town.

But no Christie Johnson at the wheel in the pilot house this time.

'Smith! Get Smith!' is the cry.

Can he take her in? Well, now! Ask a man who has had steamers sink on him in half the lakes from Temiscaming to the Bay, if he can take her in? Ask a man who has run a York boat down the rapids of the Moose when the ice is moving, if he can grip the steering wheel of the *Mariposa Belle*? So there she steams safe and sound to the town wharf!

Look at the lights and the crowd! If only the federal census taker could count us now! Hear them calling and shouting back and forward from the deck to the shore! Listen! There is the rattle of the shore ropes as they get them ready, and there's the Mariposa band—actually forming in a circle on the upper deck just as she docks, and the leader with his baton —one—two—ready now—

'O Can-a-da!'

Snow

FREDERICK PHILIP GROVE (1871–1948)

Towards morning the blizzard had died down, though it was still far from daylight. Stars without number blazed in the dark blue sky which presented that brilliant and uncompromising appearance always characterizing, on the northern plains of America, those nights in the dead of winter when the thermometer dips to its lowest levels.

In the west Orion was sinking to the horizon. It was between five and six o'clock.

In the bush-fringe of the Big Marsh, sheltered by thick but bare bluffs of aspens, stood a large house, built of logs, whitewashed, solid—such as a settler who is still single would put up only when he thinks of getting married. It, too, looked ice-cold, frozen in the night. Not a breath stirred where it stood; a thin thread of whitish smoke, reaching up to the level of the tree-tops, seemed to be suspended into the chimney rather than to issue from it.

Through the deep snow of the yard, newly packed, a man was fighting his way to the door. Arrived there, he knocked and knocked, first tapping with his knuckles, then hammering with his fists.

Two, three minutes passed. Then a sound awoke in the house, as of somebody stirring, getting out of bed.

The figure on the door-slab—a medium-sized, slim man in sheepskin and high rubber boots into which his trousers were tucked, with the ear-flaps of his cap pulled down—stood and waited, bent over, hands thrust into the pockets of the short coat, as if he wished to shrink into the smallest possible space so as to offer the smallest possible surface to the attack of the cold. In order to get rid of the dry, powdery snow which filled every crease of his foot-gear and trousers, he stamped his feet. His chin was drawn deep into the turned-up collar on whose points his breath had settled in the form of a thick layer of hoarfrost.

At last a bolt was withdrawn inside.

The face of a man peered out, just discernible in the starlight.

Then the door was opened; in ominous silence the

figure from the outside entered, still stamping its feet.

Not a word was spoken till the door had been closed. Then a voice sounded through the cold and dreary darkness of the room.

'Redcliff hasn't come home. He went to town about noon and expected to get back by midnight. We're afraid he's lost.'

The other man, quite invisible in the dark, had listened, his teeth chattering with the cold. 'Are you sure he started out from town?'

'Well,' the new-comer answered hesitatingly, 'one of the horses came to the yard.'

'One of his horses?'

'Yes. One of those he drove. The woman worked her way to my place to get help.'

The owner of the house did not speak again. He went, in the dark, to the door in the rear and opened it. There, he groped about for matches and, finding them, lighted a lamp. In the room stood a big stove, a coal-stove of the self-feeder type; but the fuel used was wood. He opened the drafts and shook the grate clear of ashes; there were two big blocks of spruce in the fire-box, smouldering away for the night. In less than a minute they blazed up.

The new-comer entered, blinking in the light of the lamp, and looked on. Before many minutes the heat from the stove began to tell.

'I'll call Bill,' the owner of the house said. He was himself of medium height or only slightly above it, but of enormous breadth of shoulder: a figure built for lifting loads. By his side the other man looked small, weakly, dwarfed.

He left the room and, returning through the cold, bare hall in front, went upstairs.

A few minutes later a tall, slender, well-built youth bolted into the room where the new-comer was waiting. Bill, Carroll's hired man, was in his underwear and carried his clothes, thrown in a heap over his arm. Without loss of time, but jumping, stamping, swinging his arms, he began at once to dress.

He greeted the visitor. 'Hello, Mike! What's that Abe tells me? Redcliff got lost?'

'Seems that way,' said Mike listlessly.

'By gringo,' Bill went on, 'I shouldn't wonder. In that storm! I'd have waited in town! Wouldn't catch me going out in that kind of weather!'

'Didn't start till late in the afternoon,' Mike Sobotski said in his shivering way.

'No. And didn't last long either,' Bill agreed while he shouldered into his overalls. 'But while she lasted . . .'

At this moment Abe Carroll, the owner of the farm, re-entered, with sheepskin, fur cap, and long woollen scarf on his arm. His deeply lined, striking, square face bore a settled frown while he held the inside of his sheepskin to the stove, to warm it up. Then, without saying a word, he got deliberately into it.

Mike Sobotski still stood bent over, shivering, though he had opened his coat and, on his side of the stove, was catching all the heat it afforded.

Abe, with the least motion needed to complete dressing, made for the door. In passing Bill, he flung out an elbow which touched the young man's arm. 'Come on,' he said; and to the other, pointing to the stove, 'Close the drafts.'

A few minutes later a noise as of rearing and snorting horses in front of the house. . . .

Mike, buttoning up his coat and pulling his mitts over his hands, went out.

They mounted three unsaddled horses. Abe leading, they dashed through the new drifts in the yard and out through the gate to the road. Here, where the shelter of the bluffs screening the house was no longer effective, a light but freshening breeze from the north-west made itself felt as if fine little knives were cutting into the flesh of their faces.

Abe dug his heels into the flank of his rearing mount. The horse was unwilling to obey his guidance, for Abe wanted to leave the road and to cut across wild land to the south-west.

The darkness was still inky black, though here and there, where the slope of the drifts slanted in the right direction, starlight was dimly reflected from the snow. The drifts were six, eight, in places ten feet high; and the snow was once more crawling up their flanks, it was so light and fine. It would fill the tracks in half an hour. As the horses plunged through, the crystals dusted up in clouds, flying aloft over horses and riders.

In less than half an hour they came to a group of two little buildings, of logs, that seemed to squat on their haunches in the snow. Having entered the yard through a gate, they passed one of the buildings and made for the other, a little stable; their horses snorting, they stopped in its lee.

Mike dismounted, throwing the halter-shank of his horse to Bill. He went to the house, which stood a hundred feet or so away. The shack was even smaller than the stable, twelve by fifteen feet perhaps. From its flue-pipe a thick, white plume of smoke blew to the south-east.

Mike returned with a lantern; the other two

sprang to the ground; and they opened the door to examine the horse which the woman had allowed to enter.

The horse was there, still excited, snorting at the leaping light and shadows from the lantern, its eyes wild, its nostrils dilated. It was covered with white frost and fully harnessed, though its traces were tied up to the back-band.

'He let him go,' said Mike, taking in these signs. 'Must have stopped and unhitched him.'

'Must have been stuck in a drift,' Bill said, assenting.

'And tried to walk it,' Abe added.

For a minute or so they stood silent, each following his own gloomy thoughts. Weird, luminous little clouds issued fitfully from the nostrils of the horse inside.

'I'll get the cutter,' Abe said at last.

'I'll get it,' Bill volunteered. 'I'll take the drivers along. We'll leave the filly here in the stable.'

'All right.'

Bill remounted, leading Abe's horse. He disappeared into the night.

Abe and Mike, having tied the filly and the other horse in their stalls, went out, closed the door, and turned to the house.

There, by the light of a little coal-oil lamp, they saw the woman sitting at the stove, pale, shivering, her teeth achatter, trying to warm her hands, which were cold with fever, and looking with lack-lustre eyes at the men as they entered.

The children were sleeping; the oldest, a girl, on the floor, wrapped in a blanket and curled up like a dog; four others in one narrow bed, with hay for a mattress, two at the head, two at the foot; the baby on, rather than in, a sort of cradle made of a wide board slung by thin ropes to the pole-roof of the shack.

The other bed was empty and unmade. The air was stifling from a night of exhalations.

'We're going to hunt for him,' Mike said quietly. 'We've sent for a cutter. He must have tried to walk.'

The woman did not answer. She sat and shivered.

'We'll take some blankets,' Mike went on. 'And some whisky if you've got any in the house.'

He and Abe were standing by the stove, opposite the woman, and warming their hands, their mitts held under their armpits.

The woman pointed with a look to a home-made little cupboard nailed to the wall and apathetically turned back to the stove. Mike went, opened the door of the cupboard, took a bottle from it, and slipped it into the pocket of his sheepskin. Then he raised the blankets from the empty bed, rolled them roughly into a bundle, dropped it, and returned to the stove where, with stiff fingers, he fell to rolling a cigarette.

Thus they stood for an hour or so.

Abe's eye was fastened on the woman. He would have liked to say a word of comfort, of hope. What was there to be said?

She was the daughter of a German settler in the bush, some six or seven miles north-east of Abe's place. Her father, an oldish, unctuous, bearded man, had, some ten years ago, got tired of the hard life in the bush where work meant clearing, picking stones, and digging stumps. He had sold his homestead and bought a prairie-farm, half a section, on crop-payments, giving notes for the equipment which he needed to handle the place. He had not been able to make it a 'go'. His bush farm had fallen back on his hands; he had lost his all and returned to the place. He had been counting on the help of his two boys— big, strapping young fellows—who were to clear much land and to raise crops which would lift the debt. But the boys had refused to go back to the bush; they could get easy work in town. Ready money would help. But the ready money had melted away in their hands. Redcliff, the old people's son-in-law, had been their last hope. They were on the point of losing even their bush farm. Here they might per- haps still have found a refuge for their old age— though Redcliff's homestead lay on the sandflats bordering on the marsh where the soil was thin, dreadfully thin; it drifted when the scrub-brush was cleared off. Still, with Redcliff living, this place had been a hope. What were they to do if he was gone? And this woman, hardly more than a girl, in spite of her six children!

The two tiny, square windows of the shack began to turn grey.

At last Abe, thinking he heard a sound, went to the door and stepped out. Bill was there; the horses were shaking the snow out of their pelts; one of them was pawing the ground.

Once more Abe opened the door and gave Mike a look for a signal. Mike gathered the bundle of blankets into his arms, pulled on his mitts, and came out.

Abe reached for the lines, but Bill objected.

'No. Let me drive. I found something.'

And as soon as the two older men had climbed in, squeezing into the scant space on the seat, he clicked his tongue.

'Get up there!' he shouted, hitting the horses'

backs with his lines. And with a leap they darted away.

Bill turned, heading back to the Carroll farm. The horses plunged, reared, snorted, and then, throwing their heads, shot along in a gallop, scattering snow-slabs right and left and throwing wing-waves of the fresh, powdery snow, especially on the lee side. Repeatedly they tried to turn into the wind, which they were cutting at right angles. But Bill plied the whip and guided them expertly.

Nothing was visible anywhere; nothing but the snow in the first grey of dawn. Then, like enormous ghosts, or like evanescent apparitions, the trees of the bluff were adumbrated behind the lingering veils of the night.

Bill turned to the south, along the straight trail which bordered Abe Carroll's farm. He kept looking out sharply to right and left. But after awhile he drew his galloping horses in.

'Whoa!' he shouted, tearing at the lines in seesaw fashion. And when the rearing horses came to a stop, excited and breathless, he added, 'I've missed it.' He turned.

'What is it?' Abe asked.

'The other horse,' Bill answered. 'It must have had the scent of our yard. It's dead . . . frozen stiff.'

A few minutes later he pointed to a huge white mound on top of a drift to the left. 'That's it,' he said, turned the horses into the wind, and stopped.

To the right, the bluffs of the farm slowly outlined themselves in the morning greyness.

The two older men alighted and, with their hands, shovelled the snow away. There lay the horse, stiff and cold, frozen into a rock-like mass.

'Must have been here a long while,' Abe said.

Mike nodded. 'Five, six hours.' Then he added, 'Couldn't have had the smell of the yard. Unless the wind has turned.'

'It has,' Abe answered, and pointed to a fold in the flank of the snow-drift which indicated that the present drift had been superimposed on a lower one whose longitudinal axis ran to the north-east.

For a moment longer they stood and pondered.

Then Abe went back to the cutter and reached for the lines. 'I'll drive,' he said.

Mike climbed in.

Abe took his bearings, looking for landmarks. They were only two or three hundred feet from his fence. That enabled him to estimate the exact direction of the breeze. He clicked his tongue. 'Get up!'

And the horses, catching the infection of a dull excitement, shot away. They went straight into the desert of drifts to the west, plunging ahead without any trail, without any landmark in front to guide them.

They went for half an hour, an hour, and longer.

None of the three said a word. Abe knew the sand-flats better than any other; Abe reasoned better than they. If anyone could find the missing man, it was Abe.

Abe's thought ran thus. The horse had gone against the wind. It would never have done so without good reason; that reason could have been no other than a scent to follow. If that was so, however, it would have gone in as straight a line as it could. The sand-flats stretched away to the south-west for sixteen miles with not a settlement, not a farm but Redcliff's. If Abe managed to strike that line of scent, it must take him to the point whence the horses had started.

Clear and glaring, with an almost indifferent air, the sun rose to their left.

And suddenly they saw the wagon-box of the sleigh sticking out of the snow ahead of them.

Abe stopped, handed Bill the lines, and got out. Mike followed. Nobody said a word.

The two men dug the tongue of the vehicle out of the snow and tried it. This was part of the old, burnt-over bush land south of the sand-flats. The sleigh was tightly wedged in between several charred stumps which stuck up through the snow. That was the reason why the man had unhitched the horses and turned them loose. What else, indeed, could he have done?

The box was filled with a drift which, toward the tail-gate, was piled high, for there three bags of flour were standing on end and leaning against a barrel half-filled with small parcels, the interstices between which were packed with mealy snow.

Abe waded all around the sleigh, reconnoitring; and as he did so, wading at the height of the upper-edge of the wagon-box, the snow suddenly gave way beneath him; he broke in; the drift was hollow.

A suspicion took hold of him; with a few quick reaches of his arm he demolished the roof of the drift all about.

And there, in the hollow, lay the man's body as if he were sleeping, a quiet expression, as of painless rest, on his face. His eyes were closed; a couple of bags were wrapped about his shoulders. Apparently he had not even tried to walk! Already chilled to the bone, he had given in to that desire for rest, for shelter at any price, which overcomes him who is doomed to freeze.

Without a word the two men carried him to the cutter and laid him down on the snow.

Bill, meanwhile, had unhitched the horses and was hooking them to the tongue of the sleigh. The two others looked on in silence. Four times the horses sprang, excited because Bill tried to make them pull with a sudden twist. The sleigh did not stir.

'Need an axe,' Mike said at last, 'to cut the stumps. We'll get the sleigh later.'

Mike hitched up again and turned the cutter. The broken snow-drifts through which they had come gave the direction.

Then they laid the stiff, dead body across the floor of their vehicle, leaving the side-doors open, for it protruded both ways. They themselves climbed up on the seat and crouched down, so as not to put their feet on the corpse.

Thus they returned to Abe Carroll's farm where, still in silence, they deposited the body in the granary.

That done, they stood for a moment as if in doubt. Then Bill unhitched the horses and took them to the stable to feed.

'I'll tell the woman,' said Mike. 'Will you go tell her father?'

Abe nodded. 'Wait for breakfast,' he added.

It was ten o'clock; and none of them had eaten since the previous night.

On the way to Altmann's place in the bush, drifts were no obstacles to driving. Drifts lay on the marsh, on the open sand-flats.

Every minute of the time Abe, as he drove along, thought of that woman in the shack: the woman, alone, with six children, and with the knowledge that her man was dead.

Altmann's place in the bush looked the picture of

peace and comfort: a large log-house of two rooms. Window-frames and doors were painted green. A place to stay with, not to leave. . . .

When Abe knocked, the woman, whom he had seen but once in his life, at the sale where they had lost their possessions, opened the door—an enormously fat woman, overflowing her clothes. The man, tall, broad, with a long, rolling beard, now grey, stood behind her, peering over her shoulder. A visit is an event in the bush!

'Come in,' he said cheerfully when he saw Abe. 'What a storm that was!'

Abe entered the kitchen which was also dining- and living-room. He sat down on the chair which was pushed forward for him and looked at the two old people, who remained standing.

Suddenly, from the expression of his face, they anticipated something of his message. No use dissembling.

'Redcliff is dead,' he said. 'He was frozen to death last night on his way home from town.'

The two old people also sat down; it looked as if their knees had given way beneath them. They stared at him, dumbly, a sudden expression of panic fright in their eyes.

'I thought you might want to go to your daughter,' Abe added sympathetically.

The man's big frame seemed to shrink as he sat there. All the unctuousness and the conceit of the handsome man dwindled out of his bearing. The woman's eyes had already filled with tears.

Thus they remained for two, three minutes.

Then the woman folded her fat, pudgy hands; her head sank low on her breast; and she sobbed, 'God's will be done!'

Mrs. Golightly and the First Convention

ETHEL WILSON (b. 1890)

MRS. GOLIGHTLY was a shy woman. She lived in Vancouver. Her husband, Tommy Golightly, was not shy. He was personable and easy to like. He was a consulting engineer who was consulted a great deal by engineering firms, construction firms, logging firms in particular, any firm that seemed to have problems connected with traction. When he was not being consulted he played golf, tennis, or bridge according to whether the season was spring, summer, autumn, or winter. Any time that was left over he spent with his wife and three small children of whom he was very fond. When he was with them, it seemed that that was what he liked best. He was a very extroverted sort of man, easy and likeable, and his little wife was so shy that it just was not fair. But what can you do?

At the period of which I write, Conventions had not begun to take their now-accepted place in life on the North American continent. I am speaking of Conventions with a capital C. Conventions with a small c have, of course, always been with us, but not as conspicuously now as formerly. In those days, when a man said rather importantly I am going to a Convention, someone was quite liable to ask What is a Convention? Everyone seemed to think that they must be quite a good thing, which of course they are. We now take them for granted.

Now Mr. Golightly was admirably adapted to going to Conventions. His memory for names and faces was good; he liked people, both in crowds and separately; he collected acquaintances who rapidly became friends. Everyone liked him.

One day he came home and said to his wife, How would you like a trip to California?

Mrs. Golightly gave a little gasp. Her face lighted up and she said, Oh Tom. . . !

There's a Western and Middle Western Convention meeting at Del Monte the first week of March, and you and I are going down said Mr. Golightly.

Mrs. Golightly's face clouded and she said in quite a different tone and with great alarm, Oh Tom. . . !

Well what? said her husband.

Mrs. Golightly began the sort of hesitation that so easily overcame her. Well, Tom, she said, I'd have to get a hat, and I suppose a suit and a dinner dress, and Emmeline isn't very good to leave with the children and you know I'm no good with crowds and people, I never know what to say and—

Well, *get* a new hat, said her husband, get one of those hats I see women wearing with long quills on. And *get* a new dress. Get *twenty* new dresses. And Emmeline's *fine* with the children and what you need's a change and I'm the only one in my profession invited from British Columbia. You get a hat with the longest feather in town and a nice dinner dress! Mr. Golightly looked fondly at his wife and saw with new eyes that she appeared anxious and not quite as pretty as she sometimes was. He kissed her and she promised that she would get the new hat, but he did not know how terrified she was of the Convention and all the crowds of people, and that she suffered at the very thought of going. She could get along all right at home, but small talk with strangers—oh poor Mrs. Golightly. These things certainly are not fair. However, she got the dress, and a new hat with the longest quill in town. She spent a long time at the hairdresser's; and how pretty she looked and how disturbed she felt! I'll break the quill every time I get into the car, Tom, she said.

Non-*sense*, said her husband, and they set off in the car for California.

Mrs. Golightly travelled in an old knitted suit and a felt hat well pulled down on her head in observance of a theory which she had inherited from her mother that you must never wear good clothes when travelling. The night before arriving at Del Monte a car passing them at high speed sideswiped them ever so little, but the small damage and fuss that resulted from that delayed them a good deal. The result was that they got late to bed that night, slept little, rose early, and had to do three hundred miles before lunch. Mrs. Golightly began to feel very tired in spite of some mounting excitement, but this did not make her forget to ask her husband to stop at the outskirts of Del Monte so that she could take her new hat out of the bag and put it on. Mr. Golightly was delighted with the way his wife was joining in the spirit of the thing. Good girl, he said, which pleased her, and neither of them noticed that nothing looked right about Mrs. Golightly except her hat, and even smart hats, worn under those circumstances, look wrong.

How impressive it was to Mrs. Golightly, supported by her hat, to approach the portals of the fashionable Del Monte Hotel. Large cars reclined in rows, some sparkling, some dimmed by a film of dust, all of them costly. Radiant men and women, expensively dressed (the inheritors of the earth evidently) strolled about without a care in the world, or basked on the patio, scrutinizing new arrivals with experienced eyes. Mrs. Golightly had already felt something formidably buoyant in the air of California, accustomed as she was to the mild, soft, and (to tell the truth) sometimes deliciously drowsy air of the British Columbia coast. The air she breathed in California somehow alarmed her. Creatures customarily breathing this air must, she thought, by nature, be buoyant, self-confident—all the things that Mrs. Golightly was not. Flowers bloomed, trees threw their shade, birds cleft the air, blue shone the sky, and Mrs. Golightly, dazzled, knocked her hat crooked as she got out of the car, and she caught the long quill on the door. She felt it snick. Oh, she thought, my darling quill!

No sooner had they alighted from their car, which was seized on all sides by hotel minions of great competence, than her husband was surrounded by prosperous men who said, Well Tom! And how's the boy! Say Tom this is great! And Tom turned from side to side greeting, expansive, the most popular man in view. Mrs. Golightly had no idea that Tom had so many business friends that loved him dearly. And then with one accord these prosperous men turned their kindly attention to Mrs. Golightly. It overwhelmed her but it really warmed her heart to feel that they were all so pleased that she had come, and that she had come so far, and although she felt shy, travel-worn and tired, she tried to do her best and her face shone sweetly with a desire to please.

Now, said the biggest of the men, the boys are waiting for you Tom. Up in one three three. Yes in

one three three. And Mrs. Golightly I want you to
meet Mrs. Allyman of the Ladies' Committee. Mrs.
Allyman meet Mrs. Tom Golightly from British
Columbia. Will you just register her please, we've
planned a good time for the ladies, Tom . . . we'll
take good care of Tom, Mrs. Golightly. And Mr.
Golightly said, But my wife . . . and then a lot of
people streamed in, and Tom and the other men
said, Well, well, *well*, so here's Ed! Say Ed . . . the
words streamed past Mrs. Golightly and Tom was
lost to her view.

A lump that felt large came in her throat because
she was so shy and Tom was not to be seen, but Mrs.
Allyman was very kind and propelled her over to a
group of ladies and said, Oh this is the lady from
British Columbia, the name is Golightly isn't it?
Mrs. Golightly I want you to meet Mrs. Finkel and
Mrs. Connelly and Mrs. Magnus and pardon me I
didn't catch the name Mrs. Sloper from Colorado. Oh
there's the President's wife Mrs. Bagg. Well Mrs.
Bagg did you locate Mr. Bagg after all, no doubt
he's in one three three. Mrs. Golightly I'd like to
have you meet Mrs. Bagg and Mrs. Simmons, Mrs.
Bagg, Mrs. Finkel, Mrs. Bagg, and Mrs. Sloper, Mrs.
Bagg. Mrs. Golightly is all the way from British
Columbia, I think that's where you come from Mrs.
Golightly? Mrs. Allyman, speaking continually,
seemed to say all this in one breath. By the time that
Mrs. Golightly's vision had cleared (although she
felt rather dizzy) she saw that all these ladies were
chic, and that they wore hats with very long quills,
longer even than hers, which made her feel much
more secure. However, her exhilaration was passing,
she realized that she was quite tired, and she said,
smiling sweetly, I *think* I'd better find my room.

The hubbub in the hotel rotunda increased and increased.

When she reached her room she found that Tom had sent the bags up, and she thought she would unpack, and lie down for a bit to get rested, and then go down and have a quiet lunch. Perhaps she would see Tom somewhere. But first she went over to the window and looked out upon the incredible radiance of blue and green and gold, and the shine of the ethereal air. She looked at the great oak trees and the graceful mimosa trees and she thought, After I've tidied up and had some lunch I'll just go and sit under one of those beautiful mimosa trees and drink in this . . . this largesse of air and scent and beauty. Mrs. Golightly had never seen anything like it. The bright air dazzled her, and made her sad and gay. Just then the telephone rang. A man's strong and purposeful voice said, Pardon me, but may I speak to Tom?

Oh I'm sorry, said Mrs. Golightly, Tom's not here.

Can you tell me where I can get him? asked the voice very urgently.

I'm so sorry . . . faltered Mrs. Golightly.

Sorry to troub . . . said the voice and the telephone clicked off.

There. The Convention had invaded the bedroom, the azure sky, and the drifting grace of the mimosa tree outside the bedroom window.

I think, said Mrs. Golightly to herself, if I had a bath it would freshen me, I'm beginning to have a headache. She went into the bathroom and gazed with pleasure on its paleness and coolness and shiningness, on the lavish array of towels, and an uneven picture entered and left her mind of the

69

bathroom at home, full, it seemed to her, of the essentials for cleaning and dosing a father and mother and three small children, non-stop. The peace! The peace of it! She lay in the hot water regarding idly and alternately the soap which floated agreeably upon the water, and the window through which she saw blue sky of an astonishing azure.

The telephone rang.

Is that Mrs. Goodman? purred a voice.

No, no, not Mrs. Goodman, said Mrs. Golightly, wrapped in a towel.

I'm *so* sorry, purred the voice.

Mrs. Golightly got thankfully into the bath and turned on some more hot water.

The telephone rang.

She scrambled out, Hello, hello?

There's a wire at the desk for Mr. Golightly, said a voice, shall we send it up?

Oh dear, oh dear, said Mrs. Golightly wrapped in a towel, well . . . not yet . . . not for half an hour.

Okay, said the voice.

She got back into the bath. She closed her eyes in disturbed and recovered bliss.

The telephone rang.

Hello, hello, said Mrs. Golightly plaintively, wrapped in a very damp towel.

Is that Mrs. Golightly? said a kind voice.

Yes, oh yes, agreed Mrs. Golightly.

Well, this is Mrs. Porter speaking and we'd be pleased if you'd join Mrs. Bagg and Mrs. Wilkins and me in the Tap Room and meet some of the ladies and have a little drink before lunch.

Oh thank you, thank you, that will just be lovely, I'd love to, said Mrs. Golightly. Away went the sky, away went the birds, away went the bath, and away went the mimosa tree.

Well, that will be lovely, said Mrs. Porter, in about half-an-hour?

Oh thank you, thank you, that will be lovely . . . ! said Mrs. Golightly, repeating herself considerably.

She put on her new grey flannel suit which was only slightly rumpled, and straightened the tip of her quill as best she could. She patted her rather aching forehead with cold water and felt somewhat refreshed. She paid particular and delicate attention to her face, and left her room looking and feeling quite pretty but agitated.

When she got down to the Tap Room everyone was having Old-Fashioneds and a little woman in grey came up and said, Pardon me but are you Mrs. Golightly from British Columbia? Mrs. Golightly, I'd like to have you meet Mrs. Bagg (our President's wife) and Mrs. Gillingham from St. Louis, Mrs. Wilkins from Pasadena, Mrs. Golightly, Mrs. Finkel and —pardon me?—Mrs. Connelly and Mrs. Allyman of Los Angeles.

Mrs. Golightly felt confused, but she smiled at each lady in turn, saying How do you do, but neglected to remember or repeat their names because she was so inexperienced. She slipped into a chair and a waiter brought her an Old-Fashioned. She then looked round and tried hard to memorize the ladies, nearly all of whom had stylish hats with tall quills on. Mrs. Bagg very smart. Mrs. Wilkins with pince-nez. Little Mrs. Porter in grey. Mrs. Simmons, Mrs. Connelly, and Mrs. Finkel in short fur capes. Mrs. Finkel was lovely, of a gorgeous pale beauty. Mrs. Golightly sipped her Old-Fashioned and tried to feel very gay indeed. She and Mrs. Connelly who came from Chicago found that each had three small children, and before they had finished talking, a waiter brought another Old-Fashioned. Then Mrs. Connelly had to speak to a lady on her other side, and Mrs. Golightly turned to the lady on her left. This lady was not talking to anyone but was quietly sipping her Old-Fashioned. By this time Mrs. Golightly was feeling unusually bold and responsible, and quite like a woman of the world. She thought to herself, Come now, everyone is being so lovely and trying to make everyone feel at home, and I must try too.

So she said to the strange lady, I don't think we met, did we? My name is Mrs. Golightly and I come from British Columbia. And the lady said, I'm pleased to meet you. I'm Mrs. Gampish and I come from Toledo, Ohio. And Mrs. Golightly said, Oh isn't this a beautiful hotel and wouldn't you like to see the gardens, and then somehow everyone was moving.

When Mrs. Golightly got up she felt as free as air, but as if she was stepping a little high. When they reached the luncheon table there must have been about a hundred ladies and of course everyone was talking. Mrs. Golightly was seated between two perfectly charming people, Mrs. Carillo from Little Rock, Arkansas, and Mrs. Clark from Phoenix, Arizona. They both said what a cute English accent she had and she had to tell them because she was so truthful that she had never been to England. It was a little hard to talk as there was an orchestra and Mrs. Golightly and Mrs. Carillo and Mrs. Clark were seated just below the saxophones. Mrs. Golightly couldn't quite make out whether she had no headache at all, or the worst headache of her life. This is lovely, she thought as she smiled back at her shouting companions, but how nice it will be to go upstairs and lie down. Just for half an hour after lunch, before I go and sit under the mimosa tree.

But when the luncheon was over, Mrs. Wilkins clapped her hands and said, Now Ladies, cars are waiting at the door and we'll assemble in the lobby for the drive. And Mrs. Golightly said, Oh hadn't I better run upstairs and see whether my husband . . . But Mrs. Wilkins said again, Now Ladies! So they all gathered in the lobby, and for one moment, one moment, Mrs. Golightly was still.

Oh, she thought, I feel awful, and I am so sleepy, and I feel a little queer. But she soon started smiling again, and they all got into motor-cars.

She got into a nice car with some other ladies whom she did not know. They all had tall quills on their hats which made it awkward. Mrs. Golightly was the smallest and sat in the middle. She turned from side to side with great politeness. Flick, flick went the quills, smiting against each other. Well, we'd better introduce ourselves, she thought. But the lady on her right had already explained that she was Mrs. Johnson from Seattle, so she turned to her left and said to the other stranger, Do tell me your name? I'm Mrs. Golightly and I come from British Columbia.

The other lady said a little stiffly, Well, I'm Mrs. Gampish and I come from Toledo, Ohio, and Mrs. Golightly felt awful and said, Oh Mrs. Gampish, how stupid of me, we met in the Tap Room, of course! So *many* people!—Oh, it's quite all right, said Mrs. Gampish rather coldly. But she and Mrs. Johnson soon found that their husbands both had gastric ulcers and so they had a very very interesting conversation. Mrs. Golightly did not join in because she had nothing to offer in the way of an ulcer, as she and Tom and the children never seemed to be ill and the ladies did not appear to need sympathy. She dodged this way and that behind Mrs. Gampish and Mrs. Johnson, interfering with their quills, and peering at gleaming Spanish villas enfolded in green, blazing masses of flowers, a crash and white spume of breakers, a twisted Monterey pine—they all rushed dazzling past the car windows—villas, pines, ocean, and all. If I were courageous or even tactful, thought Mrs. Golightly, I could ask to sit beside the window where I want to be, and these ladies could talk in comfort (the talk had moved from ulcers to their sons' fraternities) which is what they wish, but she knew that she was not skilful in such matters, and it would not do. Oh, she yearned, if I could ever be a woman of the world and achieve these simple matters!

Then all the cars stopped at a place called Point Lobos, and everybody got out.

Mrs. Golightly sped swiftly alone toward the cliffs. She stood on a high rock overlooking the vast ocean, and the wind roared and whistled about her. She took off her hat as the whistling, beating broken quill seemed to impede her. She looked down and could hardly believe the beauty that lay below her. Green ocean crashed and broke in towering spray on splintered rocky islets, on the cliffs where she stood, and into swirling, sucking, rock-bound bays and caves. In the translucent green waves played joyous bands of seals, so joyous that they filled her with rapture. Bellowing seals clambered upon the rocks, but the din of wind and ocean drowned their bellowing. The entrancement of sea and sky and wind and the strong playing bodies of the seals so transported Mrs. Golightly that she forgot to think, Oh I must tell the children, and how Tom would love this! She was one with the rapture of that beautiful unexpected moment. She felt someone beside her and turned. There was Mrs. Carillo with a shining face. They shouted at each other, laughing with joy, but could not hear each other, and stood arm in arm braced against the wind, looking down at the playing bands of seals.

As the party assembled again, Mrs. Golightly stepped aside and waited for Mrs. Gampish and Mrs. Johnson to get in first. Then she got in, and sat down beside the window. Conversation about Point Lobos and the seals became general, and Mrs. Johnson, who was in the middle, found herself turning from side to side, bending and catching her quill. They then became quiet, and the drive home was peaceful. I shall never forget, thought Mrs. Golightly, as the landscape and seascape flashed past her rather tired eyes, the glory of Point Lobos, and the strong bodies of the seals playing in the translucent water. Whatever happens to me on earth, I shall never never forget it.

When she arrived at the hotel she discovered that she was nearly dead with excitement and noise and fatigue and when Tom came in she said, because she was so simple and ignorant, Oh darling, can we have dinner somewhere quietly tonight, I must tell you about all those seals. And Tom looked quite shocked, and he said, Seals? But darling, aren't you having a good time? I was just talking to Mr. Bagg and he tells me that you made a great hit with his wife. This is a Convention you know, he said reprovingly, and you can't do *that* kind of thing! Seals

indeed! Where's your programme? Yes, Ladies'
Dinner in the Jacobean Room, and I'll be at the
Men's. And Mrs. Golightly said, Oh Tom. . . . Yes,
of course, I know, how stupid of me. . . . I'm having
the *loveliest* time, Tom, and we had the *loveliest*
drive, and now I'm really going to have a proper
bath and a rest before I dress. And Tom said, *Fine!*
But can I have the bathroom first because . . . and
then the telephone rang and Tom said Yes? Yes,
Al, what's that? In the Tap Room? In fifteen
minutes? Make it twenty Al, I want to bath and
change. Okay Al. . . . That was Al, dear. I'll have to
hurry but you have a good rest. And then the telephone rang and it was Mrs. Wilkins and she said,
Oh Mrs. Golightly will you join Mrs. Porter and me
and some of the ladies in my room one seven five for
cocktails at six o'clock. I do hope it won't rush you. One
seven five. Oh that will be lovely.—Oh, yes, that will
be lovely, said Mrs. Golightly. She put her hands to
her face and then she took out her blue dinner dress
and began pressing it, and away went the bath and
away went the rest and away went the mimosa tree.
And Tom came out of the bathroom and said, Why
ever aren't you lying down. That's the trouble with
you, you never will rest! Well so long darling, have
a good time. And he went, and she finished pressing
her dress and put it on.

The next time Mrs. Golightly saw Tom was downstairs in the hotel lobby as she waited with some of
the other ladies to go into the ladies' dinner. Tom
was in the middle of a group of men who walked
down the centre of the lobby. They walked almost
rolling with grandeur or something down the lobby,
owning it, sufficient unto themselves, laughing together at their own private jokes and unaware of

anyone else. But Mr. Golightly's eyes fell on his wife.
He saw how pretty she looked and was delighted
with her. He checked the flow of men down the lobby
and stepped forward and said, Terry I want you to
meet Mr. Flanagan, Bill this is my wife. And a lively
and powerful small man seized Mrs. Golightly's
hand and held it and looked admiringly at her and
said, Well, Mrs. Golightly, I certainly am pleased to
meet you. I've just got Tom here to promise that
you and he will come and stay with Mrs. Flanagan
and me this fall when the shooting's good up at our
little place in Oregon—now, no argument, it's all
settled, you're coming! What a genial host! It would
be a pleasure to stay with Mr. Flanagan.

Tom beamed in a pleased way, and Mrs. Golightly's face sparkled with pleasure. Oh Mr. Flanagan, she said, how kind! Tom and I will just *love*
to come. (Never a word or thought about What
shall we do with the children—just We'd love to
come.) So *that's* settled, said Mr. Flanagan breezily
and the flow of men down the hotel lobby was
resumed.

At dinner Mrs Golightly sat beside a nice woman
from San Francisco called Mrs. de Kay who had
once lived in Toronto so of course they had a lot in
common. Before dinner everyone had had one or
two Old-Fashioneds, and as the mists cleared a bit,
Mrs. Golightly had recognized Mrs. Bagg, Mrs. Connelly, dear Mrs. Carillo, and beautiful Mrs. Finkel.
How lovely was Mrs. Finkel sitting in blonde serenity
amidst the hubbub, in silence looking around her
with happy gentle gaze. You could never forget Mrs.
Finkel. Her face, her person, her repose, her shadowed
eyes invited scrutiny. You gazed with admiration
and sweetly she accepted your admiration. While all

around her were vivacious, Mrs. Finkel sat still. But now Mrs. Finkel and Mrs. Carillo were far down the table and Mrs. Golightly conversed with Mrs. de Kay as one woman of the world to another. How well I'm coming along! she thought, and felt puffed up.

During the sweet course she became hot with shame! She had not spoken a word to the lady on her left who wore a red velvet dress. She turned in a gushing way and said to the lady in the red dress who, she realized, was not speaking to anyone at the moment. Isn't this a delightful dinner! We haven't had a chance of a word with each other, have we, and I don't believe we've met, but I'm Mrs. Golightly from British Columbia.

The lady in the red cut-velvet dress turned towards Mrs. Golightly and said clearly, I am Mrs. Gampish, and I come from Toledo, Ohio. Their eyes met.

Mrs. Golightly remained silent. Blushes flamed over her. She thought, This is, no doubt, some dreadful dream from which I shall soon awake. And still the chatter and clatter and music went on. Mrs. Golightly could not think of anything to say. Mrs. Gampish continued to eat her dessert. Mrs. Golightly attempted to smile in a society way, but it was no good, and she couldn't say a thing.

After dinner there was bridge and what do you suppose? Mrs. Golightly was set to play with Mrs. Magnus and Mrs. Finkel and Mrs. Gampish. Trembling a little, she stood up.

I think I will go to bed, she said. She could not bear to think of Mrs. Gampish being compelled to play bridge with her.

No, *I* shall go to bed, said Mrs. Gampish.

No, do let me go to bed, cried Mrs. Golightly, I simply insist on going to bed.

And *I* insist on going to bed too, said Mrs. Gampish firmly, in any case I have a headache. Mrs. Magnus and Mrs. Finkel looked on in amazement.

No, no, I shall go to bed, said Mrs. Golightly in distress.

No, *I* shall go to bed, said Mrs. Gampish. It was very absurd.

Mrs. Bagg hurried up. Everything all set here? she said in a hostess voice.

Mrs. Gampish and Mrs. Golightly said, speaking together, I am going to bed.

Oh, don't *both* go to bed, pleaded Mrs. Bagg, unaware of any special feeling. If one of you must go to bed, do please one of you stay, and I will make the fourth.

Mrs. Golightly considered and acted quickly. If Mrs. Gampish *really* wants to go to bed, she said, timidly but with effect, I will stay . . . a slight headache . . . she said bravely fluttering her fingers and batting her eyelashes which were rather long.

Mrs. Gampish did not argue any more. She said good night to the ladies and left.

Oh do excuse me a minute, said Mrs. Golightly, flickering her eyelashes, and she caught Mrs. Gampish at the elevator. Mrs. Gampish looked at her with distaste.

I want to tell you, Mrs. Gampish, said Mrs. Golightly with true humility, and speaking very low, that I have never been to a Convention before, and I want to confess to you my stupidity. I am not really rude, only stupid and so shy although I have three children that I am truly in a whirl. Will you be able ever to forgive me? . . . It would be very kind of you if you feel that you could. Oh, please do try.

There was a silence between them as the elevators came and went. Then Mrs. Gampish gave a wan smile.

You are too earnest, my child, she said. (Oh how good you are! breathed Mrs. Golightly.) I wouldn't myself know one person in this whole Convention—except Mrs. Finkel and no one could forget her, continued Mrs. Gampish, and I never knew you each time you told me who you were *until* you told me, so you needn't have worried. If you want to know why I'm going to bed, it's because I don't like bridge and anyway, I *do* have a headache.

Oh I'm so glad you *really* have a headache, no I mean I'm so sorry, and I think you're perfectly sweet, Mrs. Gampish, and if ever you come to Canada . . . and she saw the faintly amused smile of Mrs. Gampish going up in the elevator. Well I never, she said, but she felt happier.

She turned and there was Tom hurrying past. Oh Tom, she called. He stopped.

Having a good time darling? he said in a hurry. D'you want to come to the meeting at Salt Lake City next year? and he smiled at her encouragingly.

Oh Tom, she said, I'd adore it! (What a changed life. Del Monte, Mr. Flanagan's shooting lodge, Salt Lake City, all in a minute, you might say.)

Well, well! said Tom in surprise and vanished.

On the way to her bedroom that night Mrs. Golightly met Mr. Flanagan walking very slowly down the hall.

How do you do Mr. Flanagan! said Mrs. Golightly gaily. She felt that he was already her host at his shooting lodge.

Mr. Flanagan stopped and looked at her seriously

as from a great distance. It was obvious that he did
not know her. How do you do, he said very carefully and with a glazed expression. Did we meet or
did we meet. In any case, how do you do. And he
continued walking with the utmost care down the
corridor.

Oh . . . , said Mrs. Golightly, her eyes wide open,
. . . oh. . . . It was probable that Mr. Flanagan invited everyone to the shooting lodge. The shooting
lodge began to vanish like smoke.

When she entered the bedroom she saw that in her
hurry before dinner she had not put her hat away.
The quill was twice bent, and it dangled. She took
scissors and cut it short There, she thought, caress-
ing and smoothing the feather, it looks all right,
doesn't it? She had felt for a moment very low, dis-
integrated, but now as she sat on the bed in her blue
dinner dress she thought, Mr. Flanagan isn't a bit
afraid to be him and Mrs. Gampish isn't a bit afraid
to be her and now I'm not a bit afraid to be me . . .
at least, not much. As she looked down, smoothing
her little short feather, a dreamy smile came on her
face. Seals swam through the green waters of her
mind. Mrs. Finkel passed and repassed in careless
loveliness. Mrs. Gampish said austerely, Too earnest,
my child, too earnest. The ghost of the mimosa tree
drifted, drifted. Salt Lake City, she thought fondly
. . . and then . . . where? . . . anticipation . . . a delicious fear . . . an unfamiliar pleasure.

Mrs. Golightly was moving out of the class for
beginners. She is much more skilful now (How agile
and confiding are her eyelashes!) and when her husband says, There's going to be a Convention in
Mexico City (or Chilliwack or Trois Rivières), she
says with delight, Oh *Tom* . . . !

The Heritage

RINGUET[1] (b. 1895)

THE man stopped for a minute at the cross-roads in obvious embarrassment. He had to make a choice: to go right ahead along the highway and eventually get lost in the bush that was shimmering on the horizon in the heat of the day, or to turn to the left along the dusty road that wound around several hillocks where the land had been cleared and seemed to come to an end at the foot of a slope, crowned by a tuft of pine-trees sleeping in the sun. There was also, on the right hand guarding the cross-roads, a low house behind a row of maples, with one wall blistered all over with gaudy advertisements.

The man chose to climb the slope where there was welcome shade under the network of branches. He took it on an angle with a heavy tired lope; passing over the carpet of pine-needles, he came to a sandy rise beyond which the ground fell away.

His new suit and bright-coloured shirt revealed a good carriage and square shoulders. Outlined against the sky they looked a little like a strong wooden yoke made to carry burdens. He had set his pack down on the ground.

Under his eyes the landscape unfolded; perhaps in front of him was the very land he was looking for. Now that he had stopped, the shadow and the cool spring wind brought some relief, for the climb had made the sudden heat almost unbearable.

[1] Translated by Morna Scott Stoddart.

The land lay before him in long undulating folds. It fell away in a sharp descent; then after a few small valleys it took a plunge into a deep gorge, and up again on the other side; beyond, fold after fold, mounting and green, it rose until the last hill was too high for him to see over. He would have had to go far to the right to do that.

At the cross-roads, down below, a cock in the barn-yard began to sing out at the top of his voice, a triumphant song of satisfied love, a resounding song that poured his joy over his whole world, the earth, the sunlight, the spring day. For a moment it filled the wide countryside, then stopped, as if astonished at having accomplished nothing. For peace returned at once, unconquered, majestic, and final. The rustle in the branches, in the light breath that touched only the very tops of the pines, right up in the sky, seemed but a part of this silence.

On the veranda of the house a woman in a smock appeared for a moment; then almost at once she was joined by a man. Shading their eyes, they watched the man standing up on the little hill, filling the landscape with his unaccustomed presence. Then they disappeared.

Moving along the rise a little, the traveller noticed something: a grey bridge crossing the gorge. The river was certainly there. He picked up his pack and went down the hill. Before entering the store, he hesitated for a while; then, shrugging his shoulders, he pushed the door open. The woman in the smock slipped behind the greasy counter where a few candies and packets of chewing tobacco were offered for sale in a glass case.

'Can you tell me if the property of the late Baptiste Langelier is anywhere near here?'

'What?'

'They told me that the land belonging to the late Baptiste Langelier was somewhere around here.'

'Oh. Baptiste Langelier's land.'

'Ya, Baptiste Langelier's land.'

He had repeated what they said mechanically, like a man used to the ways of these simple folk.

'Well,' she continued, 'it's Baptiste Langelier's land you want to know about?'

He did not reply.

The woman disappeared behind a blanket heavy with dust hanging like a curtain over a doorway. After a minute a man came out. He looked at the stranger with an inquiring air.

The latter repeated again without any trace of impatience:

'I want to know where Baptiste Langelier's land is.'

'Baptiste Langelier? But he's dead. He's been dead some time.'

'Yes, I know. But his land?'

'All right, I'll tell you. Take the road on the left at the bottom of the hill. It's quite easy to find. It's the third place after the fork in the road.'

'Fine. Thanks very much.'

When he was away down the road, the man and the woman were still at the window behind the curtain.

'Perhaps it's really him,' said the woman.

'Looks like it is,' replied the man.

It was him all right.

When old Baptiste Langelier died suddenly, in February, everyone had been wondering who would inherit his property, for he was a bachelor and had no relatives, as far as they knew, either in the township or farther afield. For some time no-one had heard a word. Then somebody from Saint-Alphonse turned up who had seen the heir; and the news came that there actually was an heir, a city fellow called Langelier too. A cousin, perhaps.

Better than that! Little by little the story came out: this new fellow was the old man's son, sure enough. But the old man had never been married, they whispered. The son of a woman Baptiste had married twenty-five years before, other people stated quite definitely. They even went into details: she was a Montreal woman, and he had only lived with her a few weeks while he was working on munitions in 1916. The only fact that everyone agreed on was that the child had been brought up by the nuns as if he were an orphan or a bastard.

Whatever was the truth of it, Albert Langelier moved in. He took possession of the house; he had the key. He took possession of the farm-buildings, sure of himself, as owner of the property. He took possession of the farm as if he did not understand anything about it at all, with a hesitating, uncertain air. And the very first day he flung open all the windows, even in the parlour.

For a few days the neighbours were worried and friendly. After all! Seeing that the house was empty, they had made a point of going and having a look at it at night, and if old Langelier had returned he would have had to look a long time for a number of things that were certainly not in their usual places.

For some time the Vadenais never dared to use their tobacco cutter, and Ma Caron, the woman in the corner house, kept the big soap-kettle hidden in the cellar.

Another neighbour, Langlois, arrived with a broad

grin, bringing back the manure-spreader; he had been keeping it in his barn in case it should get stolen.

In the same way an old horse came back, also two cows and a pig which thoughtful souls had sheltered so that they would not die of cold and hunger. That had cost them something in feed. The new-comer frowned, but he never argued; he paid up. It seemed a bit queer to him.

As for the chickens, they must have been eaten by foxes for nobody could tell what had become of them.

At Grands-Pins the land is poor and no good for ordinary farming, so for a long time it was almost abandoned. It was only when they began to plant tobacco that people came and settled there, people as poor as the land itself. In hardship and poverty at first, and then a little more easily, tobacco-growing will keep families alive even at Grands-Pins.

Old Langelier had been one of the first to try it. As he was no longer young and expected only a few years of peace as the reward of his toil, he had not had to spend a great deal. He had built quite a good dryer, the usual square building with two ovens heated from outside. He contented himself with a few thousand seedlings which he had grown from seed indoors on his old iron stove during the dead days of February. But when the time came to set them out he had paid a neighbour's boy or a passing labourer for a few days' work. He did the same in the busy cutting season.

He was proud of his tobacco, a strain he had pre-served for years. Jealously he collected his seeds. Like everyone else, he covered seven or eight plants and let them come to maturity tied up in paper bags. But he had his own ideas. For instance he would never gather the seeds except when there was an east wind.

In the kitchen Albert Langelier found the long boxes for the seedlings, but they were all dead. There was nothing left but dusty powdered earth, dead earth, with a few withered threads—all that was left of the old man's famous strain.

Winter had rusted the stove, and around it were lying a lot of empty cans; he gave them a kick and brought in his own cans, full ones.

Coming in at the back door, the usual entrance, you went through the kitchen into a sort of parlour with nothing in it but two horse-hair chairs that were losing their stuffing and a rickety sideboard. An old calendar on the wall still showed the February page, the one the old man had been unable to tear off.

Of the two bedrooms upstairs, Albert chose the smaller where it was not so dark. The old man must have slept there, for on the bed there was a crumpled sheet and, dragging on the floor in the dust, a dirty blanket. The new-comer thought he might feel more at home in this room where evidently someone had lived before him.

Absent-mindedly he rummaged through the furniture, opening the dresser drawers one by one. A big pine cupboard occupied all one wall. He glanced in it: a broken glass, a crust of mouldy bread, and under the cobwebs in the corner, an old number of the People's Almanac. There was a bit of rag too with which he wiped the shelves before stowing his gear away. Then he saw sticking out of a crack a piece of paper. He took it out and began to read it. It was a fragment of a letter:

'. . . at Montreal, I couldn't see you. I was staying

with friends. But I would have liked to, because I needed to see you. I should have listened to you and done like Violette, instead of going off like that. But if you will keep your promise, it'll be all right. I have been to the Sisters to see . . .'

The letter was torn here:

'not too bad. But I managed to buy . . .'

'pants, and a cap . . .'

'make sense . . .'

He looked at the back, but the damp had made the ink run and he could not make out the words.

Sitting on the foot of the bed with the letter in his hands he read it again and began to wonder. Was it talking about him, of the child he had been, the poor child, shut up in an orphanage, the only place he could remember from his childhood?

He could not recall ever having seen his mother; and the Sisters had made a point of telling him that she had made no provision for him, that the convent got nothing from anyone to pay for his keep.

He glanced at the paper again, then threw it on the ground in the bachelor's careless way. But no, he must not do that, for this was his house. His house. He slipped the paper into his shirt-pocket.

What was the good of wondering? Why call up ghosts from the past when he would never even know their faces? Just before, he had instinctively looked for some photograph on the parlour walls that might show him his father's features. From this father he had received only two gifts, but they were remarkable ones: first life itself, but a life that no-one welcomed. As soon as he had realized this, it had hurt him, hurt him so much that he had never started a life of his own, a real life, the product of his own hands, faltering at first perhaps, but gaining confidence and going ahead. The second gift was this unexpected heritage. At first he had refused to believe in it, so convinced was he of his own incurable bad luck. He heard of it in the middle of the off-season when he was out of work, waiting for the ice to go out and navigation to start so that he could go back to his job as a longshoreman. Every year was the same: he would earn big wages in the summer but spend them all as he got them; every fall would find him gazing out at the last liner going down the river before the freeze-up, and all he would have in his pocket would be his last week's pay.

When he inherited eight hundred dollars in a lump sum in the month of March, he thought he was a rich man; he had also been left a farm somewhere, at Grands-Pins, away at the back of beyond. That was the silly part of it. He would certainly never see that farm.

In a day or two he had gone through a hundred dollars and never regretted it. It was a wonderful noisy celebration, and the memory of it would last him the rest of his life. Then a friend offered him a chance to go in with him and another man in a bootlegging venture where all they needed was a bit of capital to buy their raw materials. After that there would be big money to burn. A piece of cake!

The very minute they began to make a bit, the police came down on them and their distiller was caught in the act.

Then Albert thought of the farm at Grands-Pins. It was so far off. Nobody would ever find him there, at the world's end. He would take refuge there from the police.

All he had to do was to live, to earn his living, like everyone else. That should not be so difficult; and since these country folk made a go of it, surely he could do as much, a bright town boy like him. 'Nobody's fool,' they called him. In this way his father, whom he had never known, had become a sort of Providence to him, intervening in the nick of time, to be regarded henceforward with almost religious gratitude.

Also he still felt he was well-off.

Of his inheritance he had nearly three hundred dollars left, which he had not had time to gamble away or squander. He had never had so much money all at once; he often touched his belt where his little roll of bills made a comforting lump.

His confidence failed him, however, in these unfamiliar fields. There was something sly about the land that muffled his footsteps; something mysterious in the bush that shrouded the river; something disturbing in the space all around that seemed to leave him isolated. To regain confidence, he endeavoured to work his land, the most tangible part of his property.

He bought seedlings from the neighbours and listened to their lengthy explanations with the expression of a man who knows more than he seems to. On the third day he was out in the fields with the horse harnessed up when he glanced back towards the house and saw someone looking in his direction. For a moment his heart was in his mouth. But no, it was all right; it was only a woman. A woman?

'Hi!' she called.

'Hi!' he replied.

He stopped the horse and climbed up towards the house while the woman came slowly down to meet him. She waited, leaning on the fence.

'Good day. I'm Butch.'

'Good day.'

'I came to tell you that when the old man was alive I used to clean up for him every morning.'

'Oh.'

'Ya, I did up the house for him. Swept the place, washed the dishes, did the washing. He used to give me two dollars a month.'

'All right.'

Puzzled, Albert looked at Butch.

For him there were only two varieties: tarts and good women. The first class wore silk stockings and lipstick and advertised their curves; you could pick them up; they knew the answers and could laugh and chatter and join in a rowdy good time on pay-days. But good women were devoted to their homes, their children, their housekeeping, their husbands; they only went out on Sundays, to church; they never drank liquor.

This was a very simple classification. But the girl in front of him did not fall into either class. She had the youth and the smiling face of the first class, and her figure was slimmer than country folk like to see as a rule. But her lips were unpainted, and looked pale; her hair was left as Nature made it and her legs were covered with common cotton stockings.

'Who did you say you were?'

'I told you. I'm Butch.'

'Butch what?'

She looked at him in surprise. Wasn't Butch enough?

'I live at the Vaillancourts', the third house down there, the green house.'

'Then Vaillancourt is your—'

'No. He's no relation. They took me in when I was little.'

'Your parents, where did they come from?'

'My parents?'

She shrugged her shoulders in astonishment. It was so long since anyone had asked her such a question.

'I just live with the Vaillancourts. My name's Saint-Ange. Marie Saint-Ange. But they all call me Butch.'

'All right. Now listen, Marie. If you'll do the same for me as you did for the old man, I'll give you your two dollars a month. Perhaps more. You don't look too bad. You know your work.'

'Sure I do.'

'And then maybe you know something about tobacco.'

He was really teasing her, but she replied quite seriously: 'Sure I know all about tobacco. It's all that we grow hereabouts. I always help, especially at planting time.'

She had evidently not understood his insinuation. After all, he told himself, she's only a country girl.

He had been there a week when he had a visit from an agent selling farm-machinery, a big man with glasses. He seemed dull on first acquaintance, but he was actually a very keen business man.

He was used to dealing with country folk and had adapted himself to their ways. He spoke their language and understood their doubts. He would never have tried to dazzle them with a line that would only have made them suspicious. He was particularly careful never to mention money until the last moment, after he had examined—or pretended to examine—the land, the machinery, the tobacco seedlings.

But this time he knew he had a different sort of

customer to deal with. Above all he had smelled out a very rare thing: cash in the hand; and rarer still, cash ready to change hands.

Together they had checked what remained of Baptiste's gear: the old manure-spreader and an old-fashioned planter.

'It's unbelievable,' repeated the agent. 'It's unbelievable that old Langelier could have grown such good tobacco with old stuff like that, just a lot of old junk. The whole lot's hardly worth anything. Every year when I came in this direction I used to call and see him. He was a fine old fellow, a real good old Canadian type—but old-fashioned, you know, very old-fashioned. I was sorry for him.'

'Sure thing. You were sorry you couldn't sell him.'

'Well, after all, that's my job. But there was something else.'

He looked mysterious, and stared around as if every plant had grown ears. Yet the highway was deserted; the only living things in all the countryside were the busy black starlings over the fields; the air was full of the strange heaviness that comes in spring from the pregnant earth and acts like a tonic on the farmer's muscles.

'Sure, there was something else. Do you know that the people here were always jealous of old Langelier?'

'Jealous? Why would they be? He never did anybody any harm, I shouldn't think.'

'Lord no. But I was going to tell you. Old Langelier's tobacco, his own tobacco, was not ordinary stuff. I've been around tobacco-farms for twenty years and I've seen a lot of tobacco, good and not so good: big red and little red and little blue; comstock

and cannelle. But never tobacco like old Langelier's. . . .'

He gave a whistle between his dingy teeth.

'He got a good price for it?' asked Albert.

'My boy, you've hit the nail on the head. If the old
man had wanted, he could have been rich in a few
years, but he wouldn't change his ways. He stuck
with his old machinery. You should have seen his
cutter, for example. It tore up the plants, it was just
a crime. It just spoiled them for sale. But he did
leave you something, didn't he? Something
good . . . ?'

He lowered his voice to a thrilling whisper.

'. . . the seed . . . of his own tobacco.'

By now they had come to the end of the field
where the slope fell sharply away among the wild
raspberry-bushes and the tiger-lilies by the stream
until it came right down to the river.

'If you want to make some money, and I mean *big*
money, you've got to have good tools. You know
that. You come from the city. The big manufac-
turers are the ones who've got the best tools, the
newest machines, aren't they? Whatever they cost
they save you money, if only in saving time—they
pay for themselves.'

In short he talked Albert into buying all he needed
in modern machinery. The terms were easy: a hundred dollars cash and the balance later.

The seedlings were coming along well. On the
agent's advice, and because he was handy with tools,
he had made a hot-bed. He spent happy days there
in the warm spring sun, and felt himself unfolding
like the tender shoots of his seedlings. He marvelled
at them as they grew, as he watched the tiny green
dots swelling, scarcely able to believe that they would

turn into leaves, broad leaves spreading like a generous hand.

Sometimes when he was up on the hillside mending his fences along the slope by the black fir-trees, he would raise his head and see a big dark cloud on the horizon. Then he would rush home to the hotbed and lift the frame to give the seedlings air, terrified that they might be stifling before the storm.

He was still a city man and there were some things he could not get over. One was his continual astonishment when faced by Nature's little tricks both beneficial and dangerous: the obstinate warfare of the weeds; the storms, where the drumroll of the thunder drowned out the voice of the wind; the hail, whose sharp crackle he learned to dislike when he realized the danger it could be to future harvests. The other thing that was new to him was his conception of the immensity of the land where his shadow covered only an infinitely small part, even when the setting sun lengthened it and made it a flat black giant on the ground.

He had kept the city man's habit of late rising. Of course he was up by six o'clock, but every time it was a new sensation to find himself about at such an hour, and especially to feel so free, so full of vigour and get-up-and-go. On the other hand he was always astonished to see his neighbours already at work before him in the soft clear light of the morning.

About nine o'clock Butch would come along. He was eager for company so he used to watch for her coming and go up to the house as soon as she went in.

'Say, Marie, have you seen my spade?'

She would jump when she heard the name she had almost forgotten, which he insisted on using.

'Now don't tell me you've forgotten something

else. In any case, since you're here, d'ya want me to make you some coffee? Did you have any breakfast?'

'I had something this morning.'

'All right. You come back in a minute or two and I'll give you something hot.'

She began to suspect that all this forgetfulness was really inspired by hunger. What surprised her even more was that he was so well-behaved, not bold at all. She started every time he appeared, imagining that she would feel two arms around her waist and have to put up a little self-defence. After all, the old fellow had been bad enough! But no. Monsieur Albert, as she still called him to the great amusement of the neighbours, had something else on his mind. He scarcely even called to her to say 'Goodnight' when his day's work was over and he was sitting on the veranda, smoking his pipe and playing with his dog. For he had adopted a dog. And what a dog!

He had found it one morning at the door, panting, filthy, full of fleas. And simply reeking of skunk as a final touch. Where had he come from? Probably from a long way off. It was easy to reconstruct the 'tragedy'. He must have chased one of these evil-smelling creatures and met the usual defence. One jet and the dog had fled away like a crazy thing, suffocating, seeking to rid himself of the intolerable stink clinging to his coat; rolling in the mud, dashing into the water, and never escaping from the shameful smell.

Albert had to chase him away, the odour was so appalling. The poor beast took refuge in the ravine, by the stream, spending hours in a pool trying to get clean and always returning to the house. So in the end they fed him, and at last accepted him.

The man, who had never had anything to do with animals, got on with this one, which seemed so strange to him that he tried to explain it to Butch, the only person he ever had a chance to talk to.

'The country's funny, all the same. Yes, it's queer how people can change.'

'Sure, you can't be the same on the land as you are in the city.'

'You said it. Who ever would have thought I'd have a dog. And he's not even a good-looking one.'

'That's true. He's not very good-looking.'

'No, he's not. But all the same, he's not dumb. In the evening, when I sit and have a smoke on the veranda, I talk to him. People need somebody to talk to.'

Butch was busy hanging out the washing which she had just finished bleaching; filling the line that stretched between the back shed and a young willow-tree, bending over the old basket to pick up the clothes, then holding them at arm's length like a flag while she put in the clothes-pins she took from her apron pocket.

She was standing with the sun behind her, out-lining her silhouette on the white sheet and making a halo of her hair stirring in the wind—a somewhat indiscreet sun, revealing her slender legs in her flimsy skirts.

Albert watched her for a minute, a wisecrack on his lips, but all he said was: 'Yes sir. I talk to my dog. I tell him about the city and I talk about myself, too. I wouldn't say he understands me, but he looks as if he does.'

'It must be lonely sometimes, though, even now you've got him.'

'Sometimes, but I'm getting used to it.'

'It's no life for a man, alone on a farm like that.' But she said that without any intention.

'Well, I'm not sure if I'll stay on the land. If things go all right I guess I'll wait a bit and sell it when the time comes.'

'Sell your land? Well, I suppose there are some people nowadays who would sell their land.'

However, he was beginning to adapt himself to his strange new life. He found his greatest satisfaction in proving to these country folk that a city fellow could farm. After all, he had got the salesman to explain his machinery, and he remembered all he had said. On the few occasions when he had gone visiting he had listened to every word about the land or tobacco-growing or the next job to be done on the farm.

What gave him most pleasure was the very irregularity of his life. Sometimes he had a holiday because of the rain; sometimes he was forced to work from early morning until late at night, especially at transplanting time. Then it really was tough.

He had hired one man, also Butch, for he knew she was strong and could stick at it; in fact she was one of the very few women in the district who could plant all day long with the men.

He spent three anxious days in the driver's seat with his back up against the water-tank warmed by the sun. Behind him, on two little seats, level with the earth, Jeremy Beland and Butch sat holding the boxes of seedlings on their knees. The blades in front would open up the furrow; they would set out a seedling, and hold it barely a second; there would be a mouthful of water for it from the tank, and then the blades behind would cover the furrow. They had to work fast and it was a back-breaking job. But in this way they planted twelve hundred seedlings the first day, fourteen hundred the second, and six hundred the third day before the rain came.

It had all been done so quickly. Yet he had felt strangely awkward. He had to keep his eyes on the horses so as to guide them straight ahead with the two planting behind. They were all keen workers and did not have much to say, but from the beginning, Jeremy let fall a few teasing remarks in his coarse but friendly way, and Butch had retorted without the slightest shyness.

Then the sun climbed high in the sky, stupefying them with its burning breath. Their actions became mechanical. From time to time the planters stole a mouthful of water intended for the seedlings and drank it from the palm of the hand with the sticky earth still clinging to it.

They took time off at midday after their lunch down by the river, which under the crushing noonday heat looked like a stream of molten tin. Albert suggested bathing, and the other man, who had at first refused, surprised at such an idea or perhaps intending to make up to Butch, finally followed him down to the waterside. They slipped into the stream among the reeds, and the glassy light shone on their hard, tough, masculine bodies. As for Butch, she was sleeping soundly.

But when the last day came, before the storm broke, it became very oppressive. They felt it blowing up and hurried with the planting. The sky was so heavy that the drops of sweat fell like rain in the furrow. And, doubtless spurred on by the electricity in the air, Jeremy started teasing the girl again and touching her knees whenever her hands were occupied.

In front of them Albert's back became strangely stiff and tense.

Several days later he noticed a cut on Butch's forehead.

'Say, Marie, have you been in a fight?'

She went on working without a word.

'I bet you've been celebrating. What on earth's that?'

'It's nothing,' she said in a quiet grey voice. He felt that something queer was going on.

'Did you fall over something?'

This time she turned and looked straight at him with her big heavy eyes.

'No, I didn't fall down. It was Jean-Jacques that did this to me.'

'Jean-Jacques?'

'Sure. One of the Vaillancourt boys, the one who's about sixteen.'

'What got into him? Is he crazy?'

'We were wrestling around.'

'Tell me about it.'

He insisted, more to keep up a conversation than out of curiosity. It came to him every now and then: he had need of human contact; he was tired of being eternally alone with Nature's chilly silence.

'So you were wrestling around,' he repeated. 'I think your Jean-Jacques is an up-and-coming young fellow. You seem to like your boy-friends young.'

'He's not my boy-friend. He's a bad lot. He chucked a cup at my head. He could have killed me.'

'What had you been doing to him?'

'He started it. I wouldn't let him kiss me in the

milk-house yesterday, so he said some awful things to me. I never did anyone any harm. I don't want anything, except to be left alone. To get his own back he said I had let the calf out into the tobacco on purpose. And when I said it was him who let it out, and that somebody else had seen him do it, he started pushing me around. And he called me names.'

'What did he call you?'

She had never talked about herself like this; she had learned to keep her troubles to herself, throwing them one by one into a great heap in some dark corner of her memory, so dark that they could not be seen or felt very often. Now Albert's questions opened up a window on this dark corner, and the whole heap of her troubles came into full view, welling up in her eyes and burning in her heart.

'What did he say to you, Marie?'

'He called me such names. Said I was no good, that I didn't have any parents.'

'Oh. What did you say?'

'I never said anything.'

They stopped talking. Marie turned to the stove where the peas were cooking for the soup. But he heard her give a little whimper now and then. At this moment the dog woke up, stretched, and yawned, showing his bright pink tongue, his black palate, and his gleaming white teeth.

'Come here, Patira.'

'Why do you call him Patira?'

'Why? I'll tell you, Marie. It's a name I saw in a book.'

'You've been reading a book?'

'Yes. I found it on a bench somewhere. There was an unlucky fellow in it, like me. He was called

Patira. He was always in trouble. That dog, when I found him, was all alone; no father or mother. So I called him Patira.'

'But this Patira's different. He's lucky enough now!'

'Maybe. What do you think, fellow? Not bad just now, is it? If only it lasts. But if you're anything like me, you'll have no luck at all.'

Marie looked at him and felt something stirring within her, something warm and gentle, a feeling of brotherhood. She patted the dog's head, and said: 'Good dog.'

And now a long dry spell came down upon the earth. The sky was constant and cruel in its splendour. Every evening a giant sun crashed down upon a horizon in flames that foretold another killing day to follow.

All day long thousands of crickets made one single shrill clamour that never stopped; it began in the morning and was never hushed until late at night, under the soft naked light of the stars. The heat, beating on the fields, bore down with all its enormous, invisible weight to crush the man's feeble harvest.

At first the streams went on running, with their careless, happy song, trusting that rain would soon come and fill up the rocky bed. Then their morning music grew fainter, until it was nothing but a murmur. Where there had been shallow pools, there were only scabrous patches that showed more cracks every day.

At first the tobacco had flourished in the burning heat; the roots went deeper and deeper and still found the water in the subsoil. Then the heat dug into the sandy ground, drying it up a little more every day. The seedlings struggled, sending out their tiny rootlets, seeking the moisture that they felt was there. Soon there was nothing to find, nothing but a hard-baked crust crumbling gradually to dust.

Then the stems weakened, and the leaves; their green had gone and their edges were curling. Every day they drooped a little more, weary, desperate, dying.

At first the country folk had waited; then they fought back. Out in the fields at daybreak they filled their buckets at the river, and measured out a mouthful of water for each plant that vanished at once as if poured through a sieve. But the sun rose high in the sky and got ahead of them. No sooner had the water touched the soil than it straightway evaporated and rushed up towards the sun. The whole family kept at it in a feverish burst of speed; then, when high noon was unmistakably triumphant, the farmer would stand still in the middle of his field, raising his sweaty brow to the copper sky, scanning the weather, looking for the smallest breath of wind that might turn to the south-east.

Sometimes the very air seemed thick, saturated with the moisture that the thirsty earth was craving; it steamed like a cauldron. One cloud appeared on the horizon, vague and small at first, but soon swallowing up the blue. Then the farmers came out of their houses, men, women, and children, gazing towards the promised storm, watching it spreading its wings like some great bird in the sky, hoping it would alight on them and on their harvest. The rainclouds would stream out on the horizon, but alas elsewhere, always elsewhere. At the last minute would come the saving rain, just when the dying earth expected no reprieve, a real downpour, but never at Grands-Pins—away over at Saint-Sulpice where the land was not so poor and not in such desperate need.

Albert gave up and enjoyed the pleasures of idleness. At first, like the rest, he had tried to save his crop, hauling to his fields under the hammer-blows of the sun the water that the heavens refused, but later he abandoned the effort. The neighbours had six, eight, ten in family; he was alone.

More than that, he was disillusioned, filled with a calm, definite distaste born of his inability to do anything at all. Now he began to realize that nature was not simple, but a book he could not read.

At first he had innocently imagined that a bright boy from the city could win out without any difficulty if these *habitants* could get ahead. All he knew of them was their calm and rather stupid-looking faces. Now he saw that the man of the fields must know more things, and more difficult things, than the man of the factory; and that he must also know how to be much more patient, more ingenious, more responsible.

Then insidiously there arose in the township a wicked wind; and over the minds of its inhabitants another sort of wind, in its effects like the one that tore up the weakened seedlings where their withered roots could not keep them anchored in the soil.

Albert had told some of them that he had never had any luck; others disliked him—distant cousins of old Baptiste who had hoped to inherit; two especially who had almost had the land staked out or bought for next to nothing.

They decided that Albert was a Jonah. The long

drought was his fault. Where had he come from? And that absurd belief in magic, never far below the surface in the country, that sleeps in the dark ravines and the secret woods and the suspicious hearts of men, appeared, as always in time of disaster. They had prayed with no result. They had sung the special service against drought, they had paid for one mass after another, with no result. There must be something standing in the way since such remedies had proved useless. And despair turned man into what he was long ago, in the distant ages: a scared and spiteful animal, ready to run and hide or to bite.

The fiendish beauty of the sky seemed to have withered all joy in their hearts. Usually simple, kindly folk, quick to joking rather than anger, they felt their spirits growing heavier with each storm that hung over their fields and never broke.

At first they showed their feelings merely by an awkward, suspicious attitude. Albert, who did not know these people, felt more and more a stranger in their midst. They still said 'Good-morning' to him when they met on the roads, but if he turned round after passing a group of farmers, he found they were staring at him and whispering.

It was Butch who explained it to him.

One morning she never turned up. When he came back from the fields where he had been languidly trying to minister to his dying plants, he found neither the girl nor the coffee that she always had waiting for him at that time of day.

She did not appear until the next day, when she served his meal in a brooding silence.

'I don't think I can come back any more, Monsieur Albert,' she said.

'Why not, Marie?'

'I just can't come.'

'You're not sick, are you?'

'No, I'm not sick.'

'Well then . . . ?'

She began washing the dishes with her back to him; he could see only her shoulders bending over the dish-pan and the big yellow bun of her hair and the golden down on the back of her neck. He forgot himself for a moment, just looking at her. He had been alone so long. Then he came back to the present, to the immediate problem.

'Why don't you want to come back? Don't I pay you enough?'

'It's not that. It gives me a bit of money . . . it's all I get, for the Vaillancourts don't give me any. I just work for my board and lodging.'

'Then what is it?'

This time she turned round, her eyes misty. He scarcely recognized her face, and for the first time he realized, now that the brightness was gone, how bright and lovely her smile had been.

'They're bad people, Monsieur Albert. Bad people, I tell you. They say . . . they say—'

'What do they say?'

'They say you're unlucky, that you've brought your bad luck with you into the parish. They say . . . they say it won't rain until you've gone away.'

'So that's it. Yes. . . .'

Through the open door Patira came in and lay down at his master's feet. Albert bent down and patted him mechanically:

'Good dog. Good dog.'

'Then the Vaillancourts say I had no business coming here.'

Outside the terrifying song of triumph from the crickets was announcing another day of heat, another day of defeat.

'There's not much sense to that,' replied Albert. Then he laughed, but it was a laugh on the surface, like a ripple on a bottomless lake.

'I know I've never been lucky. But Marie, it doesn't make sense, does it?'

Butch hesitated; she started fussing with her wash-rag so as not to look at him in the face. 'I don't know. Really, I don't know. But all the same, there's something queer about weather like this. Nobody's ever seen anything like it. You never know.'

It went on for a few days more. The neighbours began stripping the plants that still survived—hard work, where all day long you are bent over, picking off the useless shoots that prevent the good leaves from growing and spreading out.

But when Albert went looking for helpers, he found none. Some replied that they had jobs already; others just looked at him, and when he did not leave they turned their backs on him.

Then he had a letter from the salesman telling him a payment would have to be made on the machines he had bought. Yet when he had signed, he had understood that he would not have to pay until after the harvest, after the crops had been sold, after he had collected his money, any time at all.

One evening, another evening when the air was like a sticky bitter paste, he felt that the end had come. He went down across the field where the yellowing stems stood in lines like withered offerings on tiny tombs. He went straight on down without looking where he was going, trampling the tobacco that rustled like silk beneath his feet.

At the bottom of the big ravine he watched the river gently sleeping, a very small river, with banks far too big for it. He stopped and ate a handful of raspberries mechanically. A blood-red sun was setting in a sea of mist. Its last rays were flaming on the meadows, not green as they should have been at that time of year, but quite yellow, ready for the torch. The air was clammy with humidity, and the sweat running down his brow was salty in his eyes. Patira stood panting beside him, and the thirsty earth drank in his saliva.

They climbed back to the house at dark, the master with his head high, the dog following to heel. They sat out on the porch until it was quite dark.

Then Albert lit his lantern. He went from room to room, closing each door behind him, drawing the blinds at every window. He made a bundle of his clothes, like the one he had brought with him, no bigger, no smaller. And when it was black night he went to bed. When he woke up, it felt as if he had not been to sleep at all; yet his watch said four o'clock in the morning.

Outside the night was ending, but there was no coolness in the morning air. He looked up at the sky, but there were no stars; the earth seemed strangely silent. What was wrong with the birds that they had stopped singing? There were a few beans left from the day before; he ate them cold, with a bit of bread and a mouthful of water.

Outside a vague pale light was glimmering in the east from below the overhanging clouds. He must be quick.

Patira was in his kennel near the door. Albert heard him stirring in his sleep, hesitated, but did not call him.

Steadily he walked to the shed, and came out carrying his axe. He looked around a moment, then went down towards the field and found himself among the tobacco plants. No, that was not the place!

He turned towards the stream where there was a hollow with green bushes in the shade. He whistled softly: a bark answered him.

When Patira reached his side, panting from his run, he struck him down with the axe, without a word, without a caress. Then he began to dig a deep hole. He did not shed a tear, but his lips were tightly closed. He threw the axe away, as far as he could, with all his strength.

Then he went back to the house, picked up his pack, and started off in the grey light of dawn.

And now, a few houses farther on, a shadow slipped out from behind a group of fir-trees. Butch must have seen him from the attic window. She had put a dress on, but her shoes were untied and her hair was loose down her back.

'Hullo. Is that you, Marie?'

'Where're you going like that?' She pointed at his swinging pack.

'Oh, sure, sure,' he said, feeling that she had guessed. 'I'm going back to the city. This is no place for me.'

He had begun to walk on. Butch hesitated a moment and then walked a few steps beside him.

'You don't mind, going off like this?'

He shrugged his shoulders and did not reply.

'I would have liked you to tell me first.'

'Why?' He tried to make a joke of it. 'Would you have gone with me?'

She stopped still a moment in silence; then she touched his shoulder gently and he too was still.

'Go with you? Go away with you?'

There was silence between them. Little noises were beginning in the Vaillancourts' house. She said softly, and the words welled up from within her like clear water from a spring: 'Perhaps. Yes. I would have gone with you . . . if you had wanted me.'

Then he looked at her, looked right at her, all of her. With eyes clearer than they had ever been before he looked, as if he had never seen her before that wretched morning: her clean mouth with its strange smile, her slender waist, the strong straight legs above her untied shoes. He felt that in all this countryside she was the only thing that was not a foreigner, the only friendly thing, the only thing that was precious to him although he had never suspected it. The only part of his possessions that he wanted to take away with him.

'All right. Are you coming?'

He saw her hesitate a moment, turning round and looking back at the house which was not her home although she had lived in it so long. He knew that if she turned back, even to go and fetch something, he would have to go on alone.

But she simply bent down and tied up her shoe-laces. Then she carefully twisted her long hair into a knot on the nape of her neck.

They set off.

They halted for the first time quite a way along the road. They had been walking almost an hour and had reached the summit of the long slope. They stopped for a while to take breath. Albert was standing, looking away to the east. She was sitting on the sand, at the side of the road.

Mechanically and with some difficulty she traced with her finger in the sand: ALBERT, BUTCH.

He looked down at what she was doing and she blushed. Then gently with his foot he rubbed out BUTCH and bending down wrote MARIE.

They got up again.

Through a hole in the mass of cloud a ray of sunlight came down on them. They looked towards the west far away. Above Grands-Pins there was a grey bank of clouds heavy with kindly rain, and in the slanting sunbeams they could see the long dark streaks of the downpour.

'See, Marie? They've got their rain!'

She added, almost in a whisper: 'They've got their rain . . . now that you're gone.'

'Yes,' said Albert steadily. 'And we've got the sunshine.'

Mist-Green Oats

RAYMOND KNISTER (1900–32)

IT was not until after he arrived home from taking his mother to the railway station that he began to realize how tired he had become. 'Now, don't work too hard while I'm away, Len,' had been her last words on kissing him, and before he left the train. While he was riding slowly homeward his thoughts had been busy hopping from one detail to another of the morning's activities: of his coming up from the field at eleven o'clock and stabling the horses, of

the bustlings of last-minute preparations, carrying
the grips out and expostulating with his mother as
she stood before the mirror straight and young-
looking in her travelling-dress, of the stirring numbers of people about the station and the platform
waiting and staring, who made him conscious of his
Sunday coat, overalls, and heavy shoes. And his
mind had leaped on ahead of her to his cousins
whom she would see, and what he thought to be
their life in the remote city, as he pictured it from
the two or three holidays he had passed there in the
course of his childhood.

In the lane at the end of the barn when he arrived
home his father was hitching his three-horse team
together, square-framed and alike in size; and throwing a word now and then to Syd Allrow who was sitting hunched on the handles of his plough which
lay on the ground behind his team of blacks. The
boy nodded to Syd, and his father, seeing his look
of surprise, said hurriedly, 'Syd's helping us a day
or two. Thought I'd get an early start. Go right on
in now, and have dinner. We'll be back in the apple
orchard when you come.'

The boy began to notice as he had not before that
his father's face had become a little thin and bitten
of apparently new wrinkles. The acute stridor of
haste and the spring work, the heavy anxiety, the
lack of help—he turned away when his father hastily
came around to that side of the team. Walking toward the house he heard Syd make some inertly
voiced remark or query.

The victuals were cold, but his dinner was awaiting him on the table in the kitchen. When a few
minutes later he began to take the dishes away he
left off abruptly, remembering that he should have

time for such tasks in the evening, when the work outside was done. Then he recommenced and finished clearing the table, for Syd would be there, they would be hungry and wish to have supper as soon as possible after coming from the field.

As he moved about he was not oppressed now by a sense of haste, by a fear, almost, of something unknown threatening their determination which yet chivied and lured the men of farms through those on-treading days of late spring. The season had been retarded by late frosts and heavy rains at seeding time, and the later work, corn-planting and ploughing, must be done quickly before the soil became intractable. Such conjunctures, with their own necessity, were at the source of what might in certain types of men evolve as a race against time as much for the sake of the race as for the prefigured prize. He mused.

This released sense must have come from the variation in the plan of the day. At this hour of the afternoon he was used to be in the field, or choring about the barn. Alone in the house Len Brinder's movements became slower as he made the turn from kitchen to pantry and back again. His mind went to the city toward which his mother was now speeding, where the streets and buildings and the spirit of them, which every one of the crowds about him seemed in a way to share, were wonderful from a distance of two years. It was impossible that the spirit and the crowds could mean anything but life rendered into different terms, understandable and entrancing. Everyone appeared to be full of active keenness, a beauty, and, for all it was deceptive, no one appeared to work. Automatically he continued moving the dishes about.

His father and Syd were both finishing a round when he arrived at the end of the apple-orchard. The horses of their teams were already beginning to show wet about their flanks, despite their hardened condition. As they came toward him the heads of his father's three horses, which were pulling a two-furrow plough, bobbed unevenly, and their loud breaths produced a further and audible discord. The noses of Syd's black team were drawn into their breasts, for they were pulling a walking-plough and the reins passed around their driver's back. There was little wind among the big mushroom-shaped apple-trees.

'Well,' said Sam Brinder from his seat, 'Syd's finishing the lands for me. Do you want to strike them out? It will be pretty hard around those old trunks, though.'

The boy did want to—'Not much difference, is there?'—and at once turned his team into line. The absence of his father's accustomed brusque unconsciousness struck him readily enough as a blandness affected for the benefit of the neighbour.

The hardness of the ground astonished him. He wondered how he could have thought of anything else since leaving his plough in the morning. He was obliged to hold the handles at a wearying angle in going around the trunks of the big trees, and to twist it back to a normal position in the space between. White dust like a smoke burst forth from between the ground and the fresh soil falling heavy upon it. All along the orchard the spurting dust preceded him, thin portions rising with a little wisp of breeze about his face. When he reached the end of the long furrow he was almost panting from the wrestle. 'This is going to be hard on horses,' he said to himself. 'The hottest day yet.' The ground seemed to have become petrified since the day before. 'I'll have to rest them oftener now, just after dinner. Later on we can go,' he thought, as he turned again for the return on the other side of the trees.

It was necessary to plough two furrows around each row of trees before the big plough could be used. As the end of the orchard was reached each time the ground seemed harder and the boy's arms more stretched and tired. As the time passed, the horses began to give signs of the strain. One of them would put his head down and make a forward rush, straightening the doubletree, while his mate seemed to hang back—then the other in turn dashed ahead, leaving his mate behind.

'Straighten 'em up there. Make 'em behave!' his father called from the riding-plough, and banished Len's own vexation with the team. He tried but languidly to bring it under control, while he thought, 'It's the ground. The horses are all right. They're willing enough.' Nothing could be more willing than a horse. He'd go until he dropped if the driver hadn't sense enough to pull him up, to keep him from foundering himself. It was the cursed soil. The ploughing shouldn't have been put off so long. It needn't have been. Why couldn't they have left some of the manure-hauling, some of the pruning, and done this first? And other people were able to get men on some terms, why couldn't his father? Then, why must he take such a busy time as last week had been to go to the city to see about the mortgage? These questions were like arrows pointing a centre in his thoughts: the feeling of being ill-used. Bad management was to blame, but he could not, yet, hold his father responsible, whom circumstances seemed to have rendered powerless. The boy's hat was sticking to his brow as though clamped there with some iron band driven down like hoops on a barrel.

Sam Brinder and Syd were talking at the end of the field. What did they have so important to talk about? They had been at the same spot when he started back from the other end. He didn't rest his horses that much. He was too interested in getting the work done to be so determined to take part in a confab. He would show them what he thought. He'd not give his horses half as much rest as they gave theirs. That would shame them, maybe, the lazy—'Ned! Dick! Get up here, you old—'

Tight-throated in the dust, wrestling bitterly with the stony soil, he went up and down the rows. These thoughts lasted him a long time and he forgot everything about him except the wrenching heavy plough and the rhythmic swinging singletrees and the creaking harness. Time and the sun seemed to stand still, breathless.

They started on again with a jerk when an hour later he heard his father hailing him through the trees.

'Go up and get us a pail of water,' Sam Brinder called. 'Your horses can stand the rest anyway, I guess.'

'Well, I'm not thirsty, but if you are, of course—'

'We've been back here longer than you have, remember,' his father added.

The boy looked at him, wrapped the lines about the plough-handles and went up the lane toward the well. Walking was queer alone now; easier, perhaps? It almost seemed to be done automatically, his body leaning slightly forward.

He went to the house, and brought the pail back to the well, drank slowly and gratefully of the cold water. . . .

He was walking down the lane at a moderate, stooped shouldered pace. The light summer clothes hung about his gaunt form. Well, the afternoon was going. Four o'clock when he had left the house. It might be nearly half-past four by the time he got back to work. Well, no. Five, ten minutes had gone now. Not more than ten more would pass before he should have taken Syd and his father their drinks. Even at that—twenty minutes after four—the afternoon was going pretty well. . . . Syd would be for supper, of course. Kind of nice, they had been alone so much since his older sister had left them and gone into an office in the city. Could it be as hot as this in the city, where one might go into the ice-cream parlours and the movie theatres? Different it would be, anyway.

In the orchard the sunlight seemed to pack the heat down below the boughs and above the earth. The boughs seemed to hold it there, and to make room in some way for more heat, which the sun still packed down. His feet in the heavy shoes seemed to be broiling; the socks hung loose about his thin ankles and over the hard, unbendable uppers. The horses needed a rest, his father had said, eh? It was they who needed the rest! He'd give them rest enough, all right, from now on. At each end of the field. If his father didn't mind, why should he try to do more than his share?

'Well,' said Syd as he reached for the dipper, standing in the furrow and looking up at him, 'how you standing it?' At the unevadable reply, 'Oh, all right,' he added:

'Getting about enough of farming? I was that way myself for a while. Seems kinda hard work after going to high-school, I s'pose.'

That was like him! When it was almost a year since Len had left high-school. 'Oh, I'm used to it by now,' the boy replied coldly.

Syd mopped his face with a patterned handkerchief, spat, swung a line, and said, 'Well, I guess I'll have to be getting along. Boss'll be makin' the fur fly if I don't.' He smiled at the joke, as a farmer's son himself, and independent of the whims of bosses. 'So you're keeping batch now? I better not bother you for supper.'

'Yes, you're to stay for supper. There's no trouble about that. Yes, mother thought she'd take a rest before the canning came on. . . .' He added, 'Gone to the city,' with a smile he suddenly felt was meant to appear brave.

'Tchka! Bill! Sam! Get outa here!'

His father said: 'You'll have to go up a little earlier than us and get supper ready.'

Len made no reply. Assent he felt was too miserably unnecessary, and he stood looking in silence back of the plough.

'Not making much of a job,' said Brinder. 'I got to stand on it most of the time. You got to be quick and keep shifting the levers. You got to have 'er just so. Some job, all right!'

As he walked across the scarred and lumpy headland the boy made an effort to feel at odds with his father, and to conjure an image proper to the aim. He saw him, a clipped-moustached and almost spruce figure, going away from the house to attend perhaps a meeting of school-trustees, to raise his voice among the other men. Trying to find in his memory cue for

a critical attitude, Len began to wonder how he himself appeared to those about him, going through the
gestures of daily living.

What were people made of anyway, he reflected,
bitterly deprecatory—but extravagances, ludicrous
to everyone but themselves.

The sweat was caked in salt upon the flanks of his
horses when he got back to them. One horse's head
was held in a natural position; the other's back and
head were level, and its weight slouched on a hind leg.

Stiffly the three plodded on again. As one long
round after another was made, night almost seemed
to be getting farther away, rather than nearing
them. To lean back in the lines as he found himself
wanting to do and allow the ploughtails to pull him
along was impossible. The point would shoot up and
the plough slide along the ground until he could get
the horses stopped. In spite of him sometimes it did
this, when it struck a stone or when it came to a
packed area of ground, and then the boy had to drag
its weight back several feet into its former position;
shouting at the horses and pulling them back at the
same time.

But at each end of the field he gave the team a
long rest, sitting on the plough-handles as the
clumsy implement lay on its side. He dangled his
legs and moved his feet about in the heavy shoes.
The soles were burning. Looking at the wrinkled
tough leather, which seemed to form impenetrable
bumps, he noticed that the toe of the right shoe was
turned up on the outside with a seemingly im-
manent bend, given it by the slope of the furrow
which he had for days been following. Every day the
same! With the impressionableness of youth he
could not believe that there had ever been a time at

which he had not been tired out. Every day the same. The weariness of last night and of the night before, the same. But this day was far from spent yet. To-night as well as the usual chores there would be work in the house.

He looked for a long time across the wide pasture at the end of the orchard. Several cattle were on its gently raised surface. Their feet seemed to be above the fence on the lower ground beyond them, which could be seen at either side of the rise. The sky was clear and high, and it seemed to give the cattle a lightness which should make possible for them any feat. It looked as though they might with one fabulous jump easily clear the fence in the distance and be free. For what—free? They would break into the green oats or wet alfalfa and kill themselves. The boy sighed and raised the plough-handles again. Over in the midst of the trees sharp sweet notes of birdsong began to come, giving the place in his present mood a chilled look. The grass became pale before his eyes and the sunlight a little milder broke among the branches as among windy streaming snowflakes.

The horses pulled evenly now. They were going with a seemingly terrible swiftness. The boy staggered and strode along behind them, wrenching the plough as it threatened to jump to the surface. They found it easier, charging through so rapidly, or else they wanted to get each stint over as quickly as possible for the rest at the end of it. Stumbling and striding along behind, Len hated them. Boy and horses began to sweat more profusely. 'They always get that way about this time. It must be getting late.' The sun was shining in his eyes.

As he reached the end his father shouted across to him, and he stopped to undo the tugs.

It was when he reached the house that the desire came to him to take off his shoes. He seemed to have walked on lumpy plates of hot greasy iron for innumerable ages. He sat down and untied them slowly, and the mere loosening of the leathern laces made the feet ache relief. He walked about the cool kitchen oilcloth in his socks. Then a fancy struck him. He opened the screen-door and went out on the lawn. He shoved his feet along in the short grass and rubbed them against each other. Such immeasurable sweet pain he had never known. At first he could scarcely bear to raise his weary feet from the depth of the grass. Presently he would lift one at a time in a strange and heavy dance, for the pleasure it was of putting it down again among the cool soft blades. The lowering sun variegated the green of the different kinds of evergreen trees back of the house, of which he always confused the names. Something of beauty which, it seemed, must have been left out of it or which he had forgotten, appeared in the closing day. Something was changed, perhaps. He did not know how long he had been there, scrubbing his soles about like brushes in the grass, and regretfully hopping, until he remembered that the men would be coming in for their supper at any minute. Beginning to wonder whether anyone had witnessed his movements, he went into the house and re-laced his shoes.

The men were eating their supper. After they had washed their hands and faces outside of the back door, throwing each dirty basinful away with a dripping hiss into the light breeze, they entered the house. Syd sat very straight on a chair by the wall, with his arms folded, and looked at nothing in particular. His black shirt was still open at the neck. Sam Brinder bustled about helping Len to complete the preparations. 'Now, the eggs. How'll ye have the eggs, Syd?'

'Doesn't make any difference to me,' Syd gravely replied.

'Come, now, you've got to say.'

'No, sir. Have 'em how you like. You're the doctor.'

'Well, suppose we have them fried?'

Now, as they ate heartily, they said little, except to urge upon each other and accept or refuse more food. The room became warm and filled with the soft sounds of their eating and the steaming kettle on the stove. There was the humming of one or two flies about and between them recurrently. Presently a prolonged lowing was heard from back of the barn. 'Cows are coming up the lane of themselves,' said Brinder. 'We won't have to go after them. Pretty good, eh, Len?'

Then the two men began to speak of the crops and the comparative state of the work on the neighbouring farms.

'We're pretty well forward with our work,' said Syd, 'but there's more of us for the amount of land.' He referred to his two brothers who were at home. 'Still, you fellows are getting along pretty well. You're getting over the ground lately, all right.'

The significance came to Len of 'you fellows', making him angry and sad. A great partnership it was, he told himself, wherein his share consisted of unrequited work. Then he thought that Syd had meant to be flattering or condoling, and though he imagined that he should be vexed with him for that, he could not. The conversation was sliding on over well-worn topics, with the slight necessary variations.

The sun's rays were horizontal now, the raised window blind let them strike on the lower part of Syd's clean-shaven tan face. It was not every night that they had company, even in this fashion. The boy liked Syd, after all. It reminded him how, many years ago as it now seemed, Syd had known of a Hallowe'en prank which he with some of the high-school boys had played on one of the farmers thereabout. And he had never told. . . . The Hallowe'en joke had been to him, as much as anything else in his boy's world, a social due.

The three sat in the room which the flat rays from the window made to seem dusk-filled, and the two elder continued talking. Len moved his fork with the ends of his fingers, tilted his tea-cup, and thought, when he thought, and did not merely fill himself vaguely with a pleasant sense of Syd's identity, of the work to be done yet.

Presently they rose, and the boy remained in the house to do the washing-up while his father did the chores.

Slowly the dishes were assembled and slowly and thoroughly wiped. Unused to the work, he took a long time to finish it. Besides, he thought, there is only more work waiting outside. 'There's always work waiting outside on a farm,' he reflected. 'There'll be plenty of it right here when we're all dead. Wherever it's all getting us to—' But he saw some of the older farmers about him, and those who were not to that extent in neediness, still working as hard and during longer hours than anyone. They had come to like it. He envied and contemned them for that. There was so much of the world to see, so much of life to discover, to compare with what one might find in oneself! Suddenly Len was confident of this.

He went out into the dusk. Innumerable crickets joined voices to produce a trill. A wind was blowing and he sniffed it gratefully. 'As fresh—as fresh, as on the sea,' he muttered, slouching toward the barn. The cattle were in the yard, spotting the gloom. He could hear their windy, coughing sigh, which was at once contrasted with the drumming snort of a horse as he burrowed about in the hay of his manger. The closed stable was loud with the grinding jaws on the tough dried stems.

There was no sign of his father about, though he gave a shout. He wished to know which of the chores remained not done. There was no answer. The milk-pails upside down showed that the milking was not yet begun. 'Likely gone home with Syd for a visit,' he grunted at once, without taking any thought of the matter. He fumbled about the harnesses in the dark. 'Thinks he'll lay the chores on me, I s'pose. I'll only unharness the horses and water them. If he doesn't like that he can do the other.'

When he returned to the house he glanced at the alarm-clock on the shelf. A quarter-past nine. He picked up a magazine and took it with a lamp into the next room. Frequently when the family went to town a magazine was brought home. Before that his reading had been restricted and this began only after Len had quit high-school. He for some time found the change grateful from his dry studies. He was drowsing with his elbows on one of the magazines when the screen-door slammed and Brinder entered the house, coming on into the room where his son was sitting. The boy, fully awake, pretended to continue his reading.

'I saw you weren't out at the barn, so I came in. You didn't get the chores all finished, did you?'

'No, I just worked 'till a little after nine, and then quit and called it a day.'

'Is that so! You could have quit when you liked, if you'd asked me. I didn't order you to do the chores, remember. I asked you how many of them had been done.'

'As many as I had time to do after doing the work in here.'

'Well, you didn't have many hours' work in here, did you? How much did you do?'

'I gave the horses water and unharnessed them.'

'Oh!'

'Why, did the time seem so long over at Allrows'?'

'Over at Allrows'?'

'Yes. Didn't you go home with Syd?'

'Well, that's a joke, that is,' said Brinder, turning away. 'I went back to the pasture after old Belle. She wouldn't bring her calf up with the other cattle.'

Len was nonplussed for an instant. His father went on: 'It'll pay not to pay so much attention to the clock when a busy time's on, you'll find.' He entered the kitchen, shutting the door behind him.

The boy did not try to check his anger at this. It was increased by his knowledge that his father's was controlled.

'I'll find, will I?' he shouted at the closed door. 'I'll find where there's an eight-hour day to be had, you can bet on that!'

He heard his father grunting in the next room, and the creak of his lantern as he jerked it shut. Then the outside door slammed behind him.

Len was painfully awake now, but he could not keep his mind on the printing before him. His imagination ran amuck through possibilities. But he did not see them as possibilities. The actuality stood before him of every movement from now until the time he should have reached the city and entered on some transcendently congenial and remunerative occupation. The vision, with its minutiae, lasted a considerable time; then another came of his going to sea. When he judged that his father would soon be coming into the house again he took up his lamp and retired to his own room.

The next morning he came downstairs bearing the blackened lamp in his hand, to find that his father had gone out, leaving a fire for cooking the breakfast. It was half-past five by the clock on the shelf, and the boy at once began preparations for the morning meal. Before the table was set his father came in with the milkpail. They greeted each other somewhat shamefacedly and busied themselves with straining the milk and taking the dishes from the shelves.

As they were sitting down to the table Mr. Brinder looked at the clock: 'It's later than it seems; that clock's away slow.' He appeared to be in a hurry, and the meal was consumed in silence. When they had finished, the father said, 'You clear up here. I'll not water the driver nor your team. If I'm gone to the field when you come out, you water them.' He went away apparently without hearing Len's monosyllabic assent.

The morning was not yet more than faintly warm. White clouds were loitering about the sky, and dew hung in the grass beside the path worn to the barn. The boy slipped the halter from the head of Lass, the driver, pride of the farm, or at any rate very much that of himself. He drove her out into the yard, where she might go for a drink. Meanwhile he began to harness the team, with which he intended to plough.

In a moment Lass entered the end of the stable in which he was working, instead of the other containing her box-stall. For months one of the rollers on the door leading out of that end of the barn had been broken, so that it had been necessary to lead her forth from the part in which the other horses were quartered. Now, as she came in by the old way, long after the door had been repaired, there was something about the whole matter, about the inertia and preoccupation which had so long made them neglect it, more than about this unnecessary use of the old mode of entry, which enraged Len immeasurably. He could not have explained his rage with its sudden choking of his throat. He leaped at the little mare shouting, 'Get out of here, you! Before I—' He reached her side and struck a blow at her muzzle. She jerked her head up, turning around, and, slipping and sprawling on the cement, went out. He at once became ashamed of himself, and when he got her into the stall gave her an extra handful of oats. They watched each other while she, ears pricked, ate it. Lass did not object, as most horses did, to the impertinence of being watched while she consumed feed.

Throughout that morning the boy was nearly as tired and even more languidly bitter than the evening before. The soil seemed as hard as ever, the horses plunged, the orchard was still longer.

Wonderful high, steep and billowing clouds were in the sky. They were like vast mounds and towers of tarnished well-lit silver. He sat on the side of the plough and looked over toward the part of the orchard at which he would finish his ploughing. The green of an oats field beyond was visible under the apple-boughs. It was even now beginning to take on a grey misty tinge. Soon the oats field would seem an unbelievable blue-grey cloud glimpsed from beneath the apple-trees. In those days the granite of oats would call the eye throughout all the country. The heads would seem to dance in the high sunlight, and fields of wheat would bow and surge in amber-lit crests. The rows of young corn would be arching to either side and touching, black-green and healthy. The smell of it, as he cultivated and the horses nipped off pieces of the heavy leaves, would be more sweet than that of flowers, and more bland. The year would pass on, the harvesting of wheat, of barley and oats, fall-ploughing again, threshing, the cutting and husking of corn, the picking of apples in the same orchard. Yes, one could see the beauty of it distantly, but when the time came he would be numbed to all with toil.

That is, this round would take place, the years pass on, if he remained on the farm. Would he, or, rather he asked himself, could he do that? Nothing very alluring was to be seen ahead in the lives of anyone about him. What was his father getting out of it?

His plough could scarcely be held in the ground at all now. The point had become worn off and rounded, and he at last went over to his father for a heavy wrench with which to break it off squarely which would for a time postpone the necessity of replacing it with a new one. Syd was starting back to the other end of the orchard, and waved a heavy arm at him. Len pretended to be busy disengaging the wrench from his father's plough, but looked up an instant later to watch the steady progress down the field of the team of blacks; and Syd held the plough-handles with an appearance of firmness and ease.

'You needn't bother going for the water this morning, I'll go after it,' his father was saying.

'Ploughs nice, finishing the lands up, don't it?' Len asked, significantly, ignoring the remark.

'Well, if you wanted to do that, why didn't you say so in the first place?'

'Oh, don't bother changing us around now! I'm getting used to the hard part.' He still looked after Syd.

'No, I won't ask him to change now.'

Len walked on, more uninterruptedly now, but shouting shrilly at the horses as they jerked ahead. Stopping midway of the field he set the clevis to make the plough go deeper. It saved him some of the effort to hold it in the ground. But the horses found it still heavier going. At the hard spots at each end big blocks of cement-like earth were turned up.

He was calculating the length of the orchard and there from the distance walked in a day, when his father came with the drink. Pulling his watch out, Sam Brinder said, 'It's not as late as it seems. I've set the clock on by my watch. It's five minutes to eleven, while the right time is twenty-five minutes to eleven. I'll holler when it's time to quit. Your team is doing all right, not sweating.'

Later as he came to the end of the field he heard his father and Syd, who happened to finish at the same time, talking together.

'Yes, and she can go, all right; nice roader,' his father was saying.

'Well, I think this other one would just suit you.'

Were they speaking of Lass? Once or twice Brinder had considered disposing of her, and Len's dread of such a possibility was such that he would never discuss it. But she might be sold now. Anything, it came to him, might happen now. His father would just like to sell her to spite him, he knew. The ache of his anger was redoubled by the memory of what had happened that morning. He recalled now his deep-founded liking for the little horse. One evening he let her out in the field with the others. How she trotted! Proudly, with arched neck and tail streaming behind, she moved about among the other horses with great high free strides. 'She can trot circles around the others', he thought. Presently she stopped, standing poised and throbbing with life, snorting, ears forward, looking at him in the doorway. And he clapped his hands and she trotted off once more. Then she became still more frolicsome. Her heels shot up again and again, and he could hear the swish of her long heavy tail as she kicked.... Yes, it would be just like him to sell her.

Time passed, as if in despite of itself. The boy plodded on, his mind enfolded in these thoughts, and consciously aware of only the flopping aside of the earth before him, of the dust and the hard gravel slope of the furrow-bottom. The fatal impressibility of youth was lapping chains about him. It seemed that he had never known anything else than this dolorous wrestle in the dust. The hard clamping of his hat-brim pained his forehead. He wiped it and the grime came off on his handkerchief. The ache in his legs was not to be forgotten, but his mind swung from the certainty of the loss of one of the few things—the only one it now seemed for which he could care. He began to wonder about the time. His shadow slanted a little to the east as he faced north: surely it was after noon. He could not remember whether the shadow slanted more in the spring or in the autumn: it was surely more than twelve o'clock.

Automatically he continued work after the accustomed respite. What was the meaning of this clock business? The clock had seemed accurate enough yesterday to catch the train by. But it had been slow this morning, and now, his father said, it was fast, and fast so much. There was something strange about all this.

But as it became later there ceased to be anything strange in the matter to Len. It was part of a plan—that couldn't be doubted. To pretend that they had begun later than usual and at the same stroke keep him at work later—it was sharp, all right. Indignation and a respect for his own penetration filled him. This, he reflected in bitterness, was what he must expect from his father henceforth. And the latter would regard it as no more than just discipline, probably. But he'd be shown. 'He'll only try that once,' the boy muttered, his face fixing and his fingers tightening on the plough-handles.

Standing at the end of the field he looked about him. Through the trees he could see his father's three square-boned horses straining onward amid the shouts of their driver. 'Sitting down, having a snap,' he thought, relishing the fact of taking this as a matter of course. Farther over, Syd was going in the opposite direction, holding his plough as steadily, it appeared, as though the ground had been softened by days of rain.

'I'll not make another round,' he reflected. 'Or it will be a good while before I do, anyway. If he thinks he can do that sort of thing he's going to get left.'

Whistling a shred of an old tune he sat down on

his plough. 'Have a good rest, Ned,' he addressed the nigh horse, 'you started early enough, anyway.'

He was aware of the long barred stretch of blue-green oats now still nearer. The high sun instead of making it more vivid seemed to give its surface a hazy quality. A dragon-fly hung motionless against the mild breeze and seeming to battle with it, wings alight with a sparkle of swift motion.

'About noon when you see them things,' the boy thought.

From three-quarters of a mile away came the sound of the Allrows' dinner-bell. Old-fashioned people. It was dinner-time, then, all right. Sometimes, though, they had dinner earlier, or later. He pictured the Allrow boys and their father, quitting work in various parts of the farm, and Mrs. Allrow, plump, easily pleased woman, with her grown-up daughters preparing the meal. How long was it since he had been over to their place? That, he reflected, was the trouble; one didn't see anyone new for weeks at a stretch. The desire for various contacts had made him impatient of the people he might have known better, had he cared. He got through the day's work, but curiosity demanded leisure and energy. People on a farm, like the men on shipboard in the old days, saw too much of each other. That was it. But that could be remedied in his case, Len reflected with a quickening of the pulses. . . . Not an inch would he drive further. His father must learn that his little trick wouldn't work. As he sat, waiting for the call, he decided that if he discovered that the clock really had been advanced, he must leave. He pictured all the details of this, his father's queries and expostulations and his own determined silence. He would pack his suit-case, take his few

dollars out of hiding and walk down the road. . . .
He kicked at the side of the furrow, gazing downward. . . . How sore his feet had been last night! . . .
But he wouldn't walk very far, only to the railway
station. For he was going to the city. No, he would
ask to be driven there in the buggy, drive Lass himself. If only one could keep himself unbound! But
there'd be that one friend he'd always miss! . . . He
would ask politely, unemotionally, and his father
would not be able to refuse. . . . He'd just step to the
house and phone central and inquire the correct
time.

His father's call struck a surprise in him, and he
rose stiffly and unhitched the horses. He noticed
that both the others were unhitching also. They
didn't intend to let him go up and prepare the
dinner alone. But he'd never let that hinder him.
He'd step to the phone in their presence and find
out the truth about this matter. Robbing from both
pockets at once!

He hurried toward the barn, determined to arrive
there first. He came to the watering-trough; and
when, after waiting for the horses to drink, he had
stabled them, he was so agitated that he was struck
with a weak surprise to hear Syd and his father
talking quietly outside while they separated their
horses. He intended to go out of the building and
directly to the house, having fed the team which he
had been driving; but he changed his mind and went
back and began to put hay in the other mangers,
then made for the house and washed before
them.

He heard their voices; their heavy feet scrub the
grass of the yard . . . knock against the step.

'It's a seven-foot cut, they tell me,' Brinder was

saying. 'Now wouldn't you thought a six-foot cut would be big enough, on a farm like that.'

'Old Dunc says he may as well get a big one now. Alfred'll be getting a tractor soon as he's gone, he says.'

'Great old joker. He don't mind having big things around, himself.'

'Then I guess he's sure he'll have the job of driving it now he's getting old,' Syd laughed. 'It'll make the boys hump, to shock behind it, though.'

'Yes, they raise pretty good crops, just the same.' Mr. Brinder was putting water in the kettle, while Syd combed his hair.

'How'll we have the eggs, boys?' The voice sounded absent from the pantry, whence the regular sweep of the bread-knife could be heard.

'Well, they were pretty fair like they were last night. . . .'

Len moved from shelves to table with clean dishes. Syd sat with his arms folded on a chair tilted against the wall. He intercepted one of the rounds by asking, 'Well, how you coming? Ground soft where you are, I s'pose!'

The boy grunted in reply and managed a half-smile.

Soon the meal was ready, and as they sat down to it he remembered that he had not gone to the phone as he had promised himself. He would do it as soon as the other two were gone, and he would be left alone to wash the dishes.

The two voices went on, with a calm interest, businesslike inevitability, and the meal was almost over before Len realized that there was something in his mind being worn down and smoothed away, as old ice is worn away by spring rain. They talked as though they had been travellers in a desert who had become parted by accident and now met to re-count all they had been through. But what they told was nothing, they meant simply to demonstrate to themselves that they were together again. Then what he thought of as the unreality of it oppressed him. A change in circumstances, the presence of strangers seemed to compel one to make little changes in one's words, in one's actions. Elements of the frank, humorous, the straightforward, of eagerness in the gallantries of conversation were there. Perhaps Syd's family would smile to recognize him. His father was different too. But weren't they both after all as much themselves in any guise as they could be?

It occurred to him that his father was seeking something in the commonplace exchange. His father had been young too, once. He tried to image that youth, his aims and desires and ways. The thought unaccustomed held him for a moment, but he could not imagine them as different from his own, and the idea came that his father had betrayed them. Then as he looked at the lines in the face, scars of weather, toil and the scarifications of experience, he began to descry the blind unwitting stupor of life, reaching for what it wanted, an ox setting foot on a kitten before its manger.

He wanted to rise and rush from the room. The sound of the two with their talking kept him from his own thoughts.

They continued to discuss the fallibilities and oddities of neighbours until the table began to look emptier, and then he noticed his father saying, 'So you think you'll not be able to help us any more, Syd?'

'Well, not just for the present,' replied Syd

pleasantly, as though correcting Mr. Brinder in an important inexactitude of statement. 'Maybe sometime after a while.' . . . So Syd was going; going too. They were both going, his conscious mind repeated, though something that had been fierce and silently stridulous began to shrink within him, and he began to wonder how much he meant that.

He rose and left the house. He went down the lane and along the road which led toward the corner where, on the main highway, their mail-box stood.

There was nothing but yesterday's paper, and a postcard from his sister. The latter contained only the most banal message, documenting the facts that its sender was alive and, it added, in good spirits; and that the boss said her vacation would come in the next month.

The relationship of the brother and sister was not known to any especial tenderness, and yet, as he thought of the sense of her presence in the first few days after her return, of the feeling while at work of somebody new waiting for him at mealtimes, he couldn't but look forward to it, and he realized and now admitted to himself that his struggle had found an issue. A dull quietude came upon his mind. He tramped back home, his heavy feet upon the hard rounded road.

He found that the men had gone to the barn when he reached the kitchen. Syd would be hitching his horses and going away.

His mother—she would be beginning her holiday among the impossible wonders of the city. He thought of the endless confidential chats she would have with his sister, his Aunt Charlotte, as they would rock together in the first afternoons, and the family would be out at work or at play. Already he began to miss her. Nearly two days were gone. But he should have, though only until realization, for expectance the last one of her absence.

Then he was struck by the triviality of what he allowed to pass as excuses for abandoning the determination he had so highly taken.

Once, clearing the table, he looked at the clock, but he did not let the reminder stay with him. As he wiped the dishes slowly, he looked at it again, and said aloud and consciously:

'What's the use? What's the weary use?'

Blind MacNair

THOMAS H. RADDALL (b. 1903)

In Shardstown they sing ballads no more. Nor will you hear a chanty, for the chantymen have vanished and the tall grass shines where once the shipyards lay under a snow of chips and shavings.

It is a village enchanted. There is the yellow dust of the street, the procession of dwellings down to the broad sheltered bay, where a fleet could anchor and only the lone fishing boat flashes a riding sail; and there is the little church and the store and the dry-rotten fish wharf asleep in the sun, all still as death. Half the houses are empty, with blinds drawn and faded and forgotten, and grass in the kitchen path.

The people are pleasant but silent. They smile and vanish. Down by the waterside, in the lee of a tottering shed, you may find an old man on a cushion of discarded net, with worn boots thrust out before him, with a frown to shield his old eyes from the shine of the sea, and a dream on his face.

'A ballad? People don't sing ballads now. A chanty? Ha! Where's the need—and no sails to haul?' If you persist he will swear great oaths that have a strong taste of the sea, and he will say, 'Och, man, yes; but that's too long ago. That's back in the time of Blind MacNair.'

And who was Blind MacNair?

Before Shardstown became enchanted, the village stood pretty much as it stands now, but alive, with a smell of new-sawed wood in the air, and the sounds of hammer and adze, and the clack-clack of calking mallets. They built good ships in Shardstown then. The hulls grew by the waterside with their bow-sprits reaching over the road. A blockmaker and three families of coopers carried on business in sheds behind their homes, and a busy sailmaker squatted with palm and needle amongst billows of canvas up there in the long sail loft. The village blacksmith made ironwork for vessels three parts of the year; in winter he shod oxen and horses and fitted sled runners and peavey hooks for the loggers.

The tall iron stack of the sawmill poured blue wood smoke at the sky, and from dawn to dark within its grey wooden walls rang the death-scream of logs. There was a wisp in every chimney then, and children played by the dusty road, and women came out of the kitchen doors and set the well wind-lasses rattling. Too many women; for in those days men went out upon the broad world in the wind ships and the world did not always give them back. The sea took many, and there was the gold rush to California, and then the gold rush to Australia; and thirty men went to the American war. All that within twenty years.

So there were lonely women in Shardstown. For a time, in one part of the long street lived six widows side by side. Three married again as the years went by; but the others were Bullens and counted unlucky, their husbands gone—blown off a topsail yard, washed overboard, stabbed by a drunken foremast hand—each within fifteen months of the wedding. In a village like Shardstown men could pick safer wives.

There was a fourth Bullen sister, the youngest, but she lived with old Chris on the Bullen farm, a lonely hillside clearing by the Revesport road, fourteen miles out of Shardstown. There was a scandal about Nellie Bullen. She had gone to work in Revesport in '60 or '61, a slim blonde girl of two-and-twenty with the self-willed Bullen mouth, and came home late in '62 and had a baby. A fine wagging of tongues there was, to be sure, in that village of too many women. But one Sunday old Chris Bullen came down in his buggy and nailed to the church door a paper for all to see—Nellie Bullen's marriage lines, with a date that defied the gossips' arithmetic.

After that the matter dropped, and nobody even remembered the husband's name, and Nellie Bullen stayed close to the lonely farm with her boy and called herself Nellie Bullen. Things like that happened very easily in the old times, when men came and went from the sea like visitors from the moon.

People sang ballads then, except on Sunday when the minister came over in a buggy from Revesport and there were hymns to be sung. And the best of the singers were chantymen from the brigs and barks and barkentines, the lovely wind ships that lay at the waterside. Nowadays men say the wind ships were hell ships and well lost; and they say the chanties had no music and the ballads no poetry. Blind they are, more blind than Blind MacNair, who knew the beauty of those things.

Och, yes, Blind MacNair, who came to Shardstown in the fall of 1872 aboard a potato schooner from Prince Edward Island. Squarebuilt he was, with brown hands and a brown face and a curly black beard, and hair long and black as night. He wore a band of green silk across his eyes and carried a stick and bundle. His black frieze trousers were called shag trousers in those days, and he had a pair of stout brown sea boots under their wide bottoms, and a sailor's red shirt tucked in the top, and he wore an old long coat with skirts that hung wrinkled and loose at his knees; but he had no hat and the sea wind stirred the black hairs of his head.

The tide was out and the ship lay low, and Blind MacNair climbed the forerigging to the level of the wharf and a sailor gave him a hand and pointed him for the wharf's end. That was the way Blind MacNair came to Shardstown, with his staff striking a hollow sound from the planks of the wharf, and the sea wind blowing the skirts of his coat, and the long hair streaming about his head, like a blind prophet out of the Bible.

Shardstown folk were shy of strangers, and Blind MacNair was an awesome man to see; so they stood off and watched him up the village street and down, without a word. But children saw the gentleness in him and sang out 'Hello,' as he passed, and Blind MacNair paused in the dust and asked their names in the deep slow voice he had. And after a time Taggart's wife—Taggart of the forge—called her youngsters to supper and saw them squatted about MacNair in the grass at the wayside.

MacNair was singing softly, and the song was *Fair Margaret and Sweet William*. That is a sad song and a sweet song; the children stayed to the end, and Taggart's wife came to the gate and listened, too. At the end she said, 'Won't you come in, man, and have a bite with us?'

MacNair rose gravely and bowed. 'Thank ye, ma'am, and I will.'

After the supper things were cleared Taggart sat with MacNair by the stove in the parlour, and while Mrs. Taggart shushed the children off to their beds the blacksmith said, 'Where's your home? If that's a fair question.'

'I've none,' said Blind MacNair; 'no more than the birds.'

'It's fall,' Taggart said, 'and the birds gone to the South for winter.'

'South!' said the blind man. ''Tis a great country, the South, but a sad one, and I've had my fill of sadness. Ten years I've been wandering, and there came on me suddenly a great longing to be in my own country. This was my landfall. There's birds must winter in the North, for that is the way of them.'

'Ah!' Taggart said. He was a tall man and spare, with a red beard square as a shovel, and his eyes were kind. 'Would ye take a bed in the garret the winter?'

'Man, man,' said MacNair, 'the winter bird's no beggar. The bush by the pasture wall, the red berry left by God on the bare wild rose, a crumb at the kitchen door if it's offered, and chance the rest. That's the winter bird, and that's Blind MacNair.'

'You're proud, man, and I respect ye for it,' Taggart said. 'There's the spare bedroom over the parlour that's fixed up fine for ministers and such.'

'Is there no loft to your stable?' demanded Mac-Nair.

'What place is that for a man?' cried Taggart's wife, for she had come into the room and stood by Taggart's chair with her hands on his shoulder.

'I'm only half a man,' said MacNair, 'and a stable was good enough for the child of God.'

So MacNair slept the winter in Taggart's loft, with the quilts from Taggart's spare bed, and caught his meals as the birds do, a dinner here and a supper there; with Fraser the blockmaker, with Lowrie the fishing captain, with Shard the ship chandler, and now and again at Taggart's—but not often, for 'I'm beholden enough for the loft,' said Blind MacNair.

He was a welcome guest wherever he went. There was never a speck on his clothes nor a whiff of the stable about him; for he was clean, that man, clean as the brook that fell from the hill, and he ate as neat as a man with eyes. Like everybody in Shards-town he had the Gaelic, and when he said the grace before meat you felt that God was in that house.

After the meal Blind MacNair would sing, with the menfolk at their pipes and the women waiting the dishes, and the children sitting about his feet. A grand strong voice he had, and could roar a chanty with the best of the sailors. But he liked ballads best; for ballads he would drop his voice to the size of the room, till it was like a man speaking music, and his voice was deep and sad on the low notes like the southerly pipes of the Presbyterian organ at Revesport.

Daytime he spent at Taggart's forge. That was Shardstown's clubroom in winter, the bellows roaring under the red coals, the old men on the benches that Taggart had made for them, and the teamsters leaning or squatting while their beasts were shod. He loved to get the men singing chanties, himself giving the by-line in a great round voice and the men roaring in on the chorus. And when they struck up a real rouser like *The Drunken Sailor*, Taggart himself would join in, singing free like a man that enjoyed himself, hammering *rang-tang-tang* on the live iron, and the golden fire spurting. Those were singing times, and Shardstown men were great men to sing; but there was never such singing as they had that winter in Taggart's forge.

With the turn of the year the cold grew and there was good snow for the log hauling. Ox bells rang up and down the beaten sled road from the woods, and the birchwood yokes creaked, and the runners squealed on the snow, and the teamsters grinned and cracked their little whips.

When March came the loggers came out of the woods. They had hauled their cut, and a turn of the wind now would bring the thaw and the break-up. And there was work now at the wharves, with schooners to fit out for the spring voyage to the Banks, and a bark from Revesport to load with shooks from McLaughlan's cooperage. There was great singing in the forge then, for the chantyman of the bark was a big, handsome negro man with a voice like the sound of great bells, and Singing Johnny Hanigan had come over from Revesport to go in the fishery.

The negro man had a great store of songs, and Singing Johnny was famous in forty miles of coast, and when the Shardstown men began to brag of Blind MacNair one thing was certain.

It came of a Saturday morning, with the old men sitting each in his place, and sailors and loggers and fishermen and ship carpenters standing or squatting wherever was room for their heels. Taggart's was a big forge and dark, though the sun flamed on the snow outside; for the inside walls and the high gloomy rafters were black with the smoke of a century, and the little windows thick with dust, and the big double doors closed for the sake of the old thin blood on the benches.

There was a smell of hot iron in that place always, and a smell of horses and oxen and scorched hooves; and now such a smell of men and tobacco as the forge had rarely known, for Singing Johnny and the negro man had set out to sing down Blind MacNair.

Taggart had Donald MacAllan's big ox in the shoeing stall when the singing began, and he went on with it, for he was no man to let pleasure meddle with business. So he thrust the ox down on its knees in the open frame of the stall, and made each foreleg fast with rope to the shoeing ledge, hoof upward, and moored the beast bow and stern like a ship, with a rope to the yoke and a high rope to the off hind foot. And he passed the broad canvas band under the hard brown belly and put the wooden pin in the windlass socket, and hoisted the beast off its hind feet for the shoeing of them.

Each part of that wooden stall was dark and smooth from the grasp of Taggart's hands, and the hands of his father and grandfather before him. The chimney stood at the back of the forge with the brick block of the fireplace waist-high before it, and the black beam of the bellows and the anvil and workbench by the window to the left of it. To the right was a litter of long iron stretched along the floor, and a bench for wheelwright work.

That space was full of men standing, the iron a-clank with the shift of their feet, and the bench laden with sitters. And the space between the fire and the big double doors was full of men too, except the ox stall in the corner where Taggart knelt at his work. And in the midst of it all sat Blind MacNair on a three-legged stool, with his coat skirts in the dust on the floor, and his big hands on his knees. And the smiling negro sat on the earthen floor, and Johnny Hanigan stood.

They began with chanties as a matter of course, to get them out of the way, singing the solo lines in turn and chanting the chorus together. The first was *Reuben Ranzo*, and they sang twenty verses about that famous dirty sailor who shipped aboard a whaler.

Then it came Johnny Hanigan's turn for the verse. He hesitated, and no wonder, for nobody had ever heard so many verses to *Reuben Ranzo*; but he saved himself in time with a poor patched-up sort of verse out of his own head that fitted the tune badly and rhymed worse.

There was no rule against such, for a good chanty-man could make a new verse to an old tune, and sometimes the verse pleased other ears. That was how chanties grew. But there was ill taste in offering a trumped-up verse, and a poor one, to sing down another man. Everyone expected MacNair to say something, for he knew no more, but he shrugged and opened his hands; and the negro man said 'No more here,' and the chalk went on the board on the wall with a mark for Singing Johnny.

Then MacNair began *Shenandoah*, and the negro man sang the next verse, and Johnny followed after. That is a great chanty, to be sung slowly, and so they sang it; you could shut your eyes and see sailormen stamping round a capstan with hard brown hands on the bars, and the chantyman perched on the cathead, and the cable coming in wet from the tide. MacNair had the last of it, for the negro man grinned and said, 'No more here,' and Singing Johnny could not say better.

So they went on through *Leave Her Johnny* and *Blow, Boys, Blow*, and *Banks of Sacramento*, and *Blow the Man Down*, and *Paddy Doyle's Boots*, and *Stormalong* and the other workaday chanties, and turned at last to the less familiar ones. And when it came to *Sally Brown*, and *Johnny Come to Hilo*, and *Bound to Alabama*, and those other cotton-rolling songs that drifted out to sea in the bosom of Mississipi, the big negro man went far ahead in the score, singing verse after verse when the others had dropped out and his mark was up on the wall, singing just for the pleasure of it, and his voice ringing through the crowded forge like a music of hammered brass.

From behind came the sounds of Taggart's work as he tapped home the little half-moon shoes on the ox, snipped the nail points with a twist of the sharp hammer claw, and cast loose the foot lashings, and took the pin from the windlass barrel and lowered the great drooling beast to its new-shod feet. But there the big ox stayed. His owner was part of that listening throng, lost to the world and the waiting sled on the hillside. And Taggart stood on the shoe-

ing ledge of the stall for better hearing, and hung
there silent with a hand on the yoke of the ox.

It was strange; the big ox patient in the corner,
and the tall red-bearded man above him, and the
silence of gathered men, and the singers chanting in
the midst, like something barbaric and old as the
world.

Outside, the sun stood at noon, but no one in
Taggart's forge gave a thought to food. Food was
a thing you got three times a day. Singing like this
might not come again in a month of Sundays.

They turned to ballads now, as men turn from
the morning chores to the real work of the day. Any
fool could sing chanties, and the man with the most
verses won the score. But with the ballad it was as
with hymns, a proper set of verses handed down
from the past, and woe to the man who altered so
much as a word. There were keen old ears on the
benches, and tongues to chide, and a score to lose
on the board of the wall.

Singing Johnny began with *Bold Jack Donohue*;
and at the song's end Blind MacNair said quietly,
'That is a good ballad and an old one, for it came
out of the country of Australia long before the
gold-finding; but ye have the names of the bush-
rangers wrong in the third verse.' And the old men
nodded and said it was so.

The negro man had a try at the third verse, but
the old men wagged their heads. Then sang Mac-
Nair; and the names, Walmsley, Weber, Underwood
rang true in the old heads; the blind man's score
went up on the board.

And they went on to *The Golden Vanitee*, and
Farewell to Ye Spanish Ladies, and *High Barbaree*,
and other old, old ballads of the sea, and Blind

MacNair held his own with Singing Johnny, and the black man held his lead. But when they came to *The Tiger and the Lion*, which tells of a sea fight in the olden time, the negro man dropped a point to Singing Johnny. And they came to *Hame, Dearie, Hame*, and the black man dropped a point to Blind MacNair, for he did not know those songs; and from then on the negro man was lost, for all his fine voice and the good nature of him.

'I never saw the nigger yet could sing ballads!' cried Singing Johnny Hanigan.

'Nor the braggart,' answered Blind MacNair, and Singing Johnny laughed; but there was no pleasure on his tongue—then or after.

So the negro man dropped out of the game, and Johnny and MacNair went on through *The Chesapeake and Shannon*, and then *The Fighting Chance*, and the score between them even. Blind MacNair sang *The Captain and the Maiden*, and Singing Johnny followed with *Young Johnson*: and MacNair sang *Lord Bateman*, and Johnny sang *The Banks of Newfoundland*.

And Blind MacNair said, 'That was a good ballad and well sung, and there's all the sorrow of the sea in the part that goes:

Oh, when they took us from the wreck we were more like ghosts than men,
They clothed us and they fed us and they took us home again.
But there was few of our company that e'er reached English land,
And the captain lost his limbs by frost on the Banks o' Newfoundland.'

And the man with the chalk scored one on the

board for Blind MacNair, for Hanigan had it 'The captain died o' frostbite on the Banks o' Newfoundland'—and all knew that was wrong. And again Singing Johnny laughed, and no pleasure in it.

Then Blind MacNair sang *The Ship Lady Sherbrooke,* which is a sad ballad of Irish folk wrecked on the voyage to Quebec. And Johnny Hanigan sang *On the Banks of the Brandywine,* a fine tune with romance and scenery and a sailor in it, and popular with the Shardstown men. But MacNair sang *Young Charlotte,* the ballad of the frozen bride, for the sad mood was on him; and the fishermen stirred uneasily, for they believed *Young Charlotte* an unlucky song, a Jonah song, and would never hear it sung aboard the vessels.

So Singing Johnny cheered them with *The Rambling Irishman,* a jolly thing that set them tapping their feet on the hard earthen floor, and Blind MacNair saw that he must keep his sadness to himself. So he sang *The Braes o' Balquhidder.*

That song has a lift to its music like the lilting of bagpipes heard afar on the hills in the morning, and the men were glad to see MacNair put his sadness down. And Johnny Hanigan, not to be outdone in a song of old Scotland, sang *The Pride of Glencoe,* a grand song about a soldier MacDonald and the lassie that waited home for him. But there was no pleasure in Johnny's singing any more, because he was behind in the score and he knew he could not sing down Blind MacNair.

The afternoon was far gone, the dinners parching on the stoves of Shardstown and the wives all peering out of doors to know what man-foolishness was afoot in Taggart's forge. The sun drooped low in a patch of mist over the western woods, with queer rays shining out to the four points of the sky's compass. That was a sign of snow; and the wind had come east and fetched now a cold breath from the sea, and set up a shudder in the rigging of ships, and moaned down every chimney in the village. There would be snow before morning.

Singing Johnny was beaten and he was hungry. He stared in the calm face of Blind MacNair and found something terrible about it, the face of an image that could sing, sing forever, and not to be moved by earthquakes. He could not sing that image down; but Johnny Hanigan had made a boast, and a boast is a hard thing to swallow when you are famous in forty miles.

'Can ye sing *The Blind Sailor*?' asked Singing Johnny.

'I can,' said Blind MacNair, and sang it. A verse of that song runs:

Before we reached the mainmast cap a heavier flash
    came on,
My God, I well remember it, my last glimpse of the sun.
Our main topmast in pieces split, all in a pelting light,
And me and four more seamen bold by lightning lost
    our sight.

'And,' asked Johnny Hanigan, 'is that how ye lost yours?'

''Twas not,' said Blind MacNair.

'How then?'

'In war,' said Blind MacNair.

'The American war—the Civil War?'

'Call it that if ye like.'

'Will ye sing for us *The Fifer of the Cumberland*?' demanded Johnny Hanigan.

'I will not,' said Blind MacNair.

'I wonder ye don't know it. 'Tis the song of a brave boy.'

'Ay, a brave boy, and a Yankee boy, and a good brave song.'

'I was on the Yankee side in that war,' Johnny Hanigan murmured, and ran his glance about the men, for half the gathering had fought in the Northern army in that war.

'No doubt,' said Blind MacNair. 'The war was across the border and nothing of ours, in a manner of speaking. But our talk was all of the North and the South, and from argument men go to deeds if their heart's in what they say. The war's past and done with now, and they were brave men all; but I fought by the side of the Southern men and I will sing no Yankee song.'

And now men noticed that Singing Johnny had come to a stoop, and now he was leaning forward, and his long fingers licking out to the face of Blind MacNair.

'I doubt ye fought in any war and I doubt you're blind!' he cried, and whipped the silk from MacNair's eyes while the whole forge gasped and stared.

MacNair might have been an image of stone. Not a muscle moved. His lips were firm. The lids of his eyes were closed, and white as a woman's, for they had known no sun since the fall of '64. Just beneath the thick black brows ran a scar from side to side, straight as a ruler—straight as a slash of a sword.

Singing Johnny stood dumb, with the green wisp in his fingers.

'I got that,' MacNair said quietly, 'from Sheridan's cavalry in the Valley of Virginia. A good fight, and my last.'

'Sorry,' mumbled Johnny Hanigan.

'Sorrow's not enough,' said Blind MacNair. He stood up then, a fine strong figure of a man, awesome with the bleached stripe in his dark skin, and the shining scar, and the white closed eyes.

'Many Nova Scotia men went to that war—ten thousand, they say—and some fought for the one side, some for the other, according to their opinions. There's no knowing now which had the right of it, for a brave man makes a brave cause, and blood's the one colour, North or South. But whichever jacket he wore, the Bluenose was an honest man and a fighting man and a credit to Nova Scotia. Now there must always be an exception to prove a rule, and there were certain ones that crossed Fundy Bay to pluck what cash they could from the agony of other men. In Boston ye could get two or three hundred dollars from the sons of the rich, to substitute on the draft, and another hundred bounty from the state. And 'twas easy to desert then to another state and 'list again with another name for another shower of Yankee dollars. Some were caught, and some got away home with their blood-money—though it couldn't buy enough soap to take the judas smell from their hands. I'm truly blind, Johnny Hanigan, but the eye of the mind sees through the stones of the wall. I will sing you a Yankee song. 'Tis a good song, and a jolly song, and a fine song for the feet on the road.' And he began:

Come all you fine young fellows, I am going to sing a
        song:
I pray you give attention and I won't detain you long.
'Tis of a fine young fellow, and Johnny was his name:
He was tried in Alexandria for the doing of this same.

Now that was a song called *The Bounty Jumper*,

known to every man in the forge, and they joined
MacNair in the chorus.

So come join my humble ditty as from town to town I
    steer.
Like every real good fellow I am always on the beer;
Like every real good fellow I prefer my whisky clear,
I'm a rambling rake of poverty and the son of a
    gamboleer.

    And Blind MacNair sang on:

Oh, he jumped in Philadelphy and he jumped into New
    York;
He jumped in the City of Boston, it was all the people's
    talk.
Oh, he jumped and he jumped all along the Yankee
    shore,
But the last place he jumped was in the Town of
    Baltimore.

It was made for the laughter of marching men,
that song; but Blind MacNair sang it with a strange
violence, like the chanting of a curse.

Singing Johnny Hanigan stood, white and red by
turns, a thin sweat on his long clever face, with the
chorus pouring upon him like scalding water. And
whenever the tune struck the high note some iron
rods vibrated thinly on the beam overhead, as if the
old forge itself had come to life for the scorn of
Johnny Hanigan.

Oh, now we'll dig poor Johnny's grave, we'll dig it wide
    and deep.
We'll bury him in the valley where the bounty jumpers
    sleep.
We'll put him in his coffin and we'll carry him along,
And we'll all join the chorus of the bounty jumper's song.

But Singing Johnny did not wait for the end. He slunk out of the forge like the shadow of a man, and nobody ever saw him in Shardstown again.

He left one of the big doors open, with a broad wedge of daylight pouring into the forge and blinding them all. There was a great silence. Then a woman's shadow fell across the floor and Nellie Bullen's voice was crying, 'Mr. Taggart! Mr. Taggart!'

Taggart stepped down from the shoeing stall and thrust through the blinking men to her.

'The mare's got a loose shoe, Mr. Taggart; will you look at it, please? The road's a glare of ice— and I must get home before the snow.'

Taggart went outside and Nellie Bullen turned to follow him, and just then James McCuish said, 'Sing us one more song MacNair, afore we go.'

Nellie Bullen paused.

She was a tall woman with grey eyes, and she had the slim proud back of the Bullen women, and thick coils of hair with a dull gold shine like a hempen hawser new from the ropewalk.

'Can ye sing *The Desolate Widow*?' asked James McCuish, for he was a thoughtless man.

'Not I,' said Blind MacNair. He faced the open door with his feet together and his hands at his trouser seams, like a soldier—or a prisoner before judgement. The cold light was full on his face.

'Any song, then! A Gaelic song—we've had no Gaelic songs today.'

'I know a song,' said Blind MacNair, 'but there's no more music in me, and no rhyme to the words. A poor thing it is.'

'Give us the hang of it,' insisted James McCuish.

'An old tale, James, old as the sorrows of the

world. A young man with a hot head, and a young wife with spirit. There's the quarrel, and the young man saying things no lassie of spirit would take, and there's the separation, with the young wife home to her own folk and the young man off to the wars. You see how old a song it is. Now in those old songs always the young man comes home a hero from the wars, and finds the wife forgiving and waiting true, and there's an end of it. But this song of mine goes wrong somehow, for the man comes blind and a beggar, no fit company for man, woman or dog. A judgement on him d'ye see?—for in the parting he'd said "May I never see you again!"—and never he will, except with the eye of the mind.'

'Cruel judgement, that, for a few foolish words,' objected Lowrie the fishing captain.

'The judgement of God?' murmured old John MacLaughlan reprovingly.

'But what's the end of the song?' asked Nellie Bullen from the doorway, and the men pressed back, none knew why, until she was standing alone in the shaft of light that fell upon MacNair, and all the men hushed in the shadows.

'It has no end, it goes on forever,' cried Blind MacNair.

'Forever?' she said. 'There's only one song goes on forever.' There was a flutter of skirts, and suddenly Nellie Bullen had her arms about Blind MacNair and her shining head on his shoulder, and her hat in the dust of the floor.

'Ah, Colin, Colin!' cried Nellie Bullen.

Tears ran down his face, strange and terrible, as if you saw water spring from a barren rock.

'I've nothing to give ye, Nellie.'

She kissed him then, and the men began stealing

out of Taggart's forge with a strange look on their faces, as if they had seen ghosts.

'Will you give your son the sound of his father's voice, Colin?'

'My son!'

'Will you sing for your wife the song that goes without end?'

Och, yes, it was a great singing that day in Taggart's forge, but long ago, and who remembers the old time now? The old Bullen farmhouse, where Nellie MacNair took her husband that night of the big March snow, is gone from the Revesport road, with nothing to mark it but a dent in the green turf.

Some in Shardstown hold the place haunted, and say how on nights of the full May moon you can hear Blind MacNair ploughing the windy hillside behind the old white Bullen horse, and singing the old Gaelic song *Mo Run Geal Dileas—My Faithful Fair One*. But that is an old wives' tale; and how could they know that song? For in Shardstown only the old men in the sunshine remember, and they sing ballads no more.

Last Spring They Came Over

MORLEY CALLAGHAN (b. 1903)

ALFRED BOWLES came to Canada from England and got a job on a Toronto paper. He was a young fellow with clear, blue eyes and heavy pimples on the lower part of his face, the son of a Baptist minister whose family was too large for his salary. He got thirty dollars a week on the paper and said it was surprisingly good screw to start. For six dollars a week he got an attic room in a brick house painted brown on Mutual Street. He ate his meals in a quick-lunch near the office. He bought a cane and a light-grey fedora.

He wasn't a good reporter but was inoffensive and obliging. After he had been working two weeks the fellows took it for granted he would be fired in a little while and were nice to him, liking the way the most trifling occurrences surprised him. He was happy to carry his cane on his arm and wear the fedora at a jaunty angle, quite the reporter. He liked to explain that he was doing well. He wrote home about it.

When they put him doing night police he felt important, phoning the fire department, hospitals, and police stations, trying to be efficient. He was getting along all right. It was disappointing when after a week the assistant city editor, Mr. H. J. Brownson, warned him to phone his home if anything important happened, and he would have another man cover it. But Bowles got to like hearing the weary, irritable voice of the assistant city editor called from his bed at three o'clock in the morning. He liked politely to call Mr. Brownson as often and as late as possible, thinking it a bit of good fun.

Alfred wrote long letters to his brother and to his father, the Baptist minister, using a typewriter, carefully tapping the keys, and occasionally laughing to himself. In a month's time he had written six letters describing the long city room, the fat belly of the city editor, and the bad words the night editor used when speaking of the Orangemen.

The night editor took a fancy to him because of the astounding puerility of his political opinions.

Alfred was always willing to talk pompously of how the British Empire had policed the world and about all Catholics being aliens, and the future of Ireland and Canada resting with the Orangemen. He flung his arms wide and talked in the hoarse voice of a bad actor, but no one would have thought of taking him seriously. He was merely having a dandy time. The night editor liked him because he was such a nice boy.

Then Alfred's brother came out from the old country, and got a job on the same paper. Some of the men started talking about cheap Limey labourers crowding the good guys out of the jobs, but Harry Bowles was frankly glad to get the thirty a week. It never occurred to him that he had a funny idea of good money. With his first pay he bought a pearl-grey hat, and a cane, but even though his face was clear and had a good colour he never looked as nice as his younger brother because his heavy nose curved up at the end. The landlady on Mutual Street moved a double bed into Alfred's room and Harry slept with his brother.

The days passed with many good times together. At first it was awkward that Alfred should be working at night and his brother in the daytime, but Harry was pleased to come down to the office every night at eleven and they went down the street to the hotel that didn't bother about the closing hour. They drank a few glasses of good beer. It became a kind of rite that had to be performed carefully. Harry would put his left foot and Alfred his right foot on the rail and leaning an elbow on the bar they would slowly survey the zig-zag line of frothing glasses the length of the long bar. Men jostled them for a place at the foot-rail.

And Alfred said: 'Well, a bit of luck.'

Harry grinning and raising his glass said: 'Righto.'

'It's the stuff that heals.'

'Down she goes.'

'It helps the night along.'

'Fill them up again.'

'Toodleoo.'

Then they would walk out of the crowded bar-room, vaguely pleased with themselves. Walking slowly and erectly along the street they talked with assurance, a mutual respect for each other's opinion making it merely an exchange of information. They talked of the Englishman in Canada, comparing his lot with that of the Englishman in South Africa and India. They had never travelled but to ask what they knew of strange lands would have made one feel uncomfortable; it was better to take it for granted that the Bowles boys knew all about the ends of the earth and had judged them carefully for in their eyes was the light of far away places. Once in a while, after walking a block or two, one of the brothers would say he would damn well like to see India and the other would say it would be simply topping.

After work and on Sundays they took a look at the places they had heard about in the city. One Sunday they got up in good time and took the boat to Niagara. Their father had written asking if they had seen the Falls and would they send some souvenirs. That day they had as nice a time as a man would want to have. Standing near the pipe rail a little way from the hotel that overlooks the Falls they watched the water-line just before the drop, smooth as a long strip of bevelled glass, and

Harry compared it favourably with a cataract in the Himalayas and a giant water-fall in Africa, just above the Congo. They took a car along the gorge and getting off near the whirlpool, picked out a little hollow near a big rock at the top of the embankment where the grass was lush and green. They stretched themselves out with hats tilted over their eyes for sun-shades. The river whirled below. They talked about the funny ways of Mr. Brownson and his short fat legs and about the crazy women who fainted at the lifted hand of the faith healer who was in the city for the week. They liked the distant rumble of the Falls. They agreed to try and save a lot of money and go west to the Pacific in a year's time. They never mentioned trying to get a raise in pay.

Afterwards they each wrote home about the trip, sending the souvenirs.

Neither one was doing well on the paper. Harry wasn't much good because he hated writing the plain copy and it was hard for him to be strictly accurate. He liked telling a good tale but it never occurred to him that he was deliberately lying. He imagined a thing and straightway felt it to be true. But it never occurred to Alfred to depart from the truth. He was accurate but lazy, never knowing when he was really working. He was taken off night police and for two weeks helped a man do courts at the City Hall. He got to know the boys at the press gallery, who smiled at his naïve sincerity and thought him a decent chap without making up their minds about him. Every noon hour Harry came to the press gallery and the brothers, sitting at typewriters, wrote long letters all about the country and the people, anything interesting, and after exchanging letters, tilting back in their swivel chairs, laughing out loud. Heaven only knows who got the letters in the long run. Neither one when in the press gallery seemed to write anything for the paper.

Some of the men tried to kid Alfred and teased him about women, asking if he found the girls in this country to his liking; but he seemed to enjoy it more than they did. Seriously he explained that he had never met a girl in this country but they looked very nice. Once Alfred and Bun Brophy, a red-headed fellow with a sharp tongue who did city hall for the paper, were alone in the gallery. Brophy had in his hands a big picture of five girls in masquerade costumes. Without explaining that he loved one of the girls Brophy asked Bowles which of the lot was the prettiest.

'You want me to settle that,' said Alfred, grinning and waving his pipe. He very deliberately selected a demure little girl with a shy smile.

Brophy was disappointed. 'Don't you think this one is pretty?' a colourful, bold-looking girl.

'Well, she's all right in her way, but she's too vivacious. I'll take this one. I like them kittenish,' Alfred said.

Brophy wanted to start an argument but Alfred said it was neither here nor there. He really didn't like women.

'You mean to say you never step out?' Brophy said.

'I've never seemed to mix with them,' he said, adding that the whole business didn't matter because he liked boys much better.

The men in the press room heard about it and some suggested nasty things to Alfred. It was hard to tease him when he wouldn't be serious. Sometimes

they asked if he took Harry out walking in the evenings. Brophy called them the heavy lovers. The
brothers didn't mind because they thought the
fellows were having a little fun.

In the fall Harry was fired. The editor in a nice
note said that he was satisfied Mr. H. W. Bowles
could not adapt himself to their methods. But everybody wondered why he hadn't been fired sooner. He
was no good on the paper.

The brothers smiled, shrugged their shoulders and
went on living together. Alfred still had his job.
Every noon hour in the City Hall press room they
were together, writing letters.

Time passed and the weather got cold. Alfred's
heavy coat came from the old country and he gave
his vest and a thin sweater to Harry, who had only
a light spring coat. As the weather got colder Harry
buttoned his coat higher up on his throat and even
though he looked cold he was neat as a pin with his
derby and cane.

Then Alfred lost his job. The editor, disgusted,
called him a fool. For the first time since coming
over last Spring he felt hurt, something inside him
was hurt and he told his brother about it, wanting
to know why people acted in such a way. He said he
had been doing night police. On the way over to
No. 1 station very late Thursday night he had met
two men from other papers. They told him about a
big fire earlier in the evening just about the time
when Alfred was accustomed to going to the hotel
to have a drink with his brother. They were willing
to give all the details and Alfred thankfully shook
hands with them and hurried back to the office to
write the story. Next morning the assistant city
editor phoned Alfred and asked how it was the

morning papers missed the story. Alfred tried to explain but Mr. Brownson said he was a damn fool for not phoning the police and making sure instead of trying to make the paper look like a pack of fools printing a fake story. The fellows who had kidded him said so too. Alfred kept asking his brother why the fellows had to do it. He seemed to be losing a good feeling for people.

Still the brothers appeared at noon time in the press room. They didn't write so many letters. They were agreeable, cheerful, on good terms with everybody. Bun Brophy every day asked how they were doing and they felt at home there. Harry would stand for a while watching the checker game always in progress, knowing that if he stood staring intently at the black and red squares, watching every deliberate move, he would be asked to sit in when it was necessary one of the players make the rounds in the hall. Once Brophy gave Harry his place and walked over to the window where Alfred stood watching the fleet of automobiles arranged in a square in the courtyard. The police wagon with a load of drunks was backing toward the cells.

'Say, Alfie, I often wonder how you guys manage,' he said.

'Oh, first rate.'

'Well, you ought to be in a bad way by now.'

'Oh no, we have solved the problem,' said Alfred in a grand way, grinning, as if talking about the British Empire.

He was eager to tell how they did it. There was a store in their block where a package of tobacco could be got for twenty cents; they did their own cooking and were able to live on ten dollars a week.

'What about coming over and having tea with us

sometime,' Alfred said. He was decidedly on his uppers but he asked Brophy to visit them and have tea.

Brophy, abashed, suggested the three of them go over to the café and have a little toast. Harry talked volubly on the way over and while having coffee. He was really a better talker than his brother. They sat in an arm-chair lunch, gripped the handles of their thick mugs, and talked about religion. The brothers were sons of a Baptist minister but never thought of going to church. It seemed that Brophy had travelled a lot during war-time and afterward in Asia Minor and India. He was telling about a great golden temple of the Sikhs at Amritsar and Harry listened carefully, asking many questions. Then they talked about newspapers until Harry started talking about the East, slowly feeling his way. All of a sudden he told about standing on a height of land near Amritsar, looking down at a temple. It couldn't have been so but he would have it that Brophy and he had seen the same temple and he described the country in the words Brophy had used. When he talked that way you actually believed that he had seen the temple.

Alfred liked listening to his brother but he said finally: 'Religion is a funny business. I tell you it's a funny business,' and for the time being no one would have thought of talking seriously about religion. Alfred had a casual way of making a cherished belief or opinion seem unimportant, a way of dismissing even the bright yarns of his brother.

After that afternoon in the café Brophy never saw Harry. Alfred came often to the City Hall but never mentioned his brother. Someone said maybe Harry had a job but Alfred laughed and said no such luck in this country, explaining casually that Harry had a bit of a cold and was resting up. In the passing days Alfred came only once in a while to the City Hall, writing his letter without enthusiasm.

The press men would have tried to help the brothers if they had heard Harry was sick. They were entirely ignorant of the matter. On a Friday afternoon at three-thirty Alfred came into the gallery and, smiling apologetically, told Brophy that his brother was dead; the funeral was to be in three-quarters of an hour; would he mind coming; it was pneumonia, he added. Brophy, looking hard at Alfred, put on his hat and coat and they went out.

It was a poor funeral. The hearse went on before along the way to the Anglican cemetery that overlooks the ravine. One old cab followed behind. There had been a heavy fall of snow in the morning and the slush on the pavement was thick. Alfred and Brophy sat in the old cab, silent. Alfred was leaning forward, his chin resting on his hands, the cane acting as a support, and the heavy pimples stood out on the lower part of his white face. Brophy was uncomfortable and chilly but he mopped his shining forehead with a big handkerchief. The window was open and the air was cold and damp.

Alfred politely asked how Mrs. Brophy was doing. Then he asked about Mr. Brownson.

'Oh, he's fine,' Brophy said. He wanted to close the window but it would have been necessary to move Alfred so he sat huddled in the corner, shivering.

Alfred asked suddenly if funerals didn't leave a bad taste in the mouth and Brophy, surprised, started talking absently about that golden temple of the Sikhs in India. Alfred appeared interested until they got to the cemetery. He said suddenly

he would have to take a look at the temple one
fine day.

They buried Harry Bowles in a grave in the
paupers' section on a slippery slope of the hill. The
earth was hard and chunky and it thumped down
on the coffin case. It snowed a little near the end.

On the way along the narrow, slippery foot-path
up the hill Alfred thanked Brophy for being
thoughtful enough to come to the funeral. There
was little to say. They shook hands and went different ways.

After a day or two Alfred again appeared in the
press room. He watched the checker game, congratulated the winner and then wrote home. The
men were sympathetic and said it was too bad about
his brother. And he smiled cheerfully and said they
were good fellows. In a little while he seemed to
have convinced them that nothing important had
really happened.

His last cent must have gone to the undertaker,
for he was particular about paying bills, but he
seemed to get along all right. Occasionally he did
a little work for the paper, a story from a night
assignment when the editor thought the staff was
being overworked.

One afternoon at two-thirty in the press gallery
Brophy saw the last of Alfred, who was sucking his
pipe, his feet up on a desk, wanting to be amused.
Brophy asked if anything had turned up. In a
playful, resigned tone, his eye on the big clock,
Alfred said he had until three to join the air force.
They wouldn't take him, he said, unless he let them
know by three.

Brophy said, 'How will you like that?'

'I don't fancy it.'

'But you're going though.'

'Well, I'm not sure. Something else may come along.' It was a quarter to three and he was sitting there waiting for a job to turn up before three.

No one saw him after that, but he didn't join the air force. Someone in the gallery said that wherever he went he probably wrote home as soon as he got there.

A Sick Call

MORLEY CALLAGHAN (b. 1903)

SOMETIMES Father Macdowell mumbled out loud and took a deep wheezy breath as he walked up and down the room and read his office. He was a huge old priest, white-headed except for a shiny baby-pink bald spot on the top of his head, and he was a bit deaf in one ear. His florid face had many fine red interlacing vein lines. For hours he had been hearing confessions and he was tired, for he always had to hear more confessions than any other priest at the cathedral; young girls who were in trouble, and wild but at times repentant young men, always wanted to tell their confessions to Father Macdowell, because nothing seemed to shock or excite him, or make him really angry, and he was even tender with those who thought they were most guilty.

While he was mumbling and reading and trying to keep his glasses on his nose, the house girl knocked on the door and said, 'There's a young lady here to see you, Father. I think it's about a sick call.'

'Did she ask for me especially?' he said in a deep but slightly cracked voice.

'Indeed she did, Father. She wanted Father Macdowell and nobody else.'

So he went out to the waiting room, where a girl
about thirty years of age, with fine brown eyes, fine
cheek bones, and rather square shoulders, was sitting
daubing her eyes with a handkerchief. She was
wearing a dark coat with a grey wolf collar. 'Good
evening, Father,' she said. 'My sister is sick. I wanted
you to come and see her. We think she's dying.'

'Be easy, child; what's the matter with her? Speak
louder. I can hardly hear you.'

'My sister's had pneumonia. The doctor's coming
back to see her in an hour. I wanted you to anoint
her, Father.'

'I see, I see. But she's not lost yet. I'll not give her
extreme unction now. That may not be necessary.
I'll go with you and hear her confession.'

'Father, I ought to let you know, maybe. Her
husband won't want to let you see her. He's not a
Catholic, and my sister hasn't been to church in a
long time.'

'Oh, don't mind that. He'll let me see her,' Father
Macdowell said, and he left the room to put on his
hat and coat.

When he returned, the girl explained that her
name was Jane Stanhope, and her sister lived only
a few blocks away. 'We'll walk and you tell me
about your sister,' he said. He put his black hat
square on the top of his head, and pieces of white
hair stuck out awkwardly at the sides. They went
to the avenue together.

The night was mild and clear. Miss Stanhope
began to walk slowly, because Father Macdowell's
rolling gait didn't get him along the street very
quickly. He walked as if his feet hurt him, though

he wore a pair of large, soft, specially constructed shapeless shoes. 'Now, my child, you go ahead and tell me about your sister,' he said, breathing with difficulty, yet giving the impression that nothing could have happened to the sister which would make him feel indignant.

There wasn't much to say, Miss Stanhope replied. Her sister had married John Williams two years ago, and he was a good, hardworking fellow, only he was very bigoted and hated all church people. 'My family wouldn't have anything to do with Elsa after she married him, though I kept going to see her,' she said. She was talking in a loud voice to Father Macdowell so he could hear her.

'Is she happy with her husband?'

'She's been very happy, Father. I must say that.'

'Where is he now?'

'He was sitting beside her bed. I ran out because I thought he was going to cry. He said if I brought a priest near the place he'd break the priest's head.'

'My goodness. Never mind, though. Does your sister want to see me?'

'She asked me to go and get a priest, but she doesn't want John to know she did it.'

Turning into a side street, they stopped at the first apartment house, and the old priest followed Miss Stanhope up the stairs. His breath came with great difficulty. 'Oh dear, I'm not getting any younger, not one day younger. It's a caution how a man's legs go back on him,' he said. As Miss Stanhope rapped on the door, she looked pleadingly at the old priest, trying to ask him not to be offended at anything that might happen, but he was smiling and looking huge in the narrow hallway. He wiped his head with his handkerchief.

The door was opened by a young man in a white shirt with no collar, with a head of thick black wavy hair. At first he looked dazed, then his eyes got bright with excitement when he saw the priest, as though he were glad to see someone he could destroy with pent-up energy. 'What do you mean, Jane?' he said. 'I told you not to bring a priest around here. My wife doesn't want to see a priest.'

'What's that you're saying, young man?'

'No one wants you here.'

'Speak up. Don't be afraid. I'm a bit hard of hearing.' Father Macdowell smiled rosily. John Williams was confused by the unexpected deafness in the priest, but he stood there, blocking the door with sullen resolution as if waiting for the priest to try to launch a curse at him.

'Speak to him, Father,' Miss Stanhope said, but the priest didn't seem to hear her; he was still smiling as he pushed past the young man, saying, 'I'll go in and sit down, if you don't mind, son. I'm here on God's errand, but I don't mind saying I'm all out of breath from climbing those stairs.'

John was dreadfully uneasy to see he had been brushed aside, and he followed the priest into the apartment and said loudly, 'I don't want you here.'

Father Macdowell said, 'Eh, eh?' Then he smiled sadly. 'Don't be angry with me, son,' he said. 'I'm too old to try and be fierce and threatening.' Looking around, he said, 'Where's your wife?' and he started to walk along the hall, looking for the bedroom.

John followed him and took hold of his arm. 'There's no sense in your wasting your time talking to my wife, do you hear?' he said angrily.

Miss Stanhope called out suddenly, 'Don't be rude, John.'

'It's he that's being rude. You mind your business,' John said.

'For the love of God let me sit down a moment with her, anyway. I'm tired,' the priest said.

'What do you want to say to her? Say it to me, why don't you?'

Then they both heard someone moan softly in the adjoining room, as if the sick woman had heard them. Father Macdowell, forgetting that the young man had hold of his arm, said, 'I'll go in and see her for a moment, if you don't mind,' and he began to open the door.

'You're not going to be alone with her, that's all,' John said, following him into the bedroom.

Lying on the bed was a white-faced, fair girl, whose skin was so delicate that her cheek bones stood out sharply. She was feverish, but her eyes rolled toward the door, and she watched them coming in. Father Macdowell took off his coat, and as he mumbled to himself he looked around the room at the mauve-silk bed light and the light wallpaper with the tiny birds in flight. It looked like a little girl's room. 'Good evening, Father,' Mrs. Williams whispered. She looked scared. She didn't glance at her husband. The notion of dying had made her afraid. She loved her husband and wanted to die loving him, but she was afraid, and she looked up at the priest.

'You're going to get well, child,' Father Macdowell said, smiling and patting her hand gently.

John, who was standing stiffly by the door, suddenly moved around the big priest, and he bent down over the bed and took his wife's hand and began to caress her forehead.

'Now, if you don't mind, my son, I'll hear your wife's confession,' the priest said.

'No, you won't,' John said abruptly. 'Her people didn't want her, and they left us together, and they're not going to separate us now. She's satisfied with me.' He kept looking down at her face as if he could not bear to turn away.

Father Macdowell nodded his head up and down and sighed. 'Poor boy,' he said. 'God bless you.' Then he looked at Mrs. Williams, who had closed her eyes, and he saw a faint tear on her cheek. 'Be sensible, my boy,' he said. 'You'll have to let me hear your wife's confession. Leave us alone awhile.'

'I'm going to stay right here,' John said, and he sat down on the end of the bed. He was working himself up and staring savagely at the priest. All of a sudden he noticed the tears on his wife's cheeks, and he muttered as though bewildered, 'What's the matter, Elsa? What's the matter, darling? Are we bothering you? Just open your eyes and we'll go out of the room and leave you alone till the doctor comes.' Then he turned and said to the priest, 'I'm not going to leave you here with her, can't you see that? Why don't you go?'

'I could revile you, my son. I could threaten you; but I ask you, for the peace of your wife's soul, leave us alone.' Father Macdowell spoke with patient tenderness. He looked very big and solid and immovable as he stood by the bed. 'I liked your face as soon as I saw you,' he said to John. 'You're a good fellow.'

John still held his wife's wrist, but he rubbed one hand through his thick hair and said angrily, 'You don't get the point, sir. My wife and I were always left alone, and we merely want to be left alone now. Nothing is going to separate us. She s been content with me. I'm sorry, sir; you'll have to speak to her with me here, or you'll have to go.'

'No; you'll have to go for a while,' the priest said patiently.

Then Mrs. Williams moved her head on the pillow and said jerkily, 'Pray for me, Father.'

So the old priest knelt down by the bed, and with a sweet unruffled expression on his florid face he began to pray. At times his breath came with a whistling noise as though a rumbling were inside him, and at other times he sighed and was full of sorrow. He was praying that young Mrs. Williams might get better, and while he prayed he knew that her husband was more afraid of losing her to the Church than losing her to death.

All the time Father Macdowell was on his knees, with his heavy prayer book in his two hands, John kept staring at him. John couldn't understand the old priest's patience and tolerance. He wanted to quarrel with him, but he kept on watching the light from overhead shining on the one baby-pink bald spot on the smooth white head, and at last he burst out, 'You don't understand, sir! We've been very happy together. Neither you nor her people came near her when she was in good health, so why should you bother her now? I don't want anything to separate us now; neither does she. She came with me. You see you'd be separating us, don't you?' He was trying to talk like a reasonable man who had no prejudices.

Father Macdowell got up clumsily. His knees hurt him, for the floor was hard. He said to Mrs. Williams in quite a loud voice, 'Did you really intend to give

up everything for this young fellow?' and he bent
down close to her so he could hear.

'Yes, Father,' she whispered.

'In Heaven's name, child, you couldn't have known
what you were doing.'

'We loved each other, Father. We've been very
happy.'

'All right. Supposing you were. What now? What
about all eternity, child?'

'Oh, Father, I'm very sick and I'm afraid.' She
looked up to try to show him how scared she was,
and how much she wanted him to give her
peace.

He sighed and seemed distressed, and at last he
said to John, 'Were you married in the church?'

'No, we weren't. Look here, we're talking pretty
loud and it upsets her.'

'Ah, it's a crime that I'm hard of hearing, I
know. Never mind, I'll go.' Picking up his coat, he
put it over his arm; then he sighed as if he were very
tired, and he said, 'I wonder if you'd just fetch me
a glass of water. I'd thank you for it.'

John hesitated, glancing at the tired old priest,
who looked so pink and white and almost cherubic
in his utter lack of guile.

'What's the matter?' Father Macdowell said.

John was ashamed of himself for appearing so
sullen, so he said hastily. 'Nothing's the matter. Just
a moment. I won't be a moment.' He hurried out of
the room.

The old priest looked down at the floor and shook
his head; and then, sighing and feeling uneasy, he
bent over Mrs. Williams, with his good ear down to
her, and he said, 'I'll just ask you a few questions in
a hurry, my child. You answer them quickly and

I'll give you absolution.' He made the sign of the cross over her and asked if she repented for having strayed from the Church, and if she had often been angry, and whether she had always been faithful, and if she had ever lied or stolen—all so casually and quickly as if it hadn't occurred to him that such a young woman could have serious sins. In the same breath he muttered, 'Say a good act of contrition to yourself and that will be all, my dear.' He had hardly taken a minute.

When John returned to the room with the glass of water in his hand, he saw the old priest making the sign of the cross. Father Macdowell went on praying without even looking up at John. When he had finished, he turned and said, 'Oh, there you are. Thanks for the water. I needed it. Well, my boy, I'm sorry if I worried you.'

John hardly said anything. He looked at his wife, who had closed her eyes, and he sat down on the end of the bed. He was too disappointed to speak.

Father Macdowell, who was expecting trouble, said, 'Don't be harsh, lad.'

'I'm not harsh,' he said mildly, looking up at the priest. 'But you weren't quite fair. And it's as though she turned away from me at the last moment. I didn't think she needed you.'

'God bless you, bless the both of you. She'll get better,' Father Macdowell said. But he felt ill at ease as he put on his coat, and he couldn't look directly at John.

Going along the hall, he spoke to Miss Stanhope, who wanted to apologize for her brother-in-law's attitude. 'I'm sorry if it was unpleasant for you, Father,' she said.

'It wasn't unpleasant,' he said. 'I was glad to meet

John. He's a fine fellow. It's a great pity he isn't a Catholic. I don't know as I played fair with him.'

As he went down the stairs, puffing and sighing, he pondered the question of whether he had played fair with the young man. But by the time he reached the street he was rejoicing amiably to think he had so successfully ministered to one who had strayed from the faith and had called out to him at the last moment. Walking along with the rolling motion as if his feet hurt him, he muttered, 'Of course they were happy as they were . . . in a worldly way. I wonder if I did come between them?'

He shuffled along, feeling very tired, but he couldn't help thinking, 'What beauty there was to his staunch love for her.' Then he added quickly, 'But it was just a pagan beauty, of course.'

As he began to wonder about the nature of this beauty, for some reason he felt inexpressibly sad.

A Priest in the Family

LEO KENNEDY (b. 1907)

MRS. HALLORAN had a nephew in the priesthood but that didn't stop her from drinking like a fish. Her husband, big Flatfoot Halloran, of the thick neck and braised-beef face, had been a patrolman on the Montreal waterfront, but gin and cahoots with the Black Hook Gang had got him off the cops some years before. Flatfoot then worked as a bouncer in a joint in St. Henry, but gin and depression laid *that* job by the heels, and Mrs. Halloran had gone tearfully back to charing. She had to admit that Flatfoot wasn't much now, since the rotgut disqualified him from even being a street-cleaner.

Anyhow, his lady chared in an office building, and in St. Timothy's Church in Irish Griffintown. Rubbing the warts on her long, lean chin, she used to lament the fact that Irish St. Timothy's was plumped down within swearing distance of the tough Italian section. What with blowsy, fat, shawled Dago women, pushcarts loaded with red and green peppers, part-time bad men and inexpensive, malodorous strumpets, Mrs. Halloran always found it a too colourful place to live in. Her nationalism and semi-respectability were tipsily belligerent most of the time.

Mrs. Halloran had a concave chest, thin grey hair, and sharp, red elbows. And how, with her drinking, this chaste matron managed to keep her place at the church, was more than her snooping neighbours could tell. But the curly-haired, plump-cheeked cleric who functioned as bursar for the establishment dealt mildly and kindly with sins of the flesh. He was, as he liked to say with a chuckle, always getting parishioners out of jail or on to the cops; and the charwoman's cautious tippling on weekdays, and flagrant jags on Saturdays, never loomed larger than peccadilloes in his tolerant mind.

Besides, her nephew was a priest.

Mrs. Halloran's nephew worked for souls in the wilds of British Columbia, and as she had never travelled farther than Ahuntsic, the good woman was somewhat vague as to the conditions of his employment and habitat. But she never let people forget there was an ordained priest in the family.

When she gossiped with friends she liked to bring the talk around to things religious. She used to say what a blessing it was to have a nephew who prayed daily for her sins. She liked to add that, though her soul was as scarlet, her Joey's monthly novena to the Holy Virgin for his poor old aunt would bring her still to glory.

She always breathed strongly of gin when she talked about religion. It provoked her to thoughts of heavenly ecstasy; the tin crucifix on her scrawny chest heaved and bobbed with the fervour of her devotion. The cord of her scapular worked out of her dress like a dirty bootlace.

Liquor inflamed her partisan spirit as well as her sense of theological fitness. It brought out a violent distaste for foreign devils. For instance, when she passed her Italian neighbour, Mrs. Castelano, on the tenement stairs, she would sneer disparagement of all Neapolitan womanhood. When the Castelano turned her broad, bulging back, Mrs. Halloran would be tempted to spit.

She would say in a thin voice to the stairs:

'May Jesus, Mary and Holy Joseph put boils on the neck of that black-faced bitch.'

At St. Timothy's, Mrs. Halloran's companion in toil was a middle-aged widow with flat, red hair and a squint. Mrs. Scully was a good soul, though rheumatic, and one Thursday, just before Lent came around, her complaint confined her to bed. The affliction was sudden and Nolan, the sexton, pulled a long face when he heard of it. Mrs. Scully's big muscles and chapped fists were needed for washing pews that day. A pyx to a poor-box, he decided, Mrs. Halloran would be tipsy herself.

Mrs. Castelano came into the refectory that morning with a tale of woe about her husband going to jail again and no money in the house.

Father Hoffman called Nolan in.

'Here's a poor soul in distress,' he said. 'Bandy Castelano has been peddling booze again. They've fixed him with a stretch this time. And it's my wish and the will of God Almighty, that Bandy's unhappy spouse should have bread on her table. So what can we give her in the way of work?'

Nolan looked critically at Mrs. Castelano's great thews and blowsy costume, and said sure she could take Mrs. Scully's place that was ill of the gout.

Father Hoffman said, 'There, Mrs. Castelano, you can work for your children and the Sacred Heart of Jesus at one and the same time. Nolan, tell this woman what to do.'

*　　*　　*　　*　　*

That afternoon Mrs. Halloran entered the precincts of St. Timothy's armed with the requisites of her trade. A pail of hot water thinly sudded, a grey cloth for washing the pews, a pail of clear water for the last ablution. She was late for work, having lingered at home to haggle with Flatfoot and bibble strength for her labours. Depositing her pails at the head of the nave, she dropped her jaw to see her loathed Italian neighbour in the Scully's stead. Mrs. Castelano was already wiping the pew woodwork, and she nodded briefly.

Mrs. Halloran bristled with surprise and resentment. She stood over her pails with arms akimbo. She loosed a tentative broadside:

'An' may I be askin' where Mrs. Scully is at today? An' for what are you workin' in her place? Is St. Timothy's a Protestant gospel-hall that God-fearin' women should be put out for such as thinks Christ is a Dago bambino?'

Her unjust and inaccurate reference to non-Catholic practice left Mrs. Castelano's moon face the blanker, but the good woman bridled at 'Dago'.

'Mrs. Scully, she's sick in her legs,' said Mrs. Castelano, her large bosom rising a little. 'She don't work. Me, I got the job to wash in the church till she's fine.'

Her glance took in the other's condition.

'When she come back, too, maybe.'

'An' is it you who're makin' aspersions at me, Mrs. Castelano? To what end may I ask? Would you be graftin' my job for your fat self? Would you be keepin' your bootlegger husband on my wages?'

Mrs. Castelano breathed deeply and gave her wet cloth a wrench.

'Me, I talk to you after,' she said, 'not now in the holy God's house. I got to work. You better work, too, yes.'

Mrs. Halloran plunged her cloth in the soapy water, and with a vixenish back turned to the Italian woman, she vigorously commenced to wipe a pew. She washed and dried, muttering to herself at intervals. She poked savagely into corners as though stabbing her enemy with a cloth-draped finger.

Miss Brown, the little dried spinster who cared for the altar flowers and linens, entered the church from the sacristy. She always wore cautiously sombre woollen suits, and hats that excited neither pity nor admiration. She had a brittle, ethereal look that may have come from handling so many hothouse flowers, and long candles made of tallow and beeswax. She walked with a slight list to the right, and one felt that a breath which could flutter a candle would douse her outright.

Miss Brown began to clear the altar of its accessories. She paid no attention to the two charwomen in the dimly lit aisle; she was thinking timidly of Father Hoffman's curly head and broadish girth. The one comfort of her arid virginity was the occasional nearness of this honest and holy man.

The charwomen regarded her birdlike movements with disfavour. They demurred at that social balance which set them at one end of the church with scrub pails, and this lopsided holier-than-thou at the altar with her paws on the monstrance.

They continued to swab down pews.

Watching Miss Brown bobbing about up front, Mrs. Halloran began to think of the duty of women to God and how her sister had credited her race and family by presenting nephew Joey to holy orders. She reflected that Miss Brown's sole offering was a fistful of Easter lilies and the dripping heel of a taper. She lingered over her own barren lot. And she thought with distaste of Mrs. Castelano's seven. The big sow!

'Mrs. Castelano,' she struck her favourite motif, 'did I ever speak of my nephew in orders, him that's an O'Connaught, my own sister's child? As I always say, a priest in the family (by God's Holy Name!) should slip me through Purgatory with just the bit of a singe.'

'Sure,' said Mrs. Castelano, plying her rag, 'you told me plenty. For me, I don't like so much those Irish priests. Young one, old one, they are not much priest. Plenty people know, yes.

'Look here, St. Timothy's. What they got? They got no Irish priest. They got Father Hoffman . . . a name for a German fella. For me, I like Italian priest. Like the Pope.'

Mrs. Halloran twisted her wash cloth violently.

'You'll be sayin' next the Lord Jesus was a Dago!
An' St. Peter and St. Paul. It was a dark day for the
blessed fisher of men when he set up the holy wood
in heathen Rome. An' blacker for St. Paul when they
chopped his head off . . . murderers, gangsters that
they were.

'No good came out of that country . . . for there's
no good in it. An' it's the blight and curse of the
Catholic Church that the Pope is a wop that can't
talk English! You'll find these words in no copy-
book, Castelano. They're private sentiments! And
did I honestly speak my mind the world would be a
better place if they'd elect a Cardinal with the green
on his pants!'

The outraged madonna flashed black eyes at her
grimacing antagonist. Cowlike and placid by ordinary, her anger gathered like clouds before thunder.
But Mrs. Halloran spluttered on:

'For what are your fat priests good, but to snore
at confession and sneeze in the font? They're wops
first and priests after, an' no amount of holy oil
will fill their souls with grace. It's the likes of them
as breaks the heart of his Eminence the Bishop, an'
keeps the Irish parishes prayin' for light to array
their schemin' hearts!'

Her voice screamed up among the organ pipes.

'You Dagos, you! Gunmen and whores! Peddlers
of bathtub gin!'

Shaking with rage, the Castelano dropped her
washcloth in the dirty water, retrieved it sopping,
and with a sudden movement slashed Mrs. Halloran
across the mouth.

She squealed and struck again and again.

The Irish woman, spitting filthy water and abuse,
fought free of the piston arm, and seizing her own

pail of slops, deluged it over the face and body of Mrs. Castelano.

Mrs. Castelano screeched at the shock of water, and was still unrecovered when Mrs. Halloran's wash-rag slapped her stingingly across the eyes. Half blinded by the blow, she whirled to where she dimly and painfully saw her antagonist to be, and struck out with cloth and fist. Mrs. Halloran evaded what blows she could and delivered what thumps and scratches she might; their turmoil filled the church with sound.

Miss Brown, with mouth agape and feet firmly rooted before the altar, thrilled with horror at the sacrilege and made futile little gestures with her hands. She had been working quietly, her mind following Father Hoffman through the routine of his day, when this pandemonium broke loose in God's tabernacle. The church was empty of faithful, and she prayed that none would come to linger with the Sacred Heart before these mad women could be quietened.

A bellow from Mrs. Halloran, whose face was now running sparsely with blood, shocked her from the static pose. She swung wide the altar gate and ran screaming to part the women.

'Father Hoffman! Mr. Nolan! They'll kill each other!'

'Love of Jesus!' Then a blow from the Latin fury caught and bowled her into a pew.

The priest and sexton, occupied elsewhere in the church building, were startled to hear these muffled cries.

'You thick cow! Take that an' that!'

'Irish pig, your man was pitch' off the cops!'

'Blood of Jesus, the woman's stabbed me!'

'You spit on fat Italian, so!'

'Father Hoffman! Father Hoffman!'

'A scandal in the church, Father . . . oh, hurry, for the love of God.'

Again attempting to part the infuriated women, little Miss Brown had her hat dragged off, her hair torn, and one eye damaged. She reeled out of the radius of whirling fists, and collapsed in a pew, weeping hysterically.

The charwomen lashed, kicked and pummelled, howling abuse and panting for breath, thumping each other's bosom and stomach, splintering finger nails on face and neck. Mrs. Halloran's right cheek was channelled with the marks of four clawed fingers; the dress of Mrs. Castelano was torn half off her shoulders, disclosing one large, badly-scratched breast, and a shoulder bruised where it had been battered by the pail.

They separated for a moment, then with loud cries flew at each other, clawing and stamping. At that moment the priest tore down the aisle with Nolan at his heels; the men took the women by the arms and dragged them apart. They then hustled the whole party into the sacristy, pausing only behind closed doors to draw a free breath.

'In the name of Judgement, what scandal is this?' the priest's eyes burned into the women one by one.

'Would you be murdering each other, and you employed in the house of God? You, Mrs. Halloran, with gin on your breath, and you, Mrs. Castelano, with your dress half off.'

A panting mountain of woman ready to subside in tears, she clumsily fastened it.

'What can a Christian say to such business?' the priest continued in righteous wrath. 'Such devil's work under St. Timothy's nose? Mrs. Castelano, did I give you a job this day that you could be tearing and clawing this woman's face, and swabbing her blood with your floor-cloth?'

The German fella's excited accent implied a south of Ireland mother.

'And Mary Mother crowned in heaven, what a battered mess you've made of Miss Brown! Miss Brown, what started this fiendish ruction, that yourself should be clawed like a tom cat? But wait . . . wait . . . this is no case for me. . . . Nolan, be calling the cop off his beat!'

The women made great outcry at this: Miss Brown bleating there was scandal enough; Mrs. Castelano wailing that her man was in the jail already, and what would her children do if she followed; Mrs. Halloran demanding what was religion coming to, when Catholic fathers turned their parishioners over to the bulls? Father Hoffman motioned Nolan out none the less, and closed the door after the vestry-man. He asked Miss Brown to tell him calmly how the row began.

Miss Brown, nursing her bruises, said dazedly that the charwomen had had an argument which briskly developed into a duel to the death. She said both women were wretches, but Mrs. Halloran had been screaming the fouler oaths. She hadn't seen who struck the first blow, but thought Mrs. Halloran a blot on the honour of any parish. She said Mrs. Castelano had bleared her eye for her, but that Mrs. Halloran would prompt a saint to murder. She said, yes, Mrs. Halloran's face was scratched, but Mrs. Castelano had been smacked hard with a pail on the . . . well, chest, and her a mother, judging from her figure.

Mrs. Castelano cried that she was a mother seven times over by God's forethought, but what ailed her figure that a skinny spinster should talk of it?

Father Hoffman said, 'Hush, be still!' and told Miss Brown to go home and tend to her wounds. He swore her to silence, promised to give the women their deserts, and with a friendly pat on the cheek that made Miss Brown's dejected spirit flicker and rise like the phoenix, ushered her out. Then, with an expression of gravity, he confronted the two culprits.

'Mrs. Castelano, I'm thinking that, in spite of your actions, you're more sinned against than sinning. God knows his House is no place for a free-for-all, but knowing you both as well as I do, I see fit to make no bother this time. But think of poor Bandy languishing, and your children's hungry mouths, before you go basting people about the head. I'll be letting you off, and more than that, I'll be letting you keep your job, but not a word of this to a soul, on your honour as a Catholic. Now go tell Mr. Nolan I said you were to stay. And you'd better come and confess to me this night.'

Mrs. Castelano went out whimpering, and the priest fixed Mrs. Halloran with a calculating eye.

'If I didn't know you and your man so well, I'd be sending you off to the jail now! You're a whitened sepulchre, Mrs. Halloran, and a blot on the roll of the parish. It's a lot of trouble you're making here, and a power of hell-fire you're fixing for the hereafter. And with a priest in the family!'

'My!'

The woman began to weep with sentimental religious fear.

'The Almighty Lord is forgiving of sin, but bitter

to those who make it a habit. You're too fond of the gin.'

'Yes, Father.'

'A woman of your years should have her eyes set on eternal life. The pleasures of this life pass like snow before the sun, and Judgement awaits us the other side of the grave. Think well of that when you'd be drinking.

'Drink, Mrs. Halloran, is one of the Church's greatest enemies, and the devil's own brew!'

He observed her emotion shrewdly.

'Are you prepared to burn in hell, my poor woman? Not for the term of your life, but for all Eternity, a length of time you can't possibly imagine?'

'No, Father! I swear to Jesus, no!'

'Swearing by the Holy Name will bring you no nearer to glory . . . but Confession will. Mrs. Halloran, I'd like to hear your confession now!'

He went to a closet and took his stole from a hook, then seated himself in an easy chair and motioned to Mrs. Halloran to kneel. The woman with terror tweaking her bowels got down beside him and blessed herself.

'Bless me, Father, for I have sinned; I confess to Almighty God and to you, Father . . .'

Her confessor heard her out and pronounced a nominal penance. The man's natural kindliness made him regard her benevolently.

'Ah, Mrs. Halloran, the Saviour loves a penitent! Your soul is now as white as the lilies of the field, but keep it so! For your soul's good and the good of your job in the church, will you promise to quit the liquor? Cut it out altogether and cast out temptation.

'I'm thinking of Father Joseph O'Connaught, and how he'd feel about a drunken aunt. It's for his sake I'm letting you keep your place, though the saints know you've tried me sorely. . . .

'Go back to your pew work . . . and lay off Mrs. Castelano. She's a good Catholic herself, for all she isn't Irish. Say your penance with devotion, and pray for Father Joseph and me.'

Mrs. Halloran thanked him with fervour. She tucked her hair up under her kerchief and went into the church. Mrs. Castelano was working already; her broad back was stiff and forbidding. Mrs. Halloran got her pails, went back and filled them, and then commenced working too. In her mind she began to rattle off the prayers of her penance.

'Hail, Mary, full of grace, the Lord is with thee, blessed art thou among women an' blessed is the fruit . . .

'He said it was because Joey is a priest. Isn't that fine now? He wouldn't fire me because of my nephew. . . .

'Of thy womb, Jesus, Holy Mary, mother of God. . . .

'I always said a priest in the family is God's own blessing. An' Joey makes a monthly novena to Mary for me. . . .

'Pray for us sinners. . . .

'Prayer *is* a blessing. Joey's prayers will get me through Purgatory sure as blazes . . . but just the same. . . .

'They've saved my bacon here below as well. . . .

'Now an' at the hour of our death, Amen.'

The Painted Door

SINCLAIR ROSS (b. 1908)

STRAIGHT across the hills it was five miles from John's farm to his father's. But in winter, with the roads impassible, a team had to make a wide detour and skirt the hills, so that from five the distance was more than trebled to seventeen.

'I think I'll walk,' John said at breakfast to his wife. 'The drifts in the hills wouldn't hold a horse, but they'll carry me all right. If I leave early I can spend a few hours helping him with his chores, and still be back by suppertime.'

Moodily she went to the window, and thawing a clear place in the frost with her breath, stood looking across the snowswept farmyard to the huddle of stables and sheds. 'There was a double wheel around the moon last night,' she countered presently. 'You said yourself we could expect a storm. It isn't right to leave me here alone. Surely I'm as important as your father.'

He glanced up uneasily, then drinking off his coffee tried to reassure her. 'But there's nothing to be afraid of—even if it does start to storm. You won't need to go near the stable. Everything's fed and watered now to last till night. I'll be back at the latest by seven or eight.'

She went on blowing against the frosted pane, carefully elongating the clear place until it was oval-shaped and symmetrical. He watched her a moment or two longer, then more insistently repeated, 'I say you won't need to go near the stable. Everything's fed and watered, and I'll see that there's plenty of wood in. That will be all right, won't it?'

'Yes—of course—I heard you—' It was a curiously cold voice now, as if the words were chilled by their contact with the frosted pane. 'Plenty to eat—plenty of wood to keep me warm—what more could a woman ask for?'

'But he's an old man—living there all alone. What is it, Ann? You're not like yourself this morning.'

She shook her head without turning. 'Pay no attention to me. Seven years a farmer's wife—it's time I was used to staying alone.'

Slowly the clear place on the glass enlarged: oval, then round, then oval again. The sun was risen above the frost mists now, so keen and hard a glitter on the snow that instead of warmth its rays seemed shedding cold. One of the two-year-old colts that had cantered away when John turned the horses out for water stood covered with rime at the stable door again, head down and body hunched, each breath a little plume of steam against the frosty air. She shivered, but did not turn. In the clear, bitter light the long white miles of prairie landscape seemed a region strangely alien to life. Even the distant farmsteads she could see served only to intensify a sense of isolation. Scattered across the face of so vast and bleak a wilderness it was difficult to conceive them as a testimony of human hardihood and endurance. Rather they seemed futile, lost. Rather they seemed to cower before the implacability of snow-swept earth and clear pale sun-chilled sky.

And when at last she turned from the window there was a brooding stillness in her face as if she had recognized this mastery of snow and cold. It troubled John. 'If you're really afraid,' he yielded, 'I won't go today. Lately it's been so cold, that's all. I just wanted to make sure he's all right in case we do have a storm.'

'I know—I'm not really afraid.' She was putting in a fire now, and he could no longer see her face. 'Pay no attention to me. It's ten miles there and back, so you'd better get started.'

'You ought to know by now I wouldn't stay away,' he tried to brighten her. 'No matter how it stormed. Twice a week before we were married I never missed —and there were bad blizzards that winter too.'

He was a slow, unambitious man, content with his farm and cattle, naïvely proud of Ann. He had been bewildered by it once, her caring for a dull-witted fellow like him; then assured at last of her affection he had relaxed against it gratefully, unsuspecting it might ever be less constant than his own. Even now, listening to the restless brooding in her voice, he felt only a quick, unformulated kind of pride that after seven years his absence for a day should still concern her. While she, his trust and earnestness controlling her again:

'I know. It's just that sometimes when you're away I get lonely. . . . There's a long cold tramp in front of you. You'll let me fix a scarf around your face.'

He nodded. 'And on my way I'll drop in at Steven's place. Maybe he'll come over tonight for a game of cards. You haven't seen anybody but me for the last two weeks.'

She glanced up sharply, then busied herself clearing the table. 'It will mean another two miles if you do. You're going to be cold and tired enough as it is. When you're gone I think I'll paint the kitchen woodwork. White this time—you remember we got the paint last fall. It's going to make the room a lot lighter. I'll be too busy to find the day long.'

'I will though,' he insisted, 'and if a storm gets up you'll feel safer, knowing that he's coming. That's what you need, Ann—someone to talk to besides me.'

She stood at the stove motionless a moment, then turned to him uneasily. 'Will you shave then, John— now—before you go?'

He glanced at her questioningly, and avoiding his eyes she tried to explain, 'I mean—he may be here before you're back—and you won't have a chance then.'

'But it's only Steven—he's seen me like this—'

'He'll be shaved, though—that's what I mean— and I'd like you too to spend a little time on yourself.'

He stood up, stroking the heavy stubble on his chin. 'Maybe I should all right, but it makes the skin too tender. Especially when I've got to face the wind.'

She nodded and began to help him dress, bringing heavy socks and a big woollen sweater from the bedroom, wrapping a scarf around his face and forehead. 'I'll tell Steven to come early,' he said, as he went out. 'In time for supper. Likely there'll be chores for me to do, so if I'm not back by six don't wait.'

From the bedroom window she watched him nearly a mile along the road. The fire had gone down when at last she turned away, and already through the house there was an encroaching chill. A blaze sprang up again when the drafts were opened, but as she went on clearing the table her movements were furtive and constrained. It was the silence weighing upon her—the frozen silence of the bitter fields and sun-chilled sky—lurking outside as if alive, relentlessly in wait, mile-deep between her now and John. She listened to it, suddenly tense, motionless. The fire crackled and the clock ticked. Always it was there. 'I'm a fool,' she whispered hoarsely, rattling the dishes in defiance, going back to the stove to put in another fire. 'Warm and safe—I'm a fool. It's a good chance when he's away to paint. The day will go quickly. I won't have time to brood.'

Since November now the paint had been waiting warmer weather. The frost in the walls on a day like this would crack and peel it as it dried, but she needed something to keep her hands occupied, something to stave off the gathering cold and loneliness. 'First of all,' she said aloud, opening the paint and mixing it with a little turpentine, 'I must get the house warmer. Fill up the stove and open the oven door so that all the heat comes out. Wad something along the window sills to keep out the drafts. Then I'll feel brighter. It's the cold that depresses.'

She moved briskly, performing each little task with careful and exaggerated absorption, binding her thoughts to it, making it a screen between herself and the surrounding snow and silence. But when the stove was filled and the windows sealed it was more difficult again. Above the quiet, steady swishing of her brush against the bedroom door the clock began to tick. Suddenly her movements became precise, deliberate, her posture self-conscious, as if someone had entered the room and were watching her. It was the silence again, aggressive, hovering. The fire spit and crackled at it. Still it was there. 'I'm a fool,' she repeated. 'All farmers' wives have to stay alone. I mustn't give in this way. I mustn't brood. A few hours now and they'll be here.'

The sound of her voice reassured her. She went on: 'I'll get them a good supper—and for coffee to-night after cards bake some of the little cakes with raisins that he likes. . . . Just three of us, so I'll watch, and let John play. It's better with four, but at least we can talk. That's all I need—someone to talk to. John never talks. He's stronger—he doesn't understand. But he likes Steven—no matter what the neighbours say. Maybe he'll have him come again, and some other young people too. It's what we need, both of us, to help keep young ourselves. . . . And then before we know it we'll be into March. It's cold still in March sometimes, but you never mind the same. At least you're beginning to think about spring.'

She began to think about it now. Thoughts that outstripped her words, that left her alone again with herself and the ever-lurking silence. Eager and hopeful first; then clenched, rebellious, lonely. Windows open, sun and thawing earth again, the urge of growing, living things. Then the days that began in the morning at half-past four and lasted till ten at night; the meals at which John gulped his food and scarcely spoke a word; the brute-tired stupid eyes he turned on her if ever she mentioned town or visiting.

For spring was drudgery again. John never hired a man to help him. He wanted a mortgage-free farm; then a new house and pretty clothes for her. Sometimes, because with the best of crops it was going to take so long to pay off anyway, she wondered whether they mightn't better let the mortgage wait a little. Before they were worn out, before their best years were gone. It was something of life she wanted, not just a house and furniture; something of John, not pretty clothes when she would be too old to wear them. But John of course couldn't understand. To him it seemed only right that she should have the clothes—only right that he, fit for nothing else, should slave away fifteen hours a day to give them to her. There was in his devotion a baffling, insurmountable humility that made him feel the need of sacrifice. And when his muscles ached, when his feet dragged stolidly with weariness, then it seemed that in some measure at least he was making amends for his big hulking body and simple mind. That by his sacrifice he succeeded only in the extinction of his personality never occurred to him. Year after year their lives went on in the same little groove. He drove his horses in the field; she milked the cows and hoed potatoes. By dint of his drudgery he saved a few months' wages, added a few dollars more each fall to his payments on the mortgage; but the only real difference that it all made was to deprive her of his companionship, to make him a little duller, older, uglier than he might otherwise have been. He never saw their lives objectively. To him it was not what he actually accomplished by means of the sacrifice that mattered, but the sacrifice itself, the gesture—something done for her sake.

And she, understanding, kept her silence. In such a gesture, however futile, there was a graciousness not to be shattered lightly. 'John,' she would begin sometimes, 'you're doing too much. Get a man to help you—just for a month—' but smiling down at her he would answer simply, 'I don't mind. Look at the hands on me. They're made for work.' While in his voice there would be a stalwart ring to tell her that by her thoughtfulness she had made him only the more resolved to serve her, to prove his devotion and fidelity.

They were useless, such thoughts. She knew. It was his very devotion that made them useless, that forbade her to rebel. Yet over and over, sometimes hunched still before their bleakness, sometimes her brush making swift sharp strokes to pace the chafe and rancour that they brought, she persisted in them.

This now, the winter, was their slack season. She could sleep sometimes till eight, and John till seven. They could linger over their meals a little, read, play cards, go visiting the neighbours. It was the time to relax, to indulge and enjoy themselves; but instead, fretful and impatient, they kept on waiting for the spring. They were compelled now, not by labour, but by the spirit of labour. A spirit that pervaded their lives and brought with idleness a sense of guilt. Sometimes they did sleep late, sometimes they did play cards, but always uneasily, always reproached by the thought of more important things that might be done. When John got up at five to attend to the fire he wanted to stay up and go out to the stable. When he sat down to a meal he hurried his food and pushed his chair away again, from habit, from sheer work-instinct, even though it was only to put more wood in the stove, or go down cellar to cut up beets and turnips for the cows.

And anyway, sometimes she asked herself, why sit trying to talk with a man who never talked? Why talk when there was nothing to talk about but crops and cattle, the weather and the neighbours? The neighbours, too—why go visiting them when still it was the same—crops and cattle, the weather and the other neighbours? Why go to the dances in the schoolhouse to sit among the older women, one of them now, married seven years, or to waltz with the work-bent, tired old farmers to a squeaky fiddle tune? Once she had danced with Steven six or seven times in the evening, and they had talked about it for as many months. It was easier to stay at home. John never danced or enjoyed himself. He was always uncomfortable in his good suit and shoes. He didn't like shaving in the cold weather oftener than once or twice a week. It was easier to stay at home, to stand at the window staring out across the bitter fields, to count the days and look forward to another spring.

But now, alone with herself in the winter silence, she saw the spring for what it really was. This spring —next spring—all the springs and summers still to come. While they grew old, while their bodies warped, while their minds kept shrivelling dry and empty like their lives. 'I mustn't,' she said aloud again. 'I married him—and he's a good man. I mustn't keep on this way. It will be noon before long, and then time to think about supper. . . . Maybe he'll come early—and as soon as John is finished at the stable we can all play cards.'

It was getting cold again, and she left her painting to put in more wood. But this time the warmth spread slowly. She pushed a mat up to the outside door, and went back to the window to pat down the woollen shirt that was wadded along the sill. Then she paced a few times round the room, then poked the fire and rattled the stove lids, then paced again. The fire crackled, the clock ticked. The silence now seemed more intense than ever, seemed to have reached a pitch where it faintly moaned. She began to pace on tiptoe, listening, her shoulders drawn together, not realizing for a while that it was the wind she heard, thin-strained and whimpering through the eaves.

Then she wheeled to the window, and with quick short breaths thawed the frost to see again. The glitter was gone. Across the drifts sped swift and snakelike little tongues of snow. She could not follow them, where they sprang from, or where they disappeared. It was as if all across the yard the snow were shivering awake—roused by the warnings of the wind to hold itself in readiness for the impending storm. The sky had become a sombre, whitish grey. It, too, as if in readiness, had shifted and lay close to earth. Before her as she watched a mane of powdery snow reared up breast-high against the darker background of the stable, tossed for a moment angrily, and then subsided again as if whipped down to obedience and restraint. But another followed, more reckless and impatient than the first. Another reeled and dashed itself against the window where she watched. Then ominously for a while there were only the angry little snakes of snow. The wind rose, creaking the troughs that were wired beneath the eaves. In the distance, sky and prairie now were merged into one another linelessly. All round her it was gathering; already in its press and whimpering there strummed a boding of eventual fury. Again she saw a mane of snow spring up, so dense and high this time that all the sheds and stables were obscured. Then others followed, whirling fiercely out of hand; and, when at last they cleared, the stables seemed in dimmer outline than before. It was the snow beginning, long lancet shafts of it, straight from the north, borne almost level by the straining wind. 'He'll be there soon,' she whispered, 'and coming home it will be in his back. He'll leave again right away. He saw the double wheel— he knows the kind of storm there'll be.'

She went back to her painting. For a while it was easier, all her thoughts half-anxious ones of John in the blizzard, struggling his way across the hills; but petulantly again she soon began, 'I knew we were going to have a storm—I told him so—but it doesn't matter what I say. Big stubborn fool—he goes his own way anyway. It doesn't matter what becomes of me. In a storm like this he'll never get home. He won't even try. And while he sits keeping his father company I can look after his stable for him, go ploughing through snowdrifts up to my knees— nearly frozen—'

Not that she meant or believed her words. It was just an effort to convince herself that she did have a grievance, to justify her rebellious thoughts, to prove John responsible for her unhappiness. She was young still, eager for excitement and distractions; and John's steadfastness rebuked her vanity, made her complaints seem weak and trivial. Fretfully she went on, 'If he'd listen to me sometimes and not be so stubborn we wouldn't be living still in a house like this. Seven years in two rooms—seven years and never a new stick of furniture. . . . There—as if another coat of paint could make it different anyway.'

She cleaned her brush, filled up the stove again, and went back to the window. There was a void white moment that she thought must be frost formed on the window pane; then, like a fitful shadow through the whirling snow, she recognized the stable roof. It was incredible. The sudden, maniac raging of the storm struck from her face all its pettishness. Her eyes glazed with fear a little; her lips blanched. 'If

he starts for home now,' she whispered silently—
'But he won't—he knows I'm safe—he knows Steven's
coming. Across the hills he would never dare.'

She turned to the stove, holding out her hands to
the warmth. Around her now there seemed a constant sway and tremor, as if the air were vibrating
with the violent shudderings of the walls. She stood
quite still, listening. Sometimes the wind struck with
sharp, savage blows. Sometimes it bore down in a
sustained, minute-long blast, silent with effort and
intensity; then with a foiled shriek of threat wheeled
away to gather and assault again. Always the eave-
troughs creaked and sawed. She started towards the
window again, then detecting the morbid trend of
her thoughts, prepared fresh coffee and forced herself to drink a few mouthfuls. 'He would never dare,'
she whispered again. 'He wouldn't leave the old man
anyway in such a storm. Safe in here—there's
nothing for me to keep worrying about. It's after
one already. I'll do my baking now, and then it will
be time to get supper ready for Steven.'

Soon, however, she began to doubt whether Steven
would come. In such a storm even a mile was enough
to make a man hesitate. Especially Steven, who, for
all his atractive qualities, was hardly the one to face
a blizzard for the sake of someone else's chores. He
had a stable of his own to look after anyway. It would
be only natural for him to think that when the storm
rose John had turned again for home. Another man
would have—would have put his wife first.

But she felt little dread or uneasiness at the prospect of spending the night alone. It was the first time
she had been left like this on her own resources, and
her reaction, now that she could face and appraise
her situation calmly, was gradually to feel it a kind

of adventure and responsibility. It stimulated her. Before nightfall she must go to the stable and feed everything. Wrap up in some of John's clothes— take a ball of string in her hand, one end tied to the door, so that no matter how blinding the storm she could at least find her way back to the house. She had heard of people having to do that. It appealed to her now because suddenly it made life dramatic. She had not felt the storm yet, only watched it for a minute through the window.

It took nearly an hour to find enough string, to choose the right socks and sweaters. Long before it was time to start out she tried on John's clothes, changing and rechanging, striding around the room to make sure there would be play enough for pitching hay and struggling over snowdrifts; then she took them off again, and for a while busied herself baking the little cakes with raisins that he liked.

Night came early. Just for a moment on the doorstep she shrank back, uncertain. The slow dimming of the light clutched her with an illogical sense of abandonment. It was like the covert withdrawal of an ally, leaving the alien miles unleashed and unrestrained. Watching the hurricane of writhing snow rage past the little house she forced herself, 'They'll never stand the night unless I get them fed. It's nearly dark already, and I've work to last an hour.'

Timidly, unwinding a little of the string, she crept out from the shelter of the doorway. A gust of wind spun her forward a few yards, then plunged her headlong against a drift that in the dense white whirl lay invisible across her path. For nearly a minute she huddled still, breathless and dazed. The snow was in her mouth and nostrils, inside her scarf and up her sleeves. As she tried to straighten a smothering scud flung itself against her face, cutting off her breath a second time. The wind struck from all sides, blustering and furious. It was as if the storm had discovered her, as if all its forces were concentrated upon her extinction. Seized with panic suddenly she threshed out a moment with her arms, then stumbled back and sprawled her length across the drift.

But this time she regained her feet quickly, roused by the whip and batter of the storm to retaliative anger. For a moment her impulse was to face the wind and strike back blow for blow; then, as suddenly as it had come, her frantic strength gave way to limpness and exhaustion. Suddenly, a comprehension so clear and terrifying that it struck all thoughts of the stable from her mind, she realized in such a storm her puny insignificance. And the realization gave her new strength, stilled this time to a desperate persistence. Just for a moment the wind held her, numb and swaying in its vise; then slowly, buckled far forward, she groped her way again towards the house.

Inside, leaning against the door, she stood tense and still a while. It was almost dark now. The top of the stove glowed a deep, dull red. Heedless of the storm, self-absorbed and self-satisfied, the clock ticked on like a glib little idiot. 'He shouldn't have gone,' she whispered silently. 'He saw the double wheel—he knew. He shouldn't have left me here alone.'

For so fierce now, so insane and dominant did the blizzard seem, that she could not credit the safety of the house. The warmth and lull around her was not real yet, not to be relied upon. She was still at the mercy of the storm. Only her body pressing hard like this against the door was staving it off. She didn't dare move. She didn't dare ease the ache and strain. 'He shouldn't have gone,' she repeated, thinking of the stable again, reproached by her helplessness. 'They'll freeze in their stalls—and I can't reach them. He'll say it's all my fault. He won't believe I tried.'

Then Steven came. Quickly, startled to quietness and control, she let him in and lit the lamp. He stared at her a moment, then flinging off his cap crossed to where she stood by the table and seized her arms. 'You're so white—what's wrong? Look at me—' It was like him in such little situations to be masterful. 'You should have known better than to go out on a day like this. For a while I thought I wasn't going to make it here myself—'

'I was afraid you wouldn't come—John left early, and there was the stable—'

But the storm had unnerved her, and suddenly at the assurance of his touch and voice the fear that had been gripping her gave way to an hysteria of relief. Scarcely aware of herself she seized his arm and sobbed against it. He remained still a moment, unyielding, then slipped his other arm around her shoulder. It was comforting and she relaxed against it, hushed by a sudden sense of lull and safety. Her shoulders trembled with the easing of the strain, then fell limp and still. 'You're shivering,'—he drew her gently towards the stove. 'There's nothing to be afraid of now, though. I'm going to do the chores for you.'

It was a quiet, sympathetic voice, yet with an undertone of insolence, a kind of mockery even, that made her draw away quickly and busy herself putting in a fire. With his lips drawn in a little smile he watched her till she looked at him again. The smile too was insolent, but at the same time companionable; Steven's smile, and therefore difficult to reprove. It lit up his lean, still-boyish face with a peculiar kind of arrogance: features and smile that were different from John's, from other men's—wilful and derisive, yet naïvely so—as if it were less the difference itself he was conscious of, than the long-accustomed privilege that thereby fell his due. He was erect, tall, square-shouldered. His hair was dark and trim, his young lips curved soft and full. While John, she made the comparison swiftly, was thick-set, heavy-jowled, and stooped. He always stood before her helpless, a kind of humility and wonderment in his attitude. And Steven now smiled on her appraisingly with the worldly-wise assurance of one for whom a woman holds neither mystery nor illusion.

'It was good of you to come, Steven,' she responded, the words running into a sudden, empty laugh. 'Such a storm to face—I suppose I should feel flattered.'

For his presumption, his misunderstanding of what had been only a momentary weakness, instead of angering quickened her, roused from latency and long disuse all the instincts and resources of her femininity. She felt eager, challenged. Something was at hand that hitherto had always eluded her, even in the early days with John, something vital, beckoning, meaningful. She didn't understand, but she knew. The texture of the moment was satisfyingly dreamlike: an incredibility perceived as such, yet acquiesced in. She was John's wife—she knew—but also she knew that Steven standing here was different from John. There was no thought or motive, no understanding of herself as the knowledge persisted. Wary and poised round a sudden little core of blind excitement she evaded him, 'But it's nearly dark—hadn't you better hurry if you're going to do the chores? Don't trouble—I can get them off myself—'

An hour later when he returned from the stable she was in another dress, hair rearranged, a little flush of colour in her face. Pouring warm water for him from the kettle into the basin she said evenly, 'By the time you're washed supper will be ready. John said we weren't to wait for him.'

He looked at her a moment, 'But in a storm like this you're not expecting John?'

'Of course.' As she spoke she could feel the colour deepening in her face. 'We're going to play cards. He was the one that suggested it.'

He went on washing, and then as they took their places at the table, resumed, 'So John's coming. When are you expecting him?'

'He said it might be seven o'clock—or a little later.' Conversation with Steven at other times had always been brisk and natural, but now suddenly she found it strained. 'He may have work to do for his father. That's what he said when he left. Why do you ask, Steven?'

'I was just wondering—it's a rough night.'

'He always comes. There couldn't be a storm bad enough. It's easier to do the chores in daylight, and I knew he'd be tired—that's why I started out for the stable.'

She glanced up again and he was smiling at her. The same insolence, the same little twist of mockery and appraisal. It made her flinch suddenly, and ask

herself why she was pretending to expect John—
why there should be this instinct of defence to force
her. This time, instead of poise and excitement, it
brought a reminder that she had changed her dress
and rearranged her hair. It crushed in a sudden
silence, through which she heard the whistling wind
again, and the creaking saw of the eaves. Neither
spoke now. There was something strange, almost
terrifying, about this Steven and his quiet, unrelent-
ing smile; but strangest of all was the familiarity: the
Steven she had never seen or encountered, and yet
had always known, always expected, always waited
for. It was less Steven himself that she felt than his
inevitability. Just as she had felt the snow, the
silence and the storm. She kept her eyes lowered, on
the window past his shoulder, on the stove, but his
smile now seemed to exist apart from him, to merge
and hover with the silence. She clinked a cup—
listened to the whistle of the storm—always it was
there. He began to speak, but her mind missed the
meaning of his words. Swiftly she was making com-
parisons again; his face so different to John's, so
handsome and young and clean-shaven. Swiftly,
helplessly, feeling the imperceptible and relentless
ascendancy that thereby he was gaining over her,
sensing sudden menace in this new, more vital life,
even as she felt drawn towards it.

The lamp between them flickered as an onslaught
of the storm sent shudderings through the room. She
rose to build up the fire again and he followed her.
For a long time they stood close to the stove, their
arms almost touching. Once as the blizzard creaked
the house she spun around sharply, fancying it was
John at the door; but quietly he intercepted her.
'Not tonight—you might as well make up your mind

to it. Across the hills in a storm like this—it would be suicide to try.'

Her lips trembled suddenly in an effort to answer, to parry the certainty in his voice, then set thin and bloodless. She was afraid now. Afraid of his face so different from John's—of his smile, of her own help-lessness to rebuke it. Afraid of the storm, isolating her here alone with him in its impenetrable fastness. They tried to play cards, but she kept starting up at every creak and shiver of the walls. 'It's too rough a night,' he repeated. 'Even for John. Just relax a few minutes—stop worrying and pay a little attention to me.'

But in his tone there was a contradiction to his words. For it implied that she was not worrying—that her only concern was lest it really might be John at the door.

And the implication persisted. He filled up the stove for her, shuffled the cards—won—shuffled—still it was there. She tried to respond to his conversa-tion, to think of the game, but helplessly into her cards instead she began to ask, Was he right? Was that why he smiled? Why he seemed to wait, ex-pectant and assured?

The clock ticked, the fire crackled. Always it was there. Furtively for a moment she watched him as he deliberated over his hand. John, even in the days before they were married, had never looked like that. Only this morning she had asked him to shave. Be-cause Steven was coming—because she had been afraid to see them side by side—because deep within herself she had known even then. The same know-ledge, furtive and forbidden, that was flaunted now in Steven's smile. 'You look cold,' he said at last, dropping his cards and rising from the table. 'We're not playing, anyway. Come over to the stove for a few minutes and get warm.'

'But first I think we'll hang blankets over the door. When there's a blizzard like this we always do.' It seemed that in sane, commonplace activity there might be release, a moment or two in which to recover herself. 'John has nails in to put them on. They keep out a little of the draft.'

He stood on a chair for her, and hung the blankets that she carried from the bedroom. Then for a moment they stood silent, watching the blankets sway and tremble before the blade of wind that spurted around the jamb. 'I forgot,' she said at last, 'that I painted the bedroom door. At the top there, see—I've smeared the blankets coming through.'

He glanced at her curiously, and went back to the stove. She followed him, trying to imagine the hills in such a storm, wondering whether John would come. 'A man couldn't live in it,' suddenly he answered her thoughts, lowering the oven door and drawing up their chairs one on each side of it. 'He knows you're safe. It isn't likely that he'd leave his father, anyway.'

'The wind will be in his back,' she persisted. 'The winter before we were married—all the blizzards that we had that year—and he never missed—'

'Blizzards like this one? Up in the hills he wouldn't be able to keep his direction for a hundred yards. Listen to it a minute and ask yourself.'

His voice seemed softer, kindlier now. She met his smile a moment, its assured little twist of appraisal, then for a long time sat silent, tense, careful again to avoid his eyes.

Everything now seemed to depend on this. It was the same as a few hours ago when she braced the door against the storm. He was watching her, smiling. She dared not move, unclench her hands, or raise her eyes. The flames crackled, the clock ticked. The storm wrenched the walls as if to make them buckle in. So rigid and desperate were all her muscles set, withstanding, that the room around her seemed to swim and reel. So rigid and strained that for relief at last, despite herself, she raised her head and met his eyes again.

Intending that it should be for only an instant, just to breathe again, to ease the tension that had grown unbearable—but in his smile now, instead of the insolent appraisal that she feared, there seemed a kind of warmth and sympathy. An understanding that quickened and encouraged her—that made her wonder why but a moment ago she had been afraid. It was as if the storm had lulled, as if she had suddenly found calm and shelter.

Or perhaps, the thought seized her, perhaps instead of his smile it was she that had changed. She who, in the long, wind-creaked silence, had emerged from the increment of codes and loyalties to her real, unfettered self. She who now felt suddenly an air of appraisal as nothing more than an understanding of the unfulfilled woman that until this moment had lain within her brooding and unadmitted, reproved out of consciousness by the insistence of an outgrown, routine fidelity.

For there had always been Steven. She understood now. Seven years—almost as long as John—ever since the night they first danced together.

The lamp was burning dry, and through the dimming light, isolated in the fastness of silence and storm, they watched each other. Her face was white and struggling still. His was handsome, clean-shaven, young. Her eyes were fanatic, believing desperately, fixed upon him as if to exclude all else, as if to find justification. His were cool, bland, drooped a little with expectancy. The light kept dimming, gathering the shadows round them, hushed, conspiratorial. He was smiling still. Her hands again were clenched up white and hard.

'But he always came,' she persisted. 'The wildest, coldest nights—even such a night as this. There was never a storm—'

'Never a storm like this one.' There was a quietness in his smile now, a kind of simplicity almost, as if to reassure her. 'You were out in it yourself for a few minutes. He would have five miles, across the hills. . . . I'd think twice myself, on such a night, before risking even one.'

Long after he was asleep she lay listening to the storm. As a check on the draft up the chimney they had left one of the stovelids partly off, and through the open bedroom door she could see the flickerings of flame and shadow on the kitchen wall. They leaped and sank fantastically. The longer she watched the more alive they seemed to be. There was one great shadow that struggled towards her threateningly, massive and black and engulfing all the room. Again and again it advanced, about to spring, but each time a little whip of light subdued it to its place among the others on the wall. Yet though it never reached her still she cowered, feeling that gathered there was all the frozen wilderness, its heart of terror and invincibility.

Then she dozed a while, and the shadow was John. Interminably he advanced. The whips of light still flicked and coiled, but now suddenly they were the swift little snakes that this afternoon she had watched twist and shiver across the snow. And they too were advancing. They writhed and vanished and came again. She lay still, paralysed. He was over her now, so close that she could have touched him. Already it seemed that a deadly tightening hand was on her throat. She tried to scream but her lips were locked. Steven beside her slept on heedlessly.

Until suddenly as she lay staring up at him a gleam of light revealed his face. And in it was not a trace of threat or anger—only calm, and stonelike hopelessness.

That was like John. He began to withdraw, and frantically she tried to call him back. 'It isn't true—not really true—listen, John—' but the words clung frozen to her lips. Already there was only the shriek of wind again, the sawing eaves, the leap and twist of shadow on the wall.

She sat up, startled now and awake. And so real had he seemed there, standing close to her, so vivid the sudden age and sorrow in his face, that at first she could not make herself understand she had been only dreaming. Against the conviction of his presence in the room it was necessary to insist over and over that he must still be with his father on the other side of the hills. Watching the shadows she had fallen asleep. It was only her mind, her imagination, distorted to a nightmare by the illogical and un-admitted dread of his return. But he wouldn't come. Steven was right. In such a storm he would never try. They were safe, alone. No one would ever know. It was only fear, morbid and irrational; only the sense of guilt that even her new-found and chal-lenged womanhood could not entirely quell.

She knew now. She had not let herself understand

or acknowledge it as guilt before, but gradually through the wind-torn silence of the night his face compelled her. The face that had watched her from the darkness with its stonelike sorrow—the face that was really John—John more than his features of mere flesh and bone could ever be.

She wept silently. The fitful gleam of light began to sink. On the ceiling and wall at last there was only a faint dull flickering glow. The little house shuddered and quailed, and a chill crept in again. Without wakening Steven she slipped out to build up the fire. It was burned to a few spent embers now, and the wood she put on seemed a long time catching light. The wind swirled through the blankets they had hung around the door, and struck her flesh like laps of molten ice. Then hollow and moaning it roared up the chimney again, as if against its will drawn back to serve still longer with the onrush of the storm.

For a long time she crouched over the stove, listening. Earlier in the evening, with the lamp lit and the fire crackling, the house had seemed a stand against the wilderness, against its frozen, blizzard-breathed implacability, a refuge of feeble walls wherein persisted the elements of human meaning and survival. Now, in the cold, creaking darkness, it was strangely extinct, looted by the storm and abandoned again. She lifted the stove lid and fanned the embers till at last a swift little tongue of flame began to lick around the wood. Then she replaced the lid, extended her hands, and as if frozen in that attitude stood waiting.

It was not long now. After a few minutes she closed the drafts, and as the flames whirled back upon each other, beating against the top of the stove and sending out flickers of light again, a warmth surged up to relax her stiffened limbs. But shivering and numb it had been easier. The bodily well-being that the warmth induced gave play again to an ever more insistent mental suffering. She remembered the shadow that was John. She saw him bent towards her, then retreating, his features pale and overcast with unaccusing grief. She re-lived their seven years together and, in retrospect, found them to be years of worth and dignity. Until crushed by it all at last, seized by a sudden need to suffer and atone, she crossed to where the draft was bitter, and for a long time stood unflinching on the icy floor.

The storm was close here. Even through the blankets she could feel a sift of snow against her face. The eaves sawed, the walls creaked. Above it all, like a wolf in howling flight, the wind shrilled lone and desolate.

And yet, suddenly she asked herself, hadn't there been other storms, other blizzards? And through the worst of them hadn't he always reached her?

Clutched by the thought she stood rooted a minute. It was hard now to understand how she could have so deceived herself—how a moment of passion could have quieted within her not only conscience, but reason and discretion too. John always came. There could never be a storm to stop him. He was strong, inured to the cold. He had crossed the hills since his boyhood, knew every creek-bed and gully. It was madness to go on like this—to wait. While there was still time she must waken Steven, and hurry him away.

But in the bedroom again, standing at Steven's side, she hesitated. In his detachment from it all, in his quiet, even breathing, there was such sanity, such realism. For him nothing had happened; nothing would. If she wakened him he would only laugh and tell her to listen to the storm. Already it was long past midnight; either John had lost his way or not set out at all. And she knew that in his devotion there was nothing foolhardy. He would never risk a storm beyond his endurance, never permit himself a sacrifice likely to endanger her lot or future. They were both safe. No one would ever know. She must control herself—be sane like Steven.

For comfort she let her hand rest a while on Steven's shoulder. It would be easier were he awake now, with her, sharing her guilt; but gradually as she watched his handsome face in the glimmering light she came to understand that for him no guilt existed. Just as there had been no passion, no conflict. Nothing but the sane appraisal of their situation, nothing but the expectant little smile, and the arrogance of features that were different from John's. She winced deeply, remembering how she had fixed her eyes on those features, how she had tried to believe that so handsome and young, so different from John's, they must in themselves be her justification.

In the flickering light they were still young, still handsome. No longer her justification—she knew now—John was the man—but wistfully still, wondering sharply at their power and tyranny, she touched them a moment with her fingertips again.

She could not blame him. There had been no passion, no guilt; therefore there could be no responsibility. Suddenly looking down at him as he slept, half-smiling still, his lips relaxed in the conscience-less complacency of his achievement, she understood that thus he was revealed in his entirety—all there ever was or ever could be. John was the man. With him lay all the future. For tonight, slowly and contritely through the day and years to come, she would try to make amends.

Then she stole back to the kitchen, and without thought, impelled by overwhelming need again, returned to the door where the draft was bitter still. Gradually towards morning the storm began to spend itself. Its terror blast became a feeble, worn-out moan. The leap of light and shadow sank, and a chill crept in again. Always the eaves creaked, tortured with wordless prophecy. Heedless of it all the clock ticked on in idiot content.

They found him the next day, less than a mile from home. Drifting with the storm he had run against his own pasture fence and overcome had frozen there, erect still, both hands clasping fast the wire.

'He was south of here,' they said wonderingly when she told them how he had come across the hills. 'Straight south—you'd wonder how he could have missed the buildings. It was the wind last night, coming every way at once. He shouldn't have tried. There was a double wheel around the moon.'

She looked past them a moment, then as if to herself said simply, 'If you knew him, though— John would try.'

It was later, when they had left her a while to be alone with him, that she knelt and touched his hand. Her eyes dimmed, still it was such a strong and patient hand; then, transfixed, they suddenly grew wide and clear. On the palm, white even against its frozen whiteness, was a little smear of paint.

The Pigeon

RALPH GUSTAFSON (b. 1909)

DEBORAH huddled terrified in her little upholstered armchair, listening. It had been her 'pouting' chair and although she was now ten years old and the chair's silly meaning outgrown, it still intimately held her small unfulfilled figure. She sat by the open window of her bedroom overlooking the front lawn.

She was alone in the large wooden house which stood on the brow of the hill outside the town—where the river plunges fearfully between the cliffs of the Magog Gorge. Her father and mother had gone out in the car shortly after supper, leaving Deborah with the usual instruction that she be in bed by eight o'clock. But it was late spring when the long daylight lingers, the air rich with lilac and the wings of swallows, and Deborah had sat quietly through the twilight, filled with the wonder of existence and the loneliness in which it seemed only to be.

Then the sound had come, alien, sudden, shattering the familiar silence into quick fragments of terror. Deborah's heart leaped. For minutes she waited, scarce daring to breathe. Again it came—violent, broken, above her head almost. Then the silence swept back over her.

It was in the attic. Deborah sat rigid, her hands clasping each other tightly, her eyes wide.

She pleaded that her mother come—but her father hardly ever brought her mother home from being out before Deborah was long in bed. She told when they were coming by the swath of light her father's car made on the ceiling as it turned from the hill into the driveway.

The darkness of the hallway behind her bedroom door grew enormous, crushing to get in. At the hallway's far end were the stairs of the attic where her father had forbidden her to play. But she had memorized every one of the floorboards which creaked in the hallway for the times when she stole up into the attic without them knowing. She would know now when what was in the attic was coming. Deborah listened with her whole body, her eyes on the back of the closed door.

Vehemently, she wished she was a boy. She could kill it with a gun. Her father had a gun but you had to be a boy to shoot a gun. Her father wished she was a boy, she knew he did by the disgust he made sometimes on his face. He had put his gun, one day, against her shoulder under her chin but her finger wouldn't pull the trigger no matter how hard she wanted not to be afraid. With his finger he made hers press it. Nothing happened to her from the explosion but he told her for God's sake why weren't you a boy, Deborah?

She was afraid, even, of the old barn at the back of the quarry though Lucy, Tom, and Freddy went too. She loved to play in the loft, but when you had to go home it was a dare to slide down the rope that hung in front of the door under the eaves. Lucy did it; but she was afraid. Freddy and Tom once when Lucy wasn't with them tied her with ropes to a tree in the woods for a scaredy-cat. Tom's father found her, and was kind and angry; but her father only laughed.

If only she had let her father make her brave

when he wanted to. She had tried about Prancer but her father didn't even think of her after that when he went out riding. Perhaps if he knew it wasn't really being afraid he wouldn't not like her so much, but she couldn't explain it as not actually being afraid, but something else, something in things outside her that she had nothing to do with their being like that. She would so like explaining she wasn't to blame. She liked doing things. It was only she was scared of how they were made to seem. Things by themselves were lovely. But he didn't like her to tell him that.

The sound came again. Deborah's eyes flew to the ceiling, her mind clutching back the terror in her throat lest it betray her. The low vibrated beating intensified. Then it ceased.

She tried to make her heart stop pounding. Her father would laugh at her then walk straight into the attic and find out.

Deborah held her breath. Her thought came enormous and complete. It would be the bravest deed of all her life if she went straight into the attic as he would want. Everything would be made different. Deborah sat, believing hard. She could tell him it was just nothing in the attic. And he would like being her father.

The silence abruptly shattered. The sound went on and on, this time, as if it would overpower the emptiness of the house. Deborah leapt to her feet with a gasp. But she stood still until it stopped, tense with her decision, her hands stretched open along the lightness of her slanting gingham skirt.

She made herself aware of all her body, then went to the bed. She put her toy bear, Nicholas For Christmas, under one arm and moved to the bed-

room door. Silently, she opened it toward her until
the space was big enough to go through.

The windowless corridor of dark stretched before
her, greyed only where her mother's and father's
bedroom door was ajar. The sudden crescendo of the
falls, opened into the house by her father's window
facing the river, roared at her ears. She paused to
make it lessen—then moved into the dark before
her. She tried to be brave. Balancing on the tips
of her sandals, avoiding the boards that creaked,
Deborah walked to the door at the end. The knob
filled all her hand but she soundlessly made the door
wide enough. The mustiness in the room smothered
at her nostrils. She went quickly past the stripped
bed where her grandmother had been dead, waited
in the far corner by the window, her heart thumping so that she felt ill. She listened, but there was
nothing. The low moon shone pale and ineffectual at
the dusty glass.

Then she pressed down the latch of the attic door.
Putting Nicholas high on the fourth step around
the right-angle the stairs made at the bottom, she
got down on her hands and knees. The attic stairs
creaked worst of all, but she hardly made any sound
the house might not have made by itself. The stairway mounted steeply between two walls, and from
above was just an oblong space in the floor. She lifted
Nicholas up beside her with each rise.

When her head reached the level of the attic
floor, Deborah stopped. If the sound came now she
wouldn't be able to help it and it would come at her
with the scream and the noise she had to make. She
closed her eyes tight against the panic. Images she
made at night tumbled green and monstrous through
her mind.

Gripping her fingers flat on the board which edged the side of the stairway, she raised her head, then looked.

The attic stretched away before her the length of the house. Slopes of white, torn with blackness where the plaster had fallen, leaned against each other hugging the silence. In each gable, and out of sight in the wing of the attic, were narrow windows muffled by the eaves. Under the leaning walls great shadows accumulated.

Forming vaguely in the long dimness, the confusion of shapes and objects were made themselves by Deborah's memory—the wooden cupboard projecting from the wall, whose lower shelf could contain Deborah herself; the white skeleton of the iron bed naked in the distance; along the walls the castaway trunks and boxes; the anonymous piles of books and pictures between.

It was Deborah's own territory of loneliness and reality, forbidden and secure—but now, as she crouched within the stairway, alien with terror and intrusion.

It came first as a swerve of greyness out from the wing against the yellow cupboard opposite. Screams tore from Deborah's throat and her terror scrambled for flight. But she had seen what it was.

The sound the wings of the pigeon made against the cupboard was the same rapid beating she had heard from below. The bird fluttered forward along the top, then with a thump against the farther wall. Its burst of desperation slanted to a stop and the pigeon dropped to the floor.

Deborah straightened up on her knees, raising her head above the floor. Her fingers still clutched the edge but slowly the panic in her faded away.

The bird stood, plump, on its two red threads of legs, unmoving, a few feet in front of Deborah's nose. Her eyes widened and she held her breath, now not because of herself but lest she frighten the bird. The shadows of the attic untangled from menace, were familiar and could be forgotten. Their seclusion and protection returned around her.

The pigeon swallowed a dry spherical coo, then took a step, its jab of neck like an iridescent after-beat, the feathers shifting colours in a smoke of grey.

Deborah made a soundless Oh, and it stopped still, the soft round of head perched a little, ready for instant discovery. She clucked her tongue, making the sound gentle and friendly. Its head tipped the other way—then it stalked off, delicately and wobblingly, across the attic floor.

Deborah got to her feet, and, arms balancing her tiptoe, followed, at a distance. Never before had she seen a pigeon so close-to nor such a beautiful one. She would keep it for her own, she decided, and wouldn't let anyone know they lived in the attic together and she would learn to talk its language so it would like to stay and she would know things no one else in the world had ever been told.

The pigeon walked into the shaft of moonlight that slanted the space before the windows in the wing of the attic. It stopped in the edge, uncertain. Carefully, Deborah bent over to take it in her hands. But before her fingers touched it the bird flew wildly upward. Deborah jumped away with fright. The bird struck against the angle of the ceiling, then beat down the ridge to the windows. Deborah looked in alarm. They were closed—except the window in front of the attic. She ran to the nearest box, dragged it beneath the window and got up on it. The blind had been raised and the upper sash pulled down. She put the heels of her hands against the top of the frame and pushed. It stuck. Desperately, she wiggled the sash from side to side with all her might. The weight gave and the window slammed.

She jumped down and went to the angle of the wall. She peeked round, but it wasn't in sight. She came out into the moonlight. The pigeon had disappeared. A great hollow longing filled her—then she saw it. It was standing in the narrow space between the two piles of double-windows against the wall.

She got one of the cushions stored in the cupboard, placed it on the floor in front of the pigeon, and looked to see if it was all right. 'You stay there,' she told it.

She ran to the well of the stairway and down the steps, banged open the door at the foot, ran down the hallway and down the front stairs.

She switched on the light in the kitchen, got a bottle of milk from the ice-box and poured some into a saucepan. She took two crusts from the bread-box, then switched off the light. Picking up the saucepan of milk, she carefully carried it upstairs, along the hall, and into the attic.

Placing the saucepan and crusts beside the cushion, she sat down, her legs under her, and watched. The pigeon just stood. Slowly she stretched out her hand toward the bird. It couldn't fly up where it was. She let the tip of her forefinger gently touch the top of its head. It was feathery soft and smooth as milk. The pigeon huddled in so that its neck was gone.

'What are you afraid for?' Deborah asked it. 'No

one is going to hurt you. I wouldn't hurt you—ever.'
Out of the loneliness within her a vast affection
welled. 'I love you!' she told it. 'I love you!' She
took her hand away, shoved herself back two times
on the floor, and pushed forward the pan and the
crusts. She made a soft sound with her lips. The
pigeon looked up askance. 'Drink your milk,' she
urged. 'Don't you want your milk?' In reply the
pigeon took a step, then a tentative peck at the crust.
Deborah watched, fascinated, furiously planning
their being together in the attic. Tomorrow she
would hold it and it would eat from her hand and
wouldn't be afraid of her.

Then, faintly reflected on the plaster, she saw the
sweep of light.

Her body tensed even before her mind reacted to
its meaning. The apprehension and guilt came suddenly all at once. She looked at her pigeon. She
would never let them find out! She scrambled to her
feet and ran across the attic to the stairs. She
slammed the door at the bottom and the one into
her grandmother's room, ran down the hall and
shut her bedroom door behind her.

She wriggled out of her clothes, kicking off her
sandals, got her nightgown. She heard her mother
coming over the lawn, but she was in bed before
she entered.

She clenched the top of the covers, following the
sounds below her. Her mother went to the kitchen
first. She would let her father in from the garage,
and they would come upstairs. She pictured God,
then prayed over and over: 'Please don't let the
pigeon make a noise! Please don't let it make a
noise!'

Her mother came up to her bedroom. Deborah

shut her eyes and lay perfectly still. Her door opened for a moment then softly closed. 'Is she asleep?' her father asked, as he went down the hall to the bathroom.

Deborah didn't let herself move until they were both in their bedroom and their door shut.

She tried frantically to think what to say why she was in the attic, if they found out and asked when she knew she mustn't play there. Her father's gun! Deborah's mind leaped in panic. That was what he would do! He would shoot the pigeon, she knew he would, if he found out and saw it. He would never let her keep it, even if it wasn't in the attic and would take it out and shoot it! She thought of the laugh he made after he shot at something. The laugh wasn't because he liked things or there was fun.

She lay thinking desperately, staring at the leaf-shadows across the ceiling, listening, two fingers of each hand crossed.

But the sound didn't come. There was only silence and the hush of the falls and, sometimes, with long stillness between, the brush of leaves as night moved within the trees outside. Perhaps it was asleep. Then wonder began if the pigeon had really and truly been a live pigeon in the attic. Perhaps it was thirsty and was drinking the velvet white milk that made no sound with its silvery bill and the rainbow around its throat. But when she climbed, climbed a million stairs to the attic it was gone. She ran looking everywhere and flung open the trunks and the boxes and turned over the shelves. But they only grinned at her and shook their heads from side to side together and she had to run back down the million stairs pleading she'd do anything only don't let it die but

when she got to the bottom of the beetling stairs
with a million steps and into the woods she had
to look down the black gun to where the pigeon
was, tiny, oh tinier than the smallest bird, held
struggling.

Deborah sat up, the scream at the top of her
throat. But her mind had tightened herself not to.
For a minute the images moved, vivid, then melted.
It was twilight outside and she heard the sparrows
in the bushes.

She jammed away the cover crumpled on her feet,
put on her gown and slippers. Her panic told her to
race against each terrible second to set her pigeon
free, away from her father's gun—but she made
herself not do it until the top of the stairs. Then
she ran the length of the attic to the front window,
clambered on the box and pulled at the sash with
her hands. It didn't move. She beat at the frame
with her fists. Then she stopped and pressed with
her fingers where the crack was between the two
sashes. It shifted and she pulled the window wide
open by the slit made at the top.

She ran where the pigeon was but it was gone.
She leaned over the double-windows and felt down
the space with her arm. She became frantic.

'Pigeon!' she cried not caring about the sound.

She went to where she had first watched it, then
to the bed, and to the cupboard. Great sobs choked
into her throat. She began looking behind the trunks
and boxes, shifting them forward so she could see
down the wall. In the tin edging of the blue trunk
her cloth belt caught and she had to pull it off until
it tore. But she thought only of getting the pigeon
away from the attic, outside. Trailing the belt in
her hand, she ran again to where the pan and crusts

were—then she saw it in the corner, behind the framed pictures.

She went to the bird, the tears blurring her eyes. 'You've got to go out. You've got to,' she told it. She reached over to pick the pigeon up. It backed wildly, then thrashed up out of the corner over Deborah's head, its wings striking her face. It flew madly against the ceiling, pushed itself along the slope.

'Go out! Go out!' she screamed. She lashed at the bird with the belt in her hand.

Suddenly the pigeon dropped away and flew across to the cupboard, beating violently against the cardboard boxes shoved on top.

Deborah ran after it, sobbing, hitting at the bird, reaching as high as she could.

The pile of shallow boxes gave way, tumbling forward, knocking the bird under them as they fell. The photographic plates spilled, scattered to the floor. The pigeon lay shivering, its neck half severed by the fragment of glass impaled in it.

Deborah stared at the scarlet opening with its spurting blood.

Then her mind went blind. She gave scream after scream as she watched, then tore herself from it. She stumbled down the attic stairs and down the hallway to her mother's door. Twisting the knob she pushed it open with her body and ran to her mother flinging herself against the side of the bed.

Her mother had raised herself when Deborah reached her.

'Debby! What is it!' She put her arms around her and pulled her to her. 'Debby!'

'I killed it!' Deborah shrieked. 'I killed it!' Then the pressure gave and she broke into violent sobs.

Her father in the other bed propped himself up by his elbow. 'Miriam! What's wrong?'

'It's Deborah. A nightmare.'

He let himself fall back. 'For Christ's sake!'

Deborah checked the violence that shook her. 'It's dying! Oh do something, do something!'

Her mother straightened Deborah up. 'There,' she soothed her. She took the handkerchief from Deborah's robe and wiped under her eyes. 'Now. Tell mother. What's dying?'

Deborah forced her sobs to leave her alone so her mother could go. 'In the attic!' she told her. 'The pigeon!'

'The pigeon! Darling, there's no pigeon in the attic. You only *dreamed* there was a pigeon.'

Deborah felt the terror surge back. 'I didn't dream it! I didn't!'

Her mother turned toward her father. 'George. Can't you *do* something? You can see the state Deborah's in.'

He groaned and sat himself up. 'For God's sake! What do you expect me to do? Scare nightmares away?'

'At least you might go into the attic and prove to the child nothing's dying.'

He clenched his lips to get his disgust across, looked at Deborah, then swung his legs out of bed.

Deborah watched him, wanting to tell him Oh hurry—please! but she couldn't tell him, not her father who was cruel.

He shoved his feet into his slippers, trailed his dressing gown and left the room.

Deborah held in balance all her existence. Her mother patted her and brushed back the hair from her face. She heard her tell her that her father would make everything all right but she knew he never would. He would find the pigeon dead and she would have to explain to him the wrong things that were not her fault that they happened. She stood in agony, the horror smouldering, staring at the open bedroom door.

Then he appeared in it. Deborah's eyes went down to the dead pigeon dangling from his hand.

'What the hell have you been doing in the attic?' he asked her.

Her mother gave a gasp as she saw what he held.

The guilt, familiar but now complete, whelmed Deborah's mind. 'I *didn't* do it! I *didn't* do it!' she told him.

'Stop yelling,' he ordered.

'George!' her mother turned to Deborah. 'It isn't your fault, I'm sure, darling.' She looked back at her father. 'Can't you see the child's hysterical?'

'Then she better get over it,' he said.

Deborah looked up from the pigeon to her father's face. The hate seared alive.

'I *never* will! I *never* will!' she screamed at him.

The Bravest Boat

MALCOLM LOWRY (1909–57)

IT was a day of spindrift and blowing sea-foam, with black clouds presaging rain driven over the mountains from the sea by a wild March wind.

But a clean silver sea light came from along the horizon where the sky itself was like glowing silver. And far away over in America the snowy volcanic peak of Mount Hood stood on high, disembodied, cut off from earth, yet much too close, which was an even surer presage of rain, as though the mountains had advanced, or were advancing.

In the park of the seaport the giant trees swayed, and taller than any were the tragic Seven Sisters, a constellation of seven noble red cedars that had grown there for hundreds of years, but were now dying, blasted, with bare peeled tops and stricken boughs. (They were dying rather than live longer near civilization. Yet though everyone had forgotten they were called after the Pleiades and thought they were named with civic pride after the seven daughters of a butcher, who seventy years before when the growing city was named Gaspool, had all danced together in a shop window, nobody had the heart to cut them down.)

The angelic wings of the seagulls circling over the tree tops shone very white against the black sky. Fresh snow from the night before lay far down the slopes of the Canadian mountains, whose freezing summits, massed peak behind spire, jaggedly traversed the country northward as far as the eye could reach. And highest of all an eagle, with the poise of a skier, shot endlessly down the world.

In the mirror, reflecting this and much beside, of an old weighing machine with the legend 'Your weight and your destiny' encircling its forehead and which stood on the embankment between the street-car terminus and a hamburger stall, in this mirror along the reedy edge of the stretch of water below known as Lost Lagoon two figures in mackintoshes were approaching, a man and a beautiful passionate-looking girl, both bare-headed, and both extremely fair, and hand-in-hand, so that you would have taken them for young lovers, but that they were alike as brother and sister, and the man, although he walked with youthful nervous speed, now seemed older than the girl.

The man, fine-looking, tall, yet thick-set, very bronzed, and on approaching still closer obviously a good deal older than the girl, and wearing one of those blue belted trenchcoats favoured by merchant marine officers of any country, though without any corresponding cap—moreover the trenchcoat was rather too short in the sleeve so that you could see some tattooing on his wrists, as he approached nearer still it seemed to be an anchor—whereas the girl's raincoat was of some sort of entrancing forest-green corduroy—the man paused every now and then to gaze into the lovely laughing face of his girl, and once or twice they both stopped, gulping in great draughts of salty clean sea and mountain air. A child smiled at them, and they smiled back. But the child belonged elsewhere, and the couple were unaccompanied.

In the lagoon swam wild swans, and many wild ducks: mallards and buffleheads and scaups, golden eyes, and cackling black coots with carved ivory bills. The little buffleheads often took flight from the water and some of them blew about like doves among the smaller trees. Under these trees lining the bank other ducks were sitting meekly on the sloping lawn, their beaks tucked into their plumage rumpled by the wind. The smaller trees were apples and hawthorns, some just opening into bloom even before they had foliage, and weeping willows, from whose branches small showers from the night's rain were scattered on the two figures as they passed.

A red-breasted merganser cruised in the lagoon,

and at this swift and angry sea bird, with his proud disordered crest, the two were now gazing with a special sympathy, perhaps because he looked lonely without his mate. Ah, they were wrong. The red-breasted merganser was now joined by his wife and on a sudden duck's impulse and with immense fuss the two wild creatures flew off to settle on another part of the lagoon. And for some reason this simple fact appeared to make these two good people—for nearly all people are good who walk in parks—very happy again.

Now at a distance they saw a small boy, accompanied by his father who was kneeling on the bank, trying to sail a toy boat in the lagoon. But the blustery March wind soon slanted the tiny yacht into trouble and the father hauled it back, reaching out with his curved stick, and set it on an upright keel again for his son.

Your weight and your destiny.

Suddenly the girl's face, at close quarters in the weighing machine's mirror, seemed struggling with tears: she unbuttoned the top button of her coat to readjust her scarf, revealing, attached to a gold chain around her neck, a small gold cross. They were quite alone now, standing on top of the embankment by the machine, save for a few old men feeding the ducks below, and the father and his son with the toy yacht, all of whom had their backs turned, while an empty tram abruptly city-bound trundled round the minute terminus square; and the man, who had been trying to light his pipe, took her in his arms and tenderly kissed her, and then pressing his face against her cheek, held her a moment closely.

The couple, having gone down obliquely to the

lagoon once more, had now passed the boy with his
boat and his father. They were smiling again. Or as
much as they could while eating hamburgers. And
they were smiling still as they passed the slender
reeds where a northwestern redwing was trying to
pretend he had no notion of nesting, the northwestern redwing who like all birds in these parts
may feel superior to man in that he is his own cus-
toms official, and can cross the wild border without
let.

Along the far side of Lost Lagoon the green
dragons grew thickly, their sheathed and cowled
leaves giving off their peculiar animal-like odor. The
two lovers were approaching the forest in which,
ahead, several footpaths threaded the ancient trees.
The park, seagirt, was very large, and like many
parks throughout the Pacific Northwest, wisely left
in places to the original wilderness. In fact, though
its beauty was probably unique, it was quite like
some American parks, you might have thought, save
for the Union Jack that galloped evermore by a
pavilion, and but for the apparition, at this moment,
passing by on the carefully landscaped road slightly
above, which led with its tunnels and detours to a
suspension bridge, of a posse of Royal Canadian
Mounted Policemen mounted royally upon the
cushions of an American Chevrolet.

Nearer the forest were gardens with sheltered beds
of snowdrops and here and there a few crocuses
lifting their sweet chalices. The man and his girl
now seemed lost in thought, breasting the buffeting
wind that blew the girl's scarf out behind her like a
pennant and blew the man's thick fair hair about
his head.

A loudspeaker, enthroned on a wagon, barked

from the city of Enochvilleport composed of dila-
pidated half-skyscrapers, at different levels, some
with all kinds of scrap-iron, even broken aeroplanes,
on their roofs, others being mouldy stock-exchange
buildings, new beer parlours crawling with ver-
minous light even in mid-afternoon and resembling
gigantic emerald-lit public lavatories for both sexes,
masonries containing English tea-shoppes where
your fortune could be told by a female relative of
Maximilian of Mexico, totem pole factories, drapers'
shops with the best Scotch tweed and opium dens
in the basement (though no bars, as if, like some
hideous old roué shuddering with every unmention-
able secret vice this city without gaiety had cackled
'No, I draw the line at that.—What would our wee
laddies come to then?'), cerise conflagrations of
cinemas, modern apartment buildings, and other
soulless Behemoths, housing, it might be, noble invisible struggles, of literature, the drama, art or
music, the student's lamp and the rejected manuscript; or indescribable poverty and degradation,
between which civic attractions were squeezed occasional lovely dark ivy-clad old houses that seemed
weeping, cut off from all light, on their knees, and
elsewhere bankrupt hospitals, and one or two solid-
stoned old banks, held up that afternoon; and among
which appeared too, at infrequent intervals, beyond
a melancholy never-striking black and white clock
that said three, dwarfed spires belonging to frame
façades with blackened rose windows, queer grimed
onion-shaped domes, and even Chinese pagodas, so
that first you thought you were in the Orient, then
Turkey or Russia, though finally, but for the fact
that some of these were churches, you would be sure
you were in hell: despite that anyone who had ever

233

really been in hell must have given Enochvilleport a nod of recognition, further affirmed by the spectacle, at first not unpicturesque, of the numerous sawmills relentlessly smoking and champing away like demons, Molochs fed by whole mountainsides of forests that never grew again, or by trees that made way for grinning regiments of villas in the background of 'our expanding and fair city', mills that shook the very earth with their tumult, filling the windy air with their sound as of a wailing and gnashing of teeth: all these curious achievements of man, together creating as we say 'the jewel of the Pacific', went as though down a great incline to a harbour more spectacular than Rio de Janeiro and San Francisco put together, with deep-sea freighters moored at every angle for miles in the roadstead, but to whose heroic prospect nearly the only human dwellings visible on this side of the water that had any air of belonging, or in which their inhabitants could be said any longer to participate, were, paradoxically, a few lowly little self-built shacks and floathouses, that might have been driven out of the city altogether, down to the water's edge into the sea itself, where they stood on piles, like fishermen's huts (which several of them apparently were), or on rollers, some dark and tumbledown, others freshly and prettily painted, these last quite evidently built or placed with some human need for beauty in mind, even if under the permanent threat of eviction, and all standing, even the most sombre, with their fluted tin chimneys smoking here and there like toy tramp steamers, as though in defiance of the town, before eternity. In Enochvilleport itself some ghastly-coloured neon signs had long since been going through their unctuous twitchings and gesticulations that nostalgia and love transforms into a poetry of longing: more happily one began to flicker: PALOMAR, LOUIS ARMSTRONG AND HIS ORCHESTRA. A huge new grey dead hotel that at sea might be a landmark of romance, belched smoke out of its turreted haunted-looking roof, as if it had caught fire, and beyond that all the lamps were blazing within the grim courtyard of the law courts, equally at sea a trysting place of the heart, outside which one of the stone lions having recently been blown up was covered reverently with a white cloth, and inside which for a month a group of stainless citizens had been trying a sixteen-year-old boy for murder.

Nearer the park the apron lights appeared on a sort of pebble-dashed Y.M.C.A.-Hall-cum-variety theatre saying TAMMUZ *The Master Hypnotist, To-nite 8:30,* and running past this the tramlines, down which another parkwise streetcar was approaching, could be seen extending almost to the department store in whose show window Tammuz' subject, perhaps a somnolent descendant of the seven sisters whose fame had eclipsed even that of the Pleiades, but whose announced ambition was to become a female psychiatrist, had been sleeping happily and publicly in a double bed for the last three days as an advance publicity stunt for tonight's performance.

Above Lost Lagoon on the road now mounting toward the suspension bridge in the distance much as a piece of jazz music mounts toward a break, a newsboy cried: 'LASH ORDERED FOR SAINT PIERRE! SIXTEEN YEAR OLD BOY, CHILDSLAYER, TO HANG! Read all about it!'

The weather too was foreboding. Yet seeing the wandering lovers the other passers-by on this side of the lagoon, a wounded soldier lying on a bench

smoking a cigarette, and one or two of those desti-
tute souls, the very old who haunt parks—since,
faced with a choice, the very old will sometimes
prefer, rather than to keep a room and starve, at
least in such a city as this, somehow to eat and live
outdoors—smiled too.

For as the girl walked along beside the man with
her arm through his and as they smiled together and
their eyes met with love, or they paused, watching
the blowing seagulls, or the ever-changing scene of
the snow-freaked Canadian mountains with their
fleecy indigo chasms, or to listen to the deep-tongued
majesty of a merchantman's echoing roar (these
things that made Enochvilleport's ferocious alder-
men imagine that it was the city itself that was
beautiful, and maybe they were half right), the
whistle of a ferryboat as it sidled across the inlet
northward, what memories might not be evoked in
a poor soldier, in the breasts of the bereaved, the old,
even, who knows, in the mounted policemen, not
merely of young love, but of lovers, as they seemed
to be, so much in love that they were afraid to lose
a moment of their time together?

Yet only a guardian angel of these two would
have known—and surely they must have possessed
a guardian angel—the strangest of all strange things
of which they were thinking, save that, since they
had spoken of it so often before, and especially,
when they had opportunity, on this day of the year,
each knew of course that the other was thinking
about it, to such an extent indeed that it was no
surprise, it only resembled the beginning of a ritual
when the man said, as they entered the main path
of the forest, through whose branches that shielded
them from the wind could be made out, from time

to time, suggesting a fragment of music manuscript, a bit of the suspension bridge itself:

'It was a day just like this that I set the boat adrift. It was twenty-nine years ago in June.'

'It was twenty-nine years ago in June, darling. And it was June twenty seventh.'

'It was five years before you were born, Astrid, and I was ten years old and I came down to the bay with my father.'

'It was five years before I was born, you were ten years old, and you came down to the wharf with your father. Your father and grandfather had made you the boat between them and it was a fine one, ten inches long, smoothly varnished and made of wood from your model airplane box, with a new strong white sail.'

'Yes, it was balsa wood from my model airplane box and my father sat beside me, telling me what to write for a note to put in it.'

'Your father sat beside you, telling you what to write,' Astrid laughed, 'and you wrote:

'Hello.

'My name is Sigurd Storlesen. I am ten years old. Right now I am sitting on the wharf at Fearnought Bay, Clallam County, State of Washington, U.S.A., 5 miles south of Cape Flattery on the Pacific side, and my Dad is beside me telling me what to write. Today is June 27, 1922. My Dad is a forest warden in the Olympic National Forest but my Grandad is the lighthouse keeper at Cape Flattery. Beside me is a small shiny canoe which you now hold in your hand. It is a windy day and my Dad said to put the canoe in the water when I have put this in and glued down the lid which is a piece of balsa wood from my model airplane box.

'Well must close this note now, but first I will ask you to tell the Seattle Star that you have found it, because I am going to start reading the paper from today and looking for a piece that says, who when and where it was found.

'Thanks. Sigurd Storlesen.'

'Yes, then my father and I put the note inside, and we glued down the lid and sealed it and put the boat on the water.'

'You put the boat on the water and the tide was going out and away it went. The current caught it right off and carried it out and you watched it till it was out of sight!'

The two had now reached a clearing in the forest where a few grey squirrels were scampering about on the grass. A dark-browed Indian in a windbreaker, utterly absorbed by his friendly task, stood with a sleek black squirrel sitting on his shoulder nibbling popcorn he was giving it from a bag. This reminded them to get some peanuts to feed the bears, whose cages were over the way.

Ursus Horribilis: and now they tossed peanuts to the sad lumbering sleep-heavy creatures—though at least these two grizzlies were together, they even had a home—maybe still too sleepy to know where they were, still wrapped in a dream of their timberfalls and wild blueberries in the Cordilleras Sigurd and Astrid could see again, straight ahead of them, between the trees, beyond a bay.

But how should they stop thinking of the little boat?

Twelve years it had wandered. Through the tempests of winter, over sunny summer seas, what tide rips had caught it, what wild sea birds, shearwaters, storm petrels, jaegers, that follow the thrashing propellers, the dark albatross of these northern waters, swooped upon it, or warm currents edged it lazily toward land—and blue-water currents sailed it after the albacore, with fishing boats like white giraffes—or glacial drifts tossed it about fuming Cape Flattery itself. Perhaps it had rested, floating in a sheltered cove, where the killer whale smote, lashed, the deep clear water; the eagle and the salmon had seen it, a baby seal stared with her wondering eyes, only for the little boat to be thrown aground, catching the rainy afternoon sun, on cruel barnacled rocks by the waves, lying aground knocked from side to side in an inch of water like a live thing, or a poor old tin can, pushed, pounded ashore, and swung around, reversed again, left high and dry, and then swept another yard up the beach, or carried under a lonely salt-grey shack, to drive a seine fisherman crazy all night with its faint plaintive knocking, before it ebbed out in the dark autumn dawn, and found its way afresh, over the deep, coming through thunder, to who will ever know what fierce and desolate un-inhabited shore, known only to the dread Wendigo, where not even an Indian could have found it, unfriended there, lost, until it was borne out to sea once more by the great brimming black tides of January, or the huge calm tides of the mid-summer moon, to start its journey all over again——

Astrid and Sigurd came to a large enclosure, set back from a walk, with two vine-leaved maple trees (their scarlet tassels, delicate precursors of their leaves, already visible) growing through the top, a sheltered cavernous part to one side for a lair, and the whole, save for the barred front, covered with stout large-meshed wire—considered sufficient protection for one of the most Satanic beasts left living on earth.

Two animals inhabited the cage, spotted like deceitful pastel leopards, and in appearance like decorated, maniacal-looking cats: their ears were provided with huge tassels and, as if this were in savage parody of the vine-leaved maples, from the brute's chin tassels also depended. Their legs were as long as a man's arm, and their paws, clothed in grey fur out of which shot claws curved like scimitars, were as big as a man's clenched fist.

And the two beautiful demonic creatures prowled and paced endlessly, searching the base of their cage, between whose bars there was just room to slip a murderous paw—always a hop out of reach an almost invisible sparrow went pecking away in the dust—searching with eternal voraciousness, yet seeking in desperation also some way out, passing and repassing each other rhythmically, as though truly damned and under some compelling enchantment.

And yet as they watched the terrifying Canadian lynx, in which seemed to be embodied in animal form all the pure ferocity of nature, as they watched, crunching peanuts themselves now and passing the bag between them, before the lovers' eyes still sailed that tiny boat, battling with the seas, at the mercy of a wilder ferocity yet, all those years before Astrid was born.

Ah, its absolute loneliness amid those wastes, those wildernesses, of rough rainy seas bereft even of sea birds, between contrary winds, or in the great dead windless swell that comes following a gale; and then with the wind springing up and blowing the spray across the sea like rain, like a vision of creation, blowing the little boat as it climbed the highlands into the skies, from which sizzled cobalt lightnings, and then sank down into the abyss, but already was climbing again, while the whole sea crested with foam like lambs' wool went furling off to leeward, the whole vast moon-driven expanse like the pastures and valleys and snow-capped ranges of a Sierra Madre in delirium, in ceaseless motion, rising and falling, and the little boat rising, and falling into a paralysing sea of white drifting fire and smoking spume by which it seemed overwhelmed: and all this time a sound, like a high sound of singing, yet as sustained in harmony as telegraph wires, or like the unbelievably high perpetual sound of the wind where there is nobody to listen, which perhaps does not exist, or the ghost of the wind in the rigging of ships long lost, and perhaps it was the sound of the wind in its toy rigging, as again the boat slanted onward: but even then what further unfathomed deeps had it oversailed, until what birds of ill omen turned heavenly for it at last, what iron birds with sabre wings skimming forever through the murk above the grey immeasurable swells, imparted mysteriously their own homing knowledge to it, the lonely buoyant little craft, nudging it with their beaks under golden sunsets in a blue sky, as it sailed close in to mountainous coasts of clouds with stars over them, or burning coasts at sunset once more, as it rounded not only the terrible spume-drenched rocks, like incinerators in sawmills, of Flattery, but other capes unknown, those twelve years, of giant pinnacles, images of barrenness and desolation, upon which the heart is thrown and impaled eternally!— And strangest of all how many ships themselves had threatened it, during that voyage of only some three score miles as the crow flies from its launching to its final port, looming out of the fog and passing by harmlessly all those years—those years too of the last sailing ships, rigged to the moonsail, sweeping by into their own oblivion—but ships cargoed with guns or iron for impending wars, what freighters now at the bottom of the sea he, Sigurd, had voyaged in for that matter, freighted with old marble and wine and cherries-in-brine, or whose engines even now were still somewhere murmuring: *Frère* Jacques! *Frère* Jacques!

What strange poem of God's mercy was this?

Suddenly across their vision a squirrel ran up a tree beside the cage and then, chattering shrilly, leaped from a branch and darted across the top of the wire mesh. Instantly, swift and deadly as lightning, one of the lynx sprang twenty feet into the air, hurtling straight to the top of the cage toward the squirrel, hitting the wire with a twang like a mammoth guitar, and simultaneously flashing through the wire its scimitar claws: Astrid cried out and covered her face.

But the squirrel, unhurt, untouched, was already running lightly along another branch, down to the tree, and away, while the infuriated lynx sprang straight up, sprang again, and again and again and again, as his mate crouched spitting and snarling below.

Sigurd and Astrid began to laugh. Then this seemed obscurely unfair to the lynx, now solemnly washing his mate's face. The innocent squirrel, for whom they felt such relief, might almost have been showing off, almost, unlike the oblivious sparrow, have been taunting the caged animal. The squirrel's hair-breadth escape—the thousand-to-one-chance—that on second thought must take place every day, seemed meaningless. But all at once it did not seem meaningless that they had been there to see it.

'You know how I watched the paper and waited,' Sigurd was saying, stooping to relight his pipe, as they walked on.

'The Seattle *Star*,' Astrid said.

'The Seattle *Star* . . . It was the first newspaper I ever read. Father always declared the boat had gone south—maybe to Mexico, and I seem to remember Grandad saying no, if it didn't break up on Tatoosh, the tide would take it right down Juan de Fuca Strait, maybe into Puget Sound itself. Well, I watched and waited for a long time and finally, as kids will, I stopped looking.'

'And the years went on——'

'And I grew up. Grandad was dead by then. And the old man, you know about him. Well, he's dead too now. But I never forgot. Twelve years! Think of it—! Why, it voyaged around longer than we've been married.'

'And we've been married seven years.'

'Seven years today——'

'It seems like a miracle!'

But their words fell like spent arrows before the target of this fact.

They were walking, as they left the forest, between two long rows of Japanese cherry trees, next month to be an airy avenue of celestial bloom. The cherry trees behind, the forest reappeared, to left and right of the wide clearing, and skirting two arms of the bay. As they approached the Pacific, down the gradual incline, on this side remote from the harbour the wind grew more boisterous: gulls, glaucous and raucous, wheeled and sailed overhead, yelling, and were suddenly far out to sea.

And it was the sea that lay before them, at the end of the slope that changed into the steep beach, the naked sea, running deeply below, without embankment or promenade, or any friendly shacks, though some prettily built homes showed to the left, with one light in a window, glowing warmly through the trees on the edge of the forest itself, as of some stalwart Columbian Adam, who had calmly stolen back with his Eve into Paradise, under the flaming sword of the civic cherubim.

The tide was low. Offshore, white horses were running round a point. The headlong onrush of the tide of beaten silver flashing over its crossflowing underset was so fast the very surface of the sea seemed racing away.

The path gave place to a cinder track in the familiar lee of an old frame pavilion, a deserted tea house boarded up since last summer. Dead leaves were slithering across the porch, past which on the slope to the right picnic benches, tables, a derelict swing, lay overturned, under a tempestuous grove of birches. It seemed cold, sad, inhuman there, and beyond, with the roar of that deep low tide. Yet there was that between the lovers which moved like a warmth, and might have thrown open the shutters, set the benches and tables aright, and filled the whole grove with the voices and children's laughter of summer. Astrid paused for a moment with a hand on Sigurd's arm while they were sheltered by the pavilion, and said, what she too had often said before, so that they always repeated these things almost like an incantation:

'I'll never forget it. That day when I was seven years old, coming to the park here on a picnic with my father and mother and brother. After lunch my brother and I came down to the beach to play. It was a fine summer day, and the tide was out, but there'd been this very high tide in the night, and you could see the lines of driftwood and seaweed where it had ebbed. . . . I was playing on the beach, and I found your boat!'

'You were playing on the beach and you found my boat. And the mast was broken.'

'The mast was broken and shreds of sail hung dirty and limp. But your boat was still whole and unhurt, though it was scratched and weatherbeaten and the varnish was gone. I ran to my mother, and she saw the sealing wax over the cockpit, and, darling, I found your note!'

'You found our note, my darling.'

Astrid drew from her pocket a scrap of paper and holding it between them they bent over (though it was hardly legible by now and they knew it off by heart) and read:

Hello.

My name is Sigurd Storlesen. I am ten years old. Right now I am sitting on the wharf at Fearnought Bay, Clallam County, State of Washington, U.S.A., 5 miles south of Cape Flattery, on the Pacific side, and my Dad is beside me telling me what to write. Today is June 27, 1922. My Dad is a forest warden in the Olympic National Forest but my Grandad is the lighthouse keeper at Cape Flattery. Beside me is a small shiny canoe which you now hold in your hand. It is a windy day and my Dad said to put the canoe in the water when I have put this in and glued down the lid which is a piece of balsa wood from my model airplane box.

Well must close this note now, but first I will ask you to tell the Seattle Star that you have found it, because I am going to start reading the paper from today and looking for a piece that says, who when and where it was found.

Thanks. Sigurd Storlesen.

They came to the desolate beach strewn with driftwood, sculptured, whorled, silvered, piled everywhere by tides so immense there was a tideline of seaweed and detritus on the grass behind them, and great logs and shingle-bolts and writhing snags, crucificial, or frozen in a fiery rage—or better, a few bits of lumber almost ready to burn, for someone to take home, and automatically they threw them up beyond the sea's reach for some passing soul, remembering their own winters of need—and more snags there at the foot of the grove and visible high on the sea-scythed forest banks on either side, in which riven trees were growing, yearning over the shore. And everywhere they looked was wreckage, the toll of winter's wrath: wrecked hencoops, wrecked floats, the wrecked side of a fisherman's hut, its boards once hammered together, with its wrenched shiplap and extruding nails. The fury had extended even to the beach itself, formed in hummocks and waves and barriers of shingle and shells they had to climb up in places. And everywhere too was the grotesque macabre fruit of the sea, with its exhilarating iodine smell, nightmarish bulbs of kelp like antiquated motor horns, trailing brown satin streamers twenty feet long, sea wrack like demons, or the discarded casements of evil spirits that had been cleansed. Then more wreckage: boots, a clock, torn fishing nets, a demolished wheelhouse, a smashed wheel lying in the sand.

Nor was it possible to grasp for more than a moment that all this with its feeling of death and destruction and barrenness was only an appearance, that beneath the flotsam, under the very shells they crunched, within the trickling overflows of winter-bournes they jumped over, down at the tide margin, existed, just as in the forest, a stirring and stretching of life, a seething of spring.

When Astrid and Sigurd were almost sheltered by an uprooted tree on one of these lower billows of beach they noticed that the clouds had lifted over the sea, though the sky was not blue but still that intense silver, so that they could see right across the Gulf and make out, or thought they could, the line of some Gulf Islands. A lone freighter with upraised derricks shipped seas on the horizon. A hint of the summit of Mount Hood remained, or it might have been clouds. They remarked too, in the south-east, on the sloping base of a hill, a triangle of storm-washed green, as if cut out of the overhanging murk there, in which were four pines, five telegraph posts, and a clearing resembling a cemetery. Behind them the icy mountains of Canada hid their savage peaks and snowfalls under still more savage clouds. And they saw that the sea was grey with whitecaps and currents charging offshore and spray blowing backwards from the rocks.

But when the full force of the wind caught them, looking from the shore, it was like gazing into chaos. The wind blew away their thoughts, their voices, almost their very senses, as they walked, crunching the shells, laughing and stumbling. Nor could they tell whether it was spume or rain that smote and stung their faces, whether spindrift from the sea or rain from which the sea was born, as now finally they were forced to a halt, standing there arm in arm. . . . And it was to this shore, through that chaos, by those currents, that their little boat with its innocent message had been brought out of the past finally to safety and a home.

But ah, the storms they had come through!

Vacation in La Voiselle

IRVING LAYTON (b. 1912)

I

GREY puffs of sand arose and moved across the hill-side; the rain peppered the road with spots of mud. Pfeffer sprinted up the derelict footway and arrived at the cottage out of breath. Dubiously, as if expecting someone to drive him off, he put down the satchel he had lugged all the way from Montreal and looked around. The veranda certainly needed a coat of fresh paint; as did the screen-door which stood open, its top hinge severed. The lurching screen-door, like a question he had to answer without delay, upset him by inviting him in abruptly. He should have had time to prepare himself; like an actor, time to arrange his face.

Yet Mme Tipue had been almost insistent.

She had run two fingers smelling faintly of eau de cologne down his bloodless cheeks.

'*Mon pauvre cher*, you are killing yourself. Look at these lines, Minettes! If I dropped a tear on them it would run to the ocean. *N'est-ce pas, mon ami?*' Mme Tipue humorously screws up her face and everyone smiles, including Hugo. 'Come, *mon enfant*, do not be an imbecile. You are not well, and besides what shall three enchanting women do in the country alone? Out of ennui, I'm sure I shall murder my daughters. Don't say another word; I command you,' she concludes with majestic vehemence, flinging out an absurdly thin arm.

Mme Tipue is right; he needs to rest. Of late, he has been seeing bits of coloured fuzz moving across his vision. It irritates him and he frequently shuts his eyes to make them disappear. When he opens them, however, they take up again their infuriating crablike motion. Still, he does not speak. Out of timidity and pride, you understand. A most unfortunate alliance. And Mme Tipue, not suspecting the reason for his silence, rubs his hand gently.

'*Mais*, it's only another bone in the soup. We can still spare that, you know.'

It was then 'Toinette had put her arm around his neck, had squeezed it, and called him her '*dear Toutou*', her '*Joujou*', and had pulled his ears roughly until he had promised to come. The little monkey! Only Pamela had said nothing. Her eyes dreaming in pockets of skin puffed up by good health, she had looked indifferent, even hostile.

Or was he imagining?

The summer cottage had a musty, kerosene odour. The books and magazines lying face downward as if their readers had hurried to something else; the stillness; the newspaper that had fallen to the floor; the heavy towels and bathrobes thrown carelessly over the backs of chairs; all this gave to the room an appearance of thoroughfare bustle, of activity suspended for the moment to be taken up again as soon as the inmates return. In a large mirror Pfeffer saw himself reflected, covered with dust. He smiled for no reason at all, or because there was a mirror in front of him. Then he called softly, 'Mme Tipue!

Mme Tipue!' He experienced the sensation which says as unmistakably as if someone had said it to him 'No one is here' and he called again, but this time more loudly, 'Mme Tipue! Mme Tipue!' He inserted himself into the fauteuil near the door. He crossed his legs. He waited. A glance outside showed him the young poplars cowering under the smash of the rain and the spongy track of mud leading to the village of La Voiselle, which was really a handful of tumbledown, wooden shacks confronting the river. Without turning his head, Hugo could discern their black outlines; in the rain they looked smaller, like a fringe of wet crows drinking.

He could not tell how long he waited. The storm had passed, but drops of rain kept thudding upon the ground from the roof and the soaked trees, and the wind smeared the wasted clouds across the sky. A few moments later he heard footsteps rustling the wet grass near the cottage and the sound of voices. He could distinguish Pamela's voice from that of her mother's; it was annoyingly guttural and masculine. It was 'Toinette, however, who saw him first.

'When did you get here?' she shouted from the doorway, really excited and glad as Hugo shyly got up from the fauteuil. '*Maman, O maman,* do come quickly! *Hugo est arrivé.*'

Mme Tipue, followed by Pamela, sailed into the room, her mouth open and her face grimacing. She seized his hand and held it.

'*Ah mon cher!* I am glad, I am so glad you have come. You will not imagine how *désolé,* how empty we have been without you. . . . Why did you not come sooner. . . . Have you been waiting long?'

'About an hour. But tell me truly, are you really

glad to see me? I won't be in your way?' Pfeffer
asked her diffidently.

'*Mais non*, Hugo. Believe me, I'm excessively glad
you have managed to come. We were just beginning
to bore each other.'

Hugo smiled.

At certain moments, even an ugly woman, if she
has lived for some time with the wind and the sun,
can be sexually attractive. Even if she is old enough
to be your mother. And perhaps just because she is
that old provided, a residue from her youth, there
still clings about her an animal smell. Mme Tipue's
hair is greying, but her shoulders are still shapely,
almost like a young girl's, almost like 'Toinette's,
and her legs are well-formed, the skin hairless and
delicate; somewhat incongruously a fold of her
stomach lips over the heavy leather belt which sup-
ports her khaki trousers, the trouser legs rolled up
above her knees.

She let go of his hand.

'Are you tired?' she asked.

'A little.'

'Ah, but why did you not come this morning! You
could have acquainted yourself with Jean Pettifer.
He's such a brilliant man and so *spirituel*. Just
imagine, they have given him the sack. *Les bêtes!*'

'That's a fact,' said 'Toinette with unusual solemnity. 'He was on vacation. The newspaper owner
phoned him long distance and said he was through.'

'Yes, through! *Finis!*' Mme Tipue added vigour-
ously. '*Quelle honte!*'

'But why?' Pfeffer asked. Vaguely he remembered
Jean Pettifer as the editor of *L'Étoile*. Mme Tipue
had spoken about him in Montreal.

'Why? Because he wrote an article. He said the

priests have the blame for the bad teeth of these French-Canadian peasants.'

Mme Tipue was a Parisienne.

'Just the same he ought to know better,' Pamela brought out. 'One should not mix in affairs not one's own.' She moved the fauteuil away from the door and sat down on it moodily.

'Nonsense, child. Pettifer is too radical for this province. Give these idiotic peasants Mass every day; that's what they want.'

She turned to Pfeffer, who seemed embarrassed by all the excited talk and wanted nothing better than to sit down and rest after miles of trudging on dusty roads.

'And what do you think, *mon enfant*? He's going to Montreal to commence his own newspaper. It's for this he has come to see us today. He really begged me to do the translations for him.'

Hugo tried to appear interested.

'What sort of newspaper will it be?'

'Oh, a very revolutionary paper, you may be sure. He told us all about it this morning. What plans! They are really immense. And so practical, too. He will not stop, Pettifer says, until our whole society has been changed, has been turned upsidedown. But no bloodshed. No Jacobinism. Nothing like that you may be sure. Oh he was so droll and so *sérieux*. We'll show, he says, those witch-doctors, the socialists, how to do things. Spread enlightenment. . . .'

Pamela broke in scornfully.

'He'll teach the peasants how to brush their teeth.'

Ignoring her, Mme Tipue went on:

'All the same he spoke very well about the taxes. Pettifer is such a clever man. He really knows everything. *Il est un économiste.*'

'Truly, *Maman*, I believe you are in love with M. Pettifer,' 'Toinette said mischievously.

'Don't be rude, child. . . . *Mon cher* Hugo, I think Providence is working for you. Pettifer shall make you his assistant. I shall speak to him about you. I see it all very clearly now. You will become a great publicist . . . a Voltaire.'

'Toinette shook her head impatiently.

'But Mouchequette, *soyez raisonnable*. Hugo cannot even write his name in French.'

'*Eh bien*, what fools my children are today! We can teach him. He shall spend the summer with us.'

Pamela sniffed. 'Voltaire!'

'Really, Pam, you are insufferable. And now come, Minettes, help your *Mouchequette* prepare the supper. *Cher* Hugo must be almost dead with hunger.'

'Toinette circled her arm around Hugo's neck and with the embarrassing glibness of a young girl drew herself up to him.

'Are you still my *Toutou*,' she demanded, 'my bad, bad *Joujou*? Will you be my adorable *Toutou* when you are a very old Voltaire?'

'I'll always be your *Toutou*,' Pfeffer said gravely.

II

There was nothing for Hugo to do but to lie on the grass, when the day was fine, and let the vital sunlight penetrate his exhausted body. Now and then he went to the beach—the girls called it a beach—really it was a thimbleful of sand in front of one of the shacks, but most of the time he preferred to stretch out on the level ground behind the cottage or sit quietly on the veranda, an unopened book on his lap, looking out at the river and the brown hills moving away from it like a herd of camels. How lucky I am, he thought. For the first time in ten years—it had been at a camp for underprivileged boys—he had left Montreal behind him. He was away from the city with its dirt and its sadness and its terrible, enervating heat; away from the dismal room of his boarding-house with its noisy, vulgar children and their screaming mothers; away from the smells of washing and garbage that came up from the throats of the unpaved yards and lanes like a nasty curse. He took a deep breath. Yes, it was a mistake to be an underling; this was life. This was the leisure that ennobled it, that made it endurable. The intellectuals that met every evening at Horn's to exchange their sense of failure for moral indignation, that palmed off on each other their boneless-ness for idealism, that talked with so much assurance of their inevitable milleniums—he was one of them —they were freaks and chatterers. What an imbecile he had been! He would act differently when he got back to the city, a million times more shrewdly. For he knew what he wanted now.

At first Pfeffer had supposed it his duty to enter-tain them, to amuse them, but he had no real gift for light, undirect conversation—the only sort Mme Tipue evidently cared for, and he sometimes won-dered anxiously during an oppressive silence at meal time why she had asked him to come. Hugo was one of whom people always say after a first meeting 'What a charming person' because a nervous irrita-bility not unfree from vanity made him flatteringly attentive and gave, contrary to the truth, an impres-sion of good-nature and virility. After a short time, the same people accused him, of course quite un-justly, of being affected where he was merely frightened. He was timid and bold, enthusiastic and critical, and since all was disorderly within him, the change from one state to the other was sudden and unaccountable. No sooner had he given himself un-reservedly to some new person when, alarmed at his daring, he withdrew into a disdainful reticence. A number of sharply unpleasant experiences, the memory of which still plagued him, had permitted him a slender insight into his nature. After the first week he had constant misgivings, especially now that he could no longer doubt that Pamela disliked him —for what reason he could only guess. Good-naturedly, or to ease his mind, he put it down to her general clumsiness and stupidity. Indeed, sometimes with her eyes wide open and staring abstractedly at nothing at all, she looked as if something inside her were ascending a spiral staircase. It was at such times that her face wore a particularly disagreeable ex-pression, one which always made Hugo uneasy whenever he noticed it.

Fortunately, the Minettes—so unlike in tempera-ment—were attached to each other and usually went for long walks by themselves which ended up with a visit at the Lachances', their nearest neighbour, whose barns and apathetic cows Pfeffer could see from the rise of ground on which the Tipue cottage was situated. When it grew dark they would sit around the table reading or Mme Tipue, recalling her resolution, would command Hugo to speak only in French. He made little progress. Since they were short of bedding, they had fixed up a cot for him in a corner of the living-room which was partitioned from Mme Tipue's bedroom by nothing else but a curtain made from some cheap print. After the girls had gone to their room upstairs and Mme Tipue had

called out to him *'Dormez bien, mon cher'* Hugo
could hear her gentle snores join with the buzz of
the insects beating irritably against the window-
screens.

This evening, having discussed the mail ex-
haustively—letters from Pettifer and Hugo's
brother, Frederic—he asked whether M. Tipue was
likely to come out for the week-end and regretted
the words as soon as they were spoken. For everyone
became embarrassed and Mme Tipue coughing
noisily looked warningly at 'Toinette and Pamela.
Evidently she was afraid they were going to speak.
Although not a quick-witted person, Hugo changed
the question for another, one about Pettifer, which
'Toinette answered impulsively. A few minutes later
he got up and went out on the veranda where he was
joined by Mme Tipue who sat down beside him,
taking his hand and patting it affectionately.

Stricken by the long afternoon the sun dropped—
a shrivelled mummy; a light wind parted the grass
like a moving snake.

'A quoi penses-tu?' she asked him.

'Rien.'

She put her hand to her mouth and looked at him
steadily.

'Your lips were—how shall I say?—stuck out like
two legs. I almost tripped over them. Are you happy,
mon enfant?'

'Of course I am,' he said quickly, 'and very, very
grateful to you, Mme Tipue. Believe me.'

'Tut! *Mais* just think, *mon cher* Hugo. That
article for *Les Idées.* Had you not written it, we
should never have known you.'

'You mean,' he corrected her, 'if 'Toinette hadn't
translated it for me. She was in the library when—'

'*Eh bien*,' Mme Tipue said, 'that child is too bold, too *moderne*, don't you think?'

Hugo was worried. Was she perhaps pointing her finger at him? He hesitated, then:

'Where is she now?' he asked.

'With Pamela, *chez Lachance*,' she said.

'At her age, Mme Tipue, girls are always like that. A little coquetry—'

'O, I don't mean there's any harm in the child. *Rien! Rien!* But sometimes I think 'Toinette—'

Hugo's voice was very tender.

'I think you're all wonderful people. It was really very kind of you—'

'Tut! Tut! I'd do the same for an abortion.' Mme Tipue smiled, and Pfeffer felt her hand tighten carefully on his own.

The Minettes had gone for a row with Albert Lachance and they could see them, 'Toinette at the oars, as the boat pulled away from the shore towards the middle of the narrow river. 'Toinette turned around to wave at them and with his free hand Pfeffer waved back. Mme Tipue looked away.

There are two sorts of people in whom other people are likely to place their confidence: those who are frank since they are believed honest, and those who are secretive because they are thought experienced. Mme Tipue looked at Hugo for a long time without saying anything. Finally she broke the silence.

'You have often asked me why M. Tipue doesn't come,' she began, and added quickly, 'or doesn't even write.'

It was, of course, not true. But she needed an opening and Hugo didn't contradict her.

'*Eh bien*, now that you're one of us, you have a right to know.'

She played with his fingers, nervously.

'We have been separated many years,' she said, 'We . . . we are entirely different from each other.' Then, as if regretting the proud, inflexible smile that pitted her lips:

'*Chacun à son goût! N'est-ce pas, mon ami?*'

Hugo nodded his head profoundly.

'*Chacun à son goût!* But he is interested only in science. His head is full of crazy inventions, enormous projects which, *pauvre diable*, he never finishes. *Quel fou!* I would rather live with a bear.' And she pressed Hugo's fingers as though to draw from them reassurance.

'You know my tastes, *cher* Hugo . . . *belles-lettres*, *littérature*.'

Anyone else but Pfeffer would have known what to answer then and there. A polite phrase would have done the trick admirably. An epigram, since Mme Tipue was so fond of them, a witty observation and everything would have passed off smoothly. Instead Hugo looked away from her towards the river and said nothing. His disposition, like the rightful heir that turns up at the last moment to deprive someone of a fortune, hustled him downstairs into a cellar full of heavy thoughts. He kept silent, although Mme Tipue was regarding him attentively. Nevertheless, she went on, her voice, perhaps because he hadn't spoken a word, growing shriller and shriller.

'You will never, never know how much I have suffered. He is *déséquilibré*.' Toinette has been saying that ever since she was eight. It is impossible to even imagine so much suffering. He never reads!

The company he keeps is always inferior so that he might have the pleasure of hearing them say, '*Ah docteur! Oui docteur!*' And Mme Tipue threw her head backwards and forwards and bowed exaggeratedly several times to show the humility the doctor flavoured. 'He knows nothing, absolutely nothing, about life's charm and gaiety and wit . . . *rien du tout*! But, then, do you suppose I desire to spend all my years alone? At my age? *C'est incroyable!* So I sent him a book—Balzac's Goriot—for his birthday. He thought I was trying to insult him!' She brought out the last word as if it were a cube of sugar she were biting into.

'*Bête!*'

Her hand trembling with emotion on his own made Hugo feel uncomfortable. Again he looked away from her, but from a corner of his eye he could see she was still scanning his features attentively. He could see the disappointment in her face taking gradual possession of her eyes and mouth. Desperately, as if his life depended upon it, he searched about for something appropriate to say. But his feet, as though they had been spitefully greased by an enemy, kept slipping down the cellar stairs each time he attempted to climb them. Down! Down Down! Mme Tipue was waiting for him to speak, to make some ironic jest; she wanted him, perhaps, even to laugh a little; he did not know how. Incapable of penetrating Hugo's difficulty with himself, she took his reticence and reserve for want of sympathy and coldness. She began to feel that she had made a fool of herself, which for a woman of Mme Tipue's vanity and self-assurance was an intolerable sensation. A feeling of dependency had added to Hugo's difficulty; like an invisible spore fruit it sent out filaments of self-mistrust which finally choked all power of natural expression. There was an awkward silence.

'*C'est drôle?*' she said at last.

'*Pas drôle*,' Pfeffer said with an effort. '*C'est tragique.*'

He had climbed the stairs and had kicked the door open but it was too late. He knew that for a certainty when Mme Tipue withdrew her hand, letting it fall primly upon the other. He yearned to say to her now: 'Mme Tipue, you imagine that I don't understand you; that I have no sympathy. Believe me, you are mistaken. But you won't. You are a woman and for you a thing does not exist until it has been given a name.' Well, perhaps it is just as well that he didn't: it might have sounded too sententious. At that late moment anything less than a felicitous inspiration would have seemed to her stupidly inept. No inspiration came and Pfeffer said miserably:

'I've run out of tobacco. I'd better go down to the village to get some before they shut.'

'Since you must,' she said drily without looking at him.

III

Nevertheless the very same night the Devil played with the two of them. The Minettes had gone upstairs to bed, 'Toinette throwing him a gay kiss across the bannister, and Mme Tipue had called out with no change in the inflexion of her voice, '*Dormez bien*, Hugo.' He lay on his cot and stared fixedly at the window letting in an emaciated light that drained weight and substantiality from the objects in the room. There was a great deal in his mind and he must have been staring like that for several minutes. He was startled, therefore, when Mme Tipue called softly:

'Are you asleep, *mon cher* Hugo?'

'No, not yet Mme Tipue. It's too hot.'

'Sh . . . the children upstairs will hear you.'

Silence. Then:

'What are you thinking about, *mon cher enfant*?'

'Of nothing. Of how hot it is.'

'For myself I'm thinking of you, *Chéri*. . . . But the Crucifix on the wall protects me.'

He heard her laughing quietly to herself. In an instant he was wide awake, feeling curiously stimulated. He sat up on the cot, rigid.

'Can't you sleep, either, *Mouchequette*?' he asked softly.

'Non, *Chéri*, I burn like the bad sinners in Hell. *O le Bon Dieu*,' she whispered, addressing the Crucifix and muffling her self-derisive laughter.

It was then Pfeffer's mind pictured the fold of stomach that lipped over the shiny black belt that supported Mme Tipue's trousers. He wanted to put his hand on it, to feel the soft flesh between his fingers. His body shivered and he clutched the rough woollen blanket tightly. And curious, flattered, and inexpressibly moved he thought:

'Well, why not . . . the poor woman.' His voice was husky.

'But the Cross? Does it not protect you?'

'*La Croix est tombée.*'

Hugo had already placed his feet upon the bare floor when he heard someone stirring at the top of the staircase. It was Pamela—he recognized her heavy steps! He hastily got under his blanket again and it was with difficulty that he fell asleep. When he did he dreamt Mme Tipue had fallen down the veranda steps, and lying stretched out obscenely on the ground was calling 'Hugo, *mon cher* Hugo, *mon enfant*.' He awoke with a start to find her words still echoing faintly in the room. He sat up. Was she still awake? The disturbed curtain behind which Mme Tipue lay on her bed sent the shadows, like enormous spiders, racing across the room. A few moments later he heard her snoring gently.

When they were alone the next day she said to him severely:

'You have nothing to say about yesterday?'

He looked up at her from the book he was reading. She saw his bewilderment.

'*Non, non,* that was a mistake! That must not happen again! *Je suis une vieille folle.* The children, *vous comprenez. . . .*'

'She wants to play the virtuous lady,' Pfeffer thought. He kept his eyes on the book.

'*Je suis une vieille folle,*' Mme Tipue repeated.

'You're a rutty bitch,' Pfeffer thought.

She sat down beside him.

'But about my husband . . . is he not mad?'

Her emotion struck him as unreal, as if she were acting a part; and indeed there was something theatrical in the gesture that accompanied her words. She waited for him to speak. Oh, if he could only murmur something clever, something full of a deep, original wisdom. He felt nervous and unhappy, fettered. He was confused by what had happened the night before; it had brought in an unexpected element. Finally he exclaimed, 'It's all a stupid mix-up, isn't it?' feeling somewhat relieved now that he had reduced the matter to a phrase, a formula.

'H'm . . . a terrible mix-up! No sense to it at all. Everything just happens . . . for the worse, *vous comprenez*. My husband, for example. . . . He'd always want strong coffee before going to bed. But strong! So I would say to him, *"Mais, voyons . . . you won't be able to sleep, chéri".'* Her eyes grew moist at the recollection and she sighed. '"You won't be able to sleep" I tell him. "Ah," he says, "be quiet, you are always complaining." He must have his stupid coffee and keep me awake when he can't sleep. *Déséquilibré! Bête!'*

When she stopped speaking Hugo's uneasiness increased. It was as though she were expecting him to repeat some wretched lines which he was fruitlessly trying to recall. With something like joy he remembered Frederic's letter.

'My brother intended to buy a larger farm this year. But he's had too many troubles. Nothing would grow. So he wrote, "Guess we'll have to feed on peanuts this winter."' Pfeffer tried frantically to get some verve into what he was saying.

'We'll feed on peanuts this winter. That's our philosophy, Mme Tipue.'

Pfeffer had no sooner uttered these words when he felt how improper, how outrageous, and how absurd they were.

'Peanuts!' Mme Tipue exclaimed. 'But my husband has no humour, no wit or life in him. He is as dry as a stick. And out of jealousy he has worked day and night to suppress my wit, my charm and. . . .' She interrupted herself angrily. 'Ah, it is plain, quite plain, you do not understand me. *Vraiment*, how can you? He has tried every way to crush me—like this!' Mme Tipue pressed the tips of her forefinger and thumb together. Fascinated, Hugo watched her gaiety and charm disappear into the tiny hole her fingers had made.

'*Mais* . . he is capable of great ideas, inspiring thoughts about society, life; then *tout-à-coup, c'est fini*. He will throw himself upon the bed and snore for six hours.'

She was now well launched and was about to say something more when 'Toinette rushed up to them.

'Hugo, you've broken out! You've broken out!' she shouted excitedly.

The chrysalis she had named after him had burst open.

'Come! Do come quickly!'

'*Vous êtes deux enfants*,' Mme Tipue said crossly, getting up from her chair and going into the kitchen.

Taking his hand, 'Toinette led him eagerly upstairs to her room. Pamela was already there. When they reached the windowpane the new-born butterfly was still grasping the shattered chrysalis, suspended from a splinter, between its thin, long legs. Its velvety wings unwrinkling slowly, the beautifully regular purple and yellow tints grew larger as they stood watching. No one spoke. Pamela, indeed, appeared hypnotized by the first unsteady movements the butterfly made to free itself from the broken case.

At last, as if poising itself for flight, it stood motionless, its wings spread out.

Pfeffer said very softly. 'Is it really named after me? Then let's take it outside and watch it fly away. . . . Its freedom is very precious.'

'No!' cried Pamela, startling Hugo and 'Toinette. 'We're going to keep it here! I want it!'

'But why . . . what for?' Hugo demanded hotly.

A cunning gleam came into Pamela's eyes.

'It's called "Hugo", isn't it? Well . . . I want it. It shall stay here.' And she reached for the butterfly.

'Toinette coaxed her, 'Now be a dear and let the *papillon* go.'

But Pfeffer was now shouting madly, 'Let it go! Let it go!'

Then with a sharp, impulsive movement he seized her hand, jerking it backward against the wall so that she screamed with the pain of it. The butterfly fell crushed from her fingers; its bruised wings fluttered nervelessly in the sunlight filtering on to the carpet.

Mme Tipue appeared suddenly in the doorway.

'What's all the noise and shouting?' she demanded angrily. 'Pamela you should be ashamed. You should have let the *pauvre papillon* go—to love and to enjoy,' she added, tempted even in her displeasure to make a happy phrase.

'It's all Pam's fault,' 'Toinette said.

Mme Tipue turned to Pfeffer.

'Just the same, Hugo, I think you are getting to be very disagreeable.'

Motionless, Pfeffer watched her with a dazed expression.

'*Oui! Oui!* You have become—how shall I say—a frightful bore. *Eh bien*, if you are not amusing yourself. . . .'

'I'm amusing myself,' Hugo muttered, unable to make out what had happened and saying the first ridiculous words that flew into his head.

'Well, you needn't raise your voice to me. I'm not Pamela, *vous savez*? Even though I do slave in the kitchen. . . . *Je ne suis pas encore votre servante.* . . . You promised. . . .'

'Promised what?' Hugo asked. He stood there

feeling ridiculous, as if someone had tipped a basin of dirty water over his head.

'*Rien!*' Mme Tipue rapped out. 'Just the same you might pay me for the extra cream you put away in such enormous quantities.'

'*Mouchequette!*' broke from 'Toinette's lips.

'Bah, he has deceived me. He has been deceiving me all along.'

At last Pfeffer found his tongue.

'You're vexed now, Mme Tipue. I don't think you mean what you just said.'

When he reached the door he heard Pamela parrotting him. 'You're vex-*ed* now.'

That night, of course, Pfeffer couldn't fall asleep. He tossed restlessly from side to side on his narrow cot and several times had to pick up the blankets that had fallen to the floor. 'I can't stay here another day' he muttered to himself over and over. He recalled the uncomfortable supper with everyone avoiding each other's eyes. Fortunately Albert Lachance had come to visit them. His mouth and chin were covered with pimples and ugly blond hairs grew between them. When he walked his wrists kept flapping against his fat belly.

'Sh! Sh!' Mme Tipue beamed on everyone. 'Albert is going to sing.'

A triumphant sneer in his small, dirty eyes, he cleared his throat noisily and began:

'*C'est une blonde aux grands yeux prometteurs,*
Une de ces femmes dont le regard vous grise. . . .'

Albert's grimaces, the manner in which he swayed his body and flapped his wrists made him appear an obscene dwarf. Hugo felt uncomfortable as at a sight at once absurd and disagreeable.

'*O, que c'est drôle! Que c'est drôle!*' burst out Mme

Tipue. As she could no longer hide her derision, she had made up her mind to laugh outright.

After Albert had gone she turned to Hugo.

'Didn't you find him funny?' she asked.

It was the first time she had spoken to him since her ill-tempered words in the afternoon. Pfeffer was relieved and grateful and yearned to say something that would bring them together once again. But his words were forced and he laughed artificially.

'Yes, he's a droll fellow . . . isn't he?'

Unable to sleep he got up and began pacing the room quietly so as not to disturb Mme Tipue's slumber. Then he sat down at the edge of the cot and wrapped the blanket around his waist. What a fool he had been! Life had always treated him like that. They just had no luck—the Pfeffers. He thought bitterly of his room on St. Dominique Street. It was impossible to go back there now. The heat . . . the heat. It seemed to him he could almost smell the stink from the garbage and the children's pee. . . . Well, she hadn't told him to go. Maybe it was only a spill and would pass as spills everywhere had a way of doing. The thought gave him some comfort. He lay down and closed his eyes but he couldn't fall asleep. There was a painful dizziness in his head, his throat felt dry. He was a sick man, a terribly sick man. He had to stay, at all costs he had to stay.

'Didn't you have a good night?' Mme Tipue asked him, noticing his tired eyes. Even Pamela appeared to be friendly. Pfeffer was relieved, almost happy again. And when 'Toinette stroked his chin and smiled at him and called him her dear Toutou, he wanted to exclaim rapturously, 'Everyone admit now, wasn't yesterday rotten? Let's pitch it out of the calendar.' He replied to Mme Tipue's question with real friendliness:

'Oh yes . . . so-so.'

But after the breakfast, when the dishes had been cleared off the table and the Minettes had gone for their walk, Mme Tipue said to him:

'Don't you think, Hugo, it would be best for all. . . .'

He understood. He looked up at her and she saw the hurt look in his eyes.

'*Circonstances*,' she said, shrugging her shoulders.

'*Mais*, we shall see you in town,' she added, and there was a real touch of earnestness in her voice.

Pfeffer went to his cot and began to pack his few articles. Even now, dully, he was trying to discover some formula that would express the whole thing perfectly; vulgarity, beggarliness, life. Mme Tipue. . . .

'You'll give my best to Pam and 'Toinette,' he said to Mme Tipue, trying to get a touch of intimacy into his words.

'*Mais*, yes Hugo. *Certainement!*' she replied warmly.

There was an awkward silence as Pfeffer picked up his satchel and stood near the screen-door. Then, insincerity or embarrassment making her effusive:

'Remember to certainly call on Pettifer,' Mme Tipue said. 'Be sure to see him, Hugo. I shall write him about you.' And then as if she thought the words would take away some of the sting, she added:

'This very day I shall write him.'

Hugo said nothing to her.

After trudging five miles to St. Gabriel, he noticed a post at the cross-roads on which were nailed two oblong signs, one beneath the other. He looked up and read:

> To Quebec—20 miles
> To Quebec—18 miles

The signs were pointing in the same direction.

'Crazy. Everything is crazy,' Pfeffer muttered. He turned down the road, and soon he was covered by the white dust his feet raised.

One, Two, Three Little Indians

HUGH GARNER (b. 1913)

After they had eaten, Big Tom pushed the cracked and dirty supper things to the back of the table and took the baby from its high chair, carefully, so as not to spill the flotsam of bread crumbs and boiled potatoes from the chair to the floor.

He undressed the youngster, talking to it in the old dialect, trying to awaken its interest. All evening it had been listless and fretful by turns, but now it seemed to be soothed by the story of Po-chee-ah and the Lynx, although it was too young to understand him as his voice slid awkwardly through the ageless folktale of his people.

For long minutes after the baby was asleep he talked on, letting the victorious words fill the small cabin so that they shut out the sounds of the Northern Ontario night: the buzz of mosquitoes, the far-off bark of a dog, the noise of the cars and transport trucks passing on the gravelled road.

The melodious hum of his voice was like a strong soporific, lulling him with the return of half-forgotten memories, strengthening him with the knowledge that once his people had been strong and brave, men with a nation of their own, encompassing a million miles of teeming forest, lake, and tamarack swamp.

When he halted his monologue to place the baby in the big brass bed in the corner, the sudden silence was loud in his ears, and he cringed a bit as the present suddenly caught up with the past.

He covered the baby with a corner of the church-donated patchwork quilt, and lit the kerosene lamp that stood on the mirrorless dressing table beside the stove. Taking a broom from the corner he swept the mealtime debris across the doorsill.

This done, he stood and watched the headlights of the cars run along the trees bordering the road, like a small boy's stick along a picket fence. From the direction of the trailer camp a hundred yards away came the sound of a car engine being gunned, and the halting note-tumbles of a clarinet from a tourist's radio. The soft summer smell of spruce needles and wood smoke blended with the evening dampness of the earth and felt good in his nostrils, so that he filled his worn lungs until he began to cough. He spat the resinous phlegm into the weed-filled yard.

It had been this summer smell, and the feeling of freedom it gave, that had brought him back to the woods after three years in the mines during the war. But only a part of him had come back, for the mining towns and the big money had done more than etch his lungs with silica. They had also brought him pain and distrust, and a wife who had learned to live in imitation of the gaudy boom-town life.

When his coughing attack subsided he peered

along the path, hoping to catch a glimpse of his wife Mary returning from her work at the trailer camp. He was becoming worried about the baby, and her presence, while it might not make the baby well, would mean there was someone else to share his fears. He could see nothing but the still blackness of the trees and their shadows interwoven in a sombre pattern across the mottled ground.

He re-entered the cabin and began washing the dishes, stopping once or twice to cover the moving form of the sleeping baby. He wondered if he could have transmitted his own wasting sickness to the lungs of his son. He stood for long minutes at the side of the bed, staring, trying to diagnose the child's restlessness into something other than what he feared.

His wife came in and placed some things on the table. He picked up a can of pork-and-beans she had bought and weighed it in the palm of his hand. 'The baby seems pretty sick,' he said.

She crossed the room and looked at the sleeping child. 'I guess it's his teeth.'

He placed the pork-and-beans on the table and walked over to his chair beside the empty stove. As he sat down he noticed for the first time that his wife was beginning to show her pregnancy. Her squat form had sunk lower so that it almost filled the shapeless dress she wore. Her brown ankles were puffed above the broken-down heels of the dirty silver dancing pumps she was wearing.

'Is the trailer camp full?' he asked.

'Nearly. Two more Americans came about half an hour ago.'

'Was Billy Woodhen around?'

'I didn't see him—only Elsie,' she answered. 'A

woman promised me a dress tomorrow if I scrub out her trailer.'

'Yeah?' He saw the happiness rise over her like a colour when she mentioned this. She was much younger than he was—twenty-two years against his thirty-nine—and her dark face had a fullness that is common to many Indian women. She was no longer pretty, and as he watched her he thought that wherever they went the squalor of their existence seemed to follow.

'It's a silk dress,' Mary said, as though the repeated mention of it brought it nearer.

'A silk dress is no damn good around here. You should get some overalls,' he said, angered by her lack of shame in accepting the cast-off garments of the trailer women.

She seemed not to notice his anger. 'It'll do for the dances next winter.'

'A lot of dancing you'll do,' he said, pointing to her swollen body. 'You'd better learn to stay around and take care of the kid.'

She busied herself over the stove, lighting it with newspapers and kindling. 'I'm going to have some fun. You should have married a grandmother.'

He filled the kettle with water from an open pail near the door. The baby began to cough, and the mother turned it on its side in the bed. 'As soon as I draw my money from Cooper, I'm going to get him some cough syrup from the store,' she said.

'It won't do any good. We should take him up to the doctor in town tomorrow.'

'I can't. I've got to stay here and work.'

He knew the folly of trying to reason with her. She had her heart set on earning the silk dress the woman had promised.

After they had drunk their tea he blew out the light. They took off some of their clothes and climbed over the baby into the bed. Long after his wife had fallen asleep he lay in the darkness listening to a ground moth beating its futile wings against the glass of the window.

They were awakened in the morning by the twittering of a small colony of tree sparrows who were feeding on the kitchen sweepings of the night before. Mary got up and went outside, returning a few minutes later carrying a handful of birch and poplar stovewood.

He waited until the beans were in the pan before rising and pulling on his pants. He stood in the doorway scratching his head and absorbing the sunlight through his bare feet upon the step.

The baby awoke while they were eating their breakfast.

'He don't look good,' Big Tom said as he dipped some brown sauce from his plate with a hunk of bread.

'He'll be all right later,' his wife insisted. She poured some crusted tinned milk from the can into a cup and mixed it with water from the kettle.

Big Tom splashed his hands and face with cold water and dried himself on a shirt that lay over the back of a chair. 'When you going to the camp—this morning?'

'This afternoon,' Mary answered.

'I'll be back by then.'

He took up a small pile of woven baskets from a corner and hung the handles over his arm. From the warming shelf of the stove he pulled a bedraggled band of cloth into which a large goose feather had

been sewn. Carrying this in his hand, he went outside and strode down the path towards the highway.

He ignored the chattering sauciness of a squirrel
that hurtled up the green ladder of a tree beside
him. Above the small noises of the woods could be
heard the roar of a transport truck braking its way
down the hill from the burnt-out sapling-covered
ridge to the north. The truck passed him as he
reached the road, and he waved a desultory greeting
to the driver, who answered him with a short blare
of the horn.

Placing the baskets in a pile on the shoulder of
the road, he adjusted the corduroy band on his head,
so that the feather stuck up at the rear. He knew that
by doing so he became part of the local colour, 'a
real Indian with a feather'n everything', and also
that it helped him sell his baskets. In the time he
had been living along the highway he had learned
to give them what they expected.

The trailer residents were not yet awake, so he sat
down on the wooden walk leading to the shower
room, his baskets resting on the ground in a half-
circle behind him.

After a few minutes a small boy descended from
the door of a trailer and stood staring at him. Then
he pushed his head back inside and spoke, pointing
in Big Tom's direction. In a moment a man's hand
parted the heavy curtains on the window and a bed-
mussed unshaven face stared out. The small boy
climbed back inside.

A little later two women approached on the duck-
board walk, one attired in a pair of buttock-pinching
brown slacks, and the other wearing a blue chenille
dressing-gown. They circled him warily and entered
the shower-room. From inside came the buzz of

whispered conversation and the louder noises of running water.

During the morning several people approached and stared at Big Tom and the baskets. He sold two small ones to an elderly woman. She seemed surprised when she asked him what tribe he belonged to, and he did not answer in a monosyllable but said, 'I belong to the Algonquins, ma'am.' He got rid of one of the big forty-five cent baskets to the mother of the small boy who had been the first one up earlier in the day.

A man took a series of photographs of him with an expensive-looking camera, pacing off the distance and being very careful in setting his lens opening and shutter speeds.

'I wish he'd look into the camera,' the man said loudly to a couple standing nearby, as though he were talking of an animal in a cage.

'You can't get any good picshus around here. Harold tried to get one of the five Dionney kids, but they wouldn't let him. The way they keep them quints hid you'd think they was made of china or somep'n,' the woman said. She glanced at her companion for confirmation.

'They want you to buy their picshus,' the man said. 'We was disappointed in 'em. They used to look cute before, when they was small, but now they're just five plain-looking kids.'

'Yeah. My Gawd, you'd never believe how homely they got, would you Harold? An' everything's pure robbery in Callander. You know, old man Dionney's minting money up there. Runs his own sooveneer stand.'

After lunch Big Tom watched Cooper prepare for

his trip to North Bay. 'Is there anybody going fishing, Mr. Cooper?' he asked.

The man took the radiator cap off the old truck and peered inside.

'Mr. Cooper!'

'Hey?' Cooper turned and looked at the Indian standing there, hands in pockets, his manner shy and deferential. He seemed to feel a vague irritation, as though sensing the overtone of servility in the Indian's attitude.

'Anybody going fishing?' Big Tom asked again.

'Seems to me Mr. Staynor said he'd like to go,' Cooper answered. His voice was kind, with the amused kindness of a man talking to a child.

The big Indian remained standing where he was, saying nothing. His old second-hand army trousers drooped around his lean loins, and his plaid shirt was open at the throat, showing a grey high-water mark of dirt where his face washings began and ended.

'What's the matter?' Cooper asked. 'You seem pretty anxious to go today.'

'My kid's sick. I want to make enough to take him to the doctor.'

Cooper walked around the truck and opened one of the doors, rattling the handle in his hand as if it were stuck. 'You should stay home with it. Make it some pine-sap syrup. No need to worry. It's as healthy as a bear cub.'

Mrs. Cooper came out of the house and eased her bulk into the truck cab. 'Where's Mary?' she asked.

'Up at the shack,' Big Tom answered.

'Tell her to scrub the washrooms before she does anything else. Mrs. Anderson, in that trailer over there, wants her to do her floors.' She pointed across

the lot to a large blue-and-white trailer parked
behind a Buick.

'I'll tell her,' he answered.

The Coopers drove between the whitewashed
stones marking the entrance to the camp, and swung
up the highway, leaving behind them a small cloud
of dust from the pulverized gravel of the road.

Big Tom fetched Mary and the baby from the
shack. He gave her Mrs. Cooper's instructions, and
she transferred the baby from her arms to his. The
child was feverish, its breath noisy and fast.

'Keep him warm,' she said. 'He's been worse since
we got up. I think he's got a touch of the flu.'

Big Tom placed his hand inside the old blanket
and felt the baby's cheek. It was dry and burning to
his palm.

He adjusted the baby's small weight in his arms
and walked across the camp and down the narrow
path to the lakeside where the boats were moored.

A man sitting in the stern sheets of a new-painted
skiff looked up and smiled at his approach. 'You
coming out with me, Tom?' he asked.

The Indian nodded.

'Are you bringing the papoose along?'

Big Tom winced at the word papoose, but he answered, 'He won't bother us. The wife is working
this afternoon.'

'Okay. I thought maybe we'd go over to the other
side of the lake today and try to get some of them
big fellows at the creek mouth. Like to try?'

'Sure,' the Indian answered. He placed the baby
along the wide seat in the stern and unshipped the
oars.

He rowed silently for the best part of an hour, the
sun beating through his shirt and causing the sweat

to trickle coldly down his back. At times his efforts
at the oars caused a constriction in his chest, and he
coughed and spat into the water.

When they reached the mouth of the creek across
the lake he let the oars drag and leaned over to look
at the baby. It was sleeping restlessly, its lips slightly
blue, and its breath laboured and harsh. Mr. Staynor
was busy with his lines and tackle in the bow of the
boat.

Tom picked the child up and felt its little body for
sweat. The baby's skin was bone dry. He picked up
the baling can from the boat bottom and dipped it
over the side. With the tips of his fingers he brushed
some of the cold water across the baby's forehead.
The child woke up, looked around at the strange
surroundings, and smiled up at the man. He gave it
a drink of water from the can. Feeling reassured
now, he placed the baby on the seat and went forward to help the fisherman with his gear.

Mr. Staynor fished for half an hour or so, catching
some small fish and a large black bass, which writhed
in the bottom of the boat. Big Tom watched its gills
gasping its death throes, and he noted the similarity
between the struggles of the fish and those of the
baby lying on the seat in the blanket.

He became frightened again after a time and he
turned to the man in the bow and said, 'We'll have
to go pretty soon. I'm afraid my kid's pretty
sick.'

'Eh! We've hardly started,' the man answered.
'Don't worry, there's not much wrong with the
papoose.'

Big Tom lifted the child from the seat and cradled
it in his arms. He opened the blanket, and shading
the baby's face, allowed the warm sun to shine on its

chest. If I could only get him to sweat, he thought, everything would be all right then.

He waited as long as he dared, noting the blueness creeping over the baby's lips, before he placed the child again on the seat and addressed the man in the bow. 'I'm going back now. You'd better pull in your line.'

The man turned and felt his way along the boat. He stood over the Indian and parted the folds of the blanket, looking at the baby. 'My God, he is sick, Tom! You'd better get him to a doctor right away!' He stepped across the writhing fish to the bow and began pulling in the line. Then he busied himself with his tackle, stealing glances now and again at the Indian and the baby.

Big Tom turned the boat around and with long straight pulls on the oars headed back across the lake. The fisherman took the child in his arms and blew cooling drafts of air against its fevered face.

As soon as they reached the jetty below the tourist camp Tom tied the boat's painter to a stump, and took the child from the other man.

Mr. Staynor handed him the fee for a full afternoon's work. 'I'm sorry the youngster is sick, Tom,' he said. 'Don't play around. Get him up to the doctor in town right away. We'll try her again tomorrow afternoon.'

Big Tom thanked him. Carrying the baby and unmindful of the grasping hands of the undergrowth he climbed the path through the trees. On reaching the parked cars and trailers he headed in the direction of the large blue-and-white one where his wife would be working.

When he knocked the door opened and a woman said, 'Yes?' He recognized her as the one who had been standing by in the morning while his picture was being taken.

'Is my wife here?' he asked.

'Your wife? Oh, I know who you mean. No, she's gone. She went down the road in a car a few minutes ago.'

The camp was almost empty, most of the tourists having gone to the small bathing beach farther down the lake. A car full of bathers was pulling away to go down to the beach. Big Tom hurried over and held up his hand until it stopped. 'Could you drive me to the doctor?' he asked. 'My baby seems pretty sick.'

There was a turning of heads within the car. A woman began talking in the back seat. The driver said, 'I'll see what I can do, Chief, after I take the girls to the beach.'

Big Tom sat down at the side of the driveway to wait. After a precious half hour had gone by, and they did not return, he got to his feet and started up the highway in the direction of town.

His long legs pounded on the loose gravel of the road, his anger and terror giving strength to his stride. He noticed that the passengers in the few cars he met were pointing at him and laughing, and suddenly he realized that he was still wearing the feather in the band around his head. He reached up, pulled it off, and threw it in the ditch.

When a car or truck came up from behind him he would step off the road and raise his hand to beg for a ride. After the first ones passed without pausing he stopped this useless, time-wasting gesture and strode straight ahead, impervious to the noise of their horns as they approached.

Now and again he placed his hand on the baby's face as he walked, reassuring himself that it was still alive. It was hours since it had cried or shown any other signs of consciousness.

Once, he stepped off the road at a small bridge over a stream, and making a crude cup with his hands, tried to get the baby to drink. He succeeded only in making it cough, harshly, so that its tiny face became livid with its efforts to breathe.

It was impossible that the baby should die. Babies did not die like this in their father's arms on a highway that ran fifteen miles north to a small town with a doctor and all the life-saving devices to prevent their death. . . .

The sun fell low behind the trees and the swarms of black flies and mosquitos began their nightly forage. He waved his hand above the fevered face of the baby, keeping them off, at the same time trying to waft a little air into the child's tortured lungs.

Suddenly, with feelings as black as hell itself, he knew that the baby was dying. He had seen too much of it not to know, now, that the child was in an advanced state of pneumonia. He stumbled along, his eyes devouring the darkening face of his son, while the hot tears ran from the corners of his eyes.

With nightfall he knew it was too late. He looked up into the sky, where the first stars were being drawn in silver on a burnished copper plate, and he cursed them, and cursed what made them possible.

To the north-west the clouds were piling up in preparation for a summer storm. Reluctantly he turned and headed back down the road in the direction he had come.

It was almost midnight before he felt his way along the path through the trees to the shack. It was hard to see anything in the teeming rain, and the water ran from his shoulders in a steady stream, unheeded, soaking the sodden bundle he still carried in his arms.

Reaching the shanty he opened the door and fell inside. He placed the body of his son on the bed in the corner. Then, groping along the newspaper-lined walls, he found some matches in his mackinaw and lit the lamp. With a glance around the room he realized that his wife had not yet returned, so he placed the lamp on the table under the window and headed out again into the rain.

At the trailer camp he sat down on the rail fence near the entrance to wait. Some light shone from the small windows of the trailers and from Cooper's house across the road. The illuminated sign said: COOPER'S TRAILER CAMP—Hot and Cold Running Water, Rest Rooms. FISHING AND BOATING—INDIAN GUIDES.

One by one, as he waited, the lights went out, until only the sign lit up a small area at the gate.

He saw the car's headlights first, about a hundred yards down the road. When it pulled to a stop he heard some giggling, and Mary and another Indian girl, Elsie Woodhen, staggered out into the rain.

A man's voice shouted through the car door, 'See you again, sweetheart. Don't forget next Saturday night.' The voice belonged to one of the French-Canadians who worked at a creosote camp across the lake.

Another male voice shouted, 'Wahoo!'

The girls clung to each other, laughing drunkenly, as the car pulled away.

They were not aware of Big Tom's approach until he grasped his wife by the hair and pulled her backwards to the ground. Elsie Woodhen screamed and ran away in the direction of the Cooper house. Big

Tom bent down as if he was going to strike at Mary's face with his fist. Then he changed his mind and let her go.

She stared into his eyes and saw what was there. Crawling to her feet and sobbing hysterically she limped along towards the shack, leaving one of her silver shoes in the mud.

Big Tom followed behind, all the anguish and frustration drained from him so that there was nothing left to carry him into another day. Heedless now of the coughing which tore his chest apart, he pushed along in the rain, hurrying to join his wife in the vigil over their dead.

The Old Woman

JOYCE MARSHALL (b. 1913)

HE has changed, Molly thought, the instant she glimpsed her husband in the station at Montreal. He has changed. . . . The thought thudded hollowly through her mind, over and over during the long train-ride into northern Quebec.

It was more than the absence of uniform. His face seemed so still, and there was something about his mouth—a sort of slackness. And at times she would turn and find him looking at her, his eyes absorbed and watchful.

'I *am* glad to see you,' he kept saying. 'I thought you would never make it, Moll.'

'I know,' she said. 'But I had to wait till Mother was really well. . . . It *has* been a long three years, hasn't it?'

Apart from repeating his gladness at her arrival, he seemed to have little to say. He was just strange with her, she tried to soothe herself. They had known each other less than a year when they married in England during the war, and he had left for Canada so soon without her. He must have found it hard to hold a picture of her, just as she had found it hard to hold a picture of him. As soon as they got home—whatever home might be in this strange romantic north to which the train was drawing them —he would be more nearly the Toddy she had known.

It was grey dawn faintly disturbed with pink when they left the train, the only passengers for this little town of Missawani, at the tip of Lake St. John. The name on the greyed shingle reassured Molly a little. How often she had spelled out the strange syllables on letters to Toddy—the double s, the unexpected single n. Somewhere beyond this huddle of low wooden shacks, she knew, was the big Mason paper mill, and Toddy's power-house—one of several that supplied it with electricity—was more than thirty miles away. There was a road, Toddy had told her, but it was closed in winter.

A sullen youth waited behind the station with the dogs. Such beautiful dogs, black brindled with cream, their mouths spread wide in what seemed to Molly happy smiles of welcome. She put a hand towards the nose of the lead-dog, but he lunged and Toddy drew her back.

'They're brutes,' he told her. 'All of them wolfish brutes.'

It was a long strange journey over the snow, first through pink-streaked grey, then into a sun that first dazzled and then inflamed the eyes.

Snow that was flung up coarse and stinging from the feet of the dogs, black brittle fir-trees, birches gleaming like white silk. No sound but the panting breath of the dogs, the dry leatherlike squeak of the snow under the sleigh's runners, and Toddy's rare French-spoken commands to the dogs.

At last he poked her back wordlessly and pointed a mittened hand over her shoulder. For an instant the picture seemed to hang suspended before Molly's eyes: the bare hill with the square red house at its top, the dam level with the top of the hill, the water-fall steaming down to a white swirl of rapids, the power-house like a squat grey cylinder at its foot.

'My old woman,' Toddy shouted, and she saw that he was pointing, not up the hill towards the house where they would live, but to the power-house below.

In England his habit of personalizing an electric generating plant had charmed her, fitting her picturesque notions of the Canadian north. But now she felt uneasiness prod her. It was such a sinister-looking building, and the sound of falling water was so loud and engulfing.

The kitchen of the red house had what Molly thought of as a 'poor' smell about it. Still, no one expected a man to be a good housewife. As soon as she could shut the door and get rid of the sound of that water, she told herself, it would be better. She looked quickly behind her, but Toddy had shut the door already. There must be a window open some-where. It couldn't be possible that the waterfall was going to live with them in the house like this. It couldn't be possible.

'Cheerful sort of sound,' said Toddy.

Molly looked at him vaguely, half hearing. A

window somewhere—there must be a window she could close.

He showed her quickly over the house, which was fairly well furnished and comfortably heated by electricity. Then he turned to her almost apologetically.

'I hope you won't mind if I go down right away,' he said. 'I'd like to see what kind of shape the old woman's got herself into while I've been away.'

He looked elated and eager, and she smiled at him.

'Go ahead,' she said, 'I'll be all right.'

After he had gone she unpacked her bags and went down to the living-room. It had a broad window, overlooking the power-house, the rapids, and a long snow-field disappearing into the black huddle of pine bush. Snow, she thought. I always thought snow was white, but it's blue. Blue and treacherous as steel. And fully for the first time she realized how cut off they were to be—cut off from town by thirty odd miles of snow and tangled bush and roadlessness.

She found a pail and mop and began to clean the kitchen. She would have it all fresh and nice by the time Toddy came back. She would have no time to look out into the almost instantly blinding glare of the snow. She might even be able to ignore the thundering of the water. She was going to have to spend a lot of time alone in this house. She would have to learn to keep busy.

Toddy did not come up till evening. The power-house was in very bad shape, he told her.

'Those French operators and assistants are a lazy bunch of bums. It's amazing how they can let things go to hell in just two days.'

Molly had set dinner on a little table in the living-room. Toddy had wolfed his meal, his face pre-occupied.

He *was* different. She hadn't just been imagining it. She had thought he would seem closer to her here, but he was more withdrawn than ever. For an instant she had a curious sense that none of this was real to him—not the dinner, nothing but the turbines and generators in the plant below.

Well, so you married this man, she told herself briskly, because you were thirty-eight and he looked nice in his officer's uniform. You followed him here because you were entranced with the idea of a strange and different place. So it is strange and different. And you have to start imagining things, just because your husband is a busy man who seems scarcely to notice that you are here.

'I'm going to make this place ever so much cosier,' she heard herself saying, in a voice so importunate she scarcely recognized it as her own.

'What—oh yes—yes, fine. Make any changes you like.'

He finished eating and stood up.

'Well, I must be going back now.'

'Back?' He wasn't even apologizing this time, she realized dully. 'Won't your old woman give you an evening off—even when your wife has just come from the old country?'

'I've still things to do,' he said. 'You needn't be lonely. There's a radio—though I'm afraid the static's pretty bad on account of the plant. And I'll be only fifty feet away.'

It was a week before he considered the power-house in suitable shape to show her. He showed her around it proudly—the squat gleaming turbines lying like fat sleepers along the floor, one of the four dismantled so that he could explain the power-generator within, the gauges on the wall.

'It's very interesting, dear,' she said, trying to understand his love for these inanimates, his glowing delight in the meshing parts.

'Perhaps now she looks so slick,' she added, 'you won't have to give her so much of your time.'

'You'd be surprised how quickly she can go wrong,' said Toddy.

He continued to spend all his hours there, from eight in the morning until late at night, with only brief spaces for meals.

Molly worked vigorously about the house and soon it was cleaned and sparkling from top to bottom. After that it was harder to keep busy. She read all the books she had brought, even the ancient magazines she found about the house. She could not go out. It was impossible to do more than keep a path cleared down to the power-house. There were no skis or snow-shoes, and Toddy could not seem to find time to teach her to drive the dogs. There were no neighbours within miles, no telephone calls or visits from milkman or baker—only one of Toddy's sweepers coming in once a fortnight with supplies and mail from Missawani.

She looked forward almost wildly to these visits, for they meant a break as well as letters from home. The men all lived on the nearby concessions—'ranges' they were called here in northern Quebec—six or seven or eight miles away, driving back and forth to the power-house by dog-team. She tried to get them to tell her about their lives and their families, but they were taciturn, just barely polite, and she felt that they simply did not like this house of which she was a part.

She tried constantly to build up some sort of close-ness between herself and Toddy. But he seemed only to become less talkative—he had always had a lot of cheerful small talk in England—and more absorbed in the power-house. He seemed to accept her presence as a fact which pleased him, but he had no com-panionship to spare for her.

'I wish,' she said to him one day, 'that you could go out with me soon and teach me to drive the dogs.'

'But where would you go?' he asked.

'Oh,' she said, 'around. Over the snow.'

'But I'm so busy,' he said. 'I'm sorry—but this is my work, and I'm so busy.'

As he spoke, she saw in his eyes again that look that had terrified her so the first day. Now she thought she recognized what it was. It was a watch-ful look, a powerful look, as if he were still in the presence of his machinery.

'But couldn't you take an afternoon? Those machines look as if they practically ran themselves. Couldn't you even take a Sunday, Toddy?'

'What if something went wrong while I was away?'

'Oh, Toddy, it can't need you every minute. I'm your wife and I need you too. You seemed so anxious for the time when I'd be able to come here. I can imagine how a person might get to hate being here alone, with that water always roaring and—'

Toddy's face became suddenly angry and wild.

'What do you mean?' he demanded.

'Just that you had three years here alone,' she began.

'I have never been bushed,' Toddy interrupted furiously. 'How dare you suggest that such a thing could ever happen to me? My God, apart from the war, I've lived in this country for twenty years.'

Bushed. The suggestion was his, and for a moment she allowed herself to think about it. She was familiar with the term. Toddy used it constantly about others who had come up north to live. He knew the country, but he had been away. And then he had returned alone to this place, where for so long every year the winter buried you, snow blinded you, the wind screamed up the hill at night, and the water thundered. . . .

'Toddy,' she said, afraid of the thought, putting it out of her mind, 'when spring comes, couldn't we get a cow or two. I *do* know about cattle—I wasn't in the Land Army all through the war for nothing. I think it would give me an interest.'

Toddy stared at her.

'Aren't you my wife?' he asked.

'Why yes—yes, of course.'

'Then how can you speak about needing an interest? Isn't there interest enough for you in simply being my wife?'

'But I'm—I'm left so much alone. You have your work, but I have so little to do.'

Toddy turned on his heel, preparing to go again to the power-house. At the door he glanced back over his shoulder, not speaking, merely watching her.

He doesn't want me to have an interest, thought Molly, her mind bruised with horror and fear. He looks at me watchfully, as if I were one of his machines. Perhaps that's what he wants me to be— a generator, quiet and docile, waiting for him here, moving only when he tells me to move.

And I am the sort of woman who must have work to do. If I don't, my mind will grow dim and misty. Already I can feel the long sweep of the snow trying to draw my thoughts out till they become diffused and vague. I can feel the sound of the water trying to crush and madden me.

After that, it seemed as if Toddy were trying to spend more time with her. Several times he sat and talked with her after dinner, telling her about the power-house and the catastrophes he had averted that day. But always his eyes would be turning to the window and the power-house showing grey and sullen against the snow.

'Oh, you can go down now, Toddy,' Molly would say. 'Obviously, that is where you wish to be.'

And then one day she found the work she wanted.

She looked up from her dishes to see Louis-Paul, one of the power-house oilers, standing in the doorway, snow leaking from his great felt boots on to the floor.

'Madame—' he said.

'Oh Louis, hello,' said Molly warmly, for she was friendlier with this slight fair youth than with any of Toddy's other workmen. They had long solemn conversations—she practising her French and he his English. 'But don't tell the Curé,' Louis would say. 'He does not like it if we speak English.'

'Did you come for my list?' Molly asked him. 'Are you going to town?'

'No, Madame, I have—how you say it?—I am today in big trouble. My Lucienne—'

'Oh, the baby—has your baby been born, Louis-Paul?'

'Yes, madame—'

With a hopeless gesture he relinquished his English. From his rapid, desperate French, Molly learned that there was something that prevented Lucienne from nursing her child, and none of the cows on any of the ranges were giving milk that winter.

'If you could come, madame, you might know—
you might do something—'

His team of yellow dogs was tied at the kitchen
stoop. Together Louis-Paul and Molly dashed across
the snow to the house at the first range. Just a little
bit of a house that Louis-Paul's father had built for
him six years ago when he divided his thin-soiled
farm and his timber-lots among his sons. Its roof
was the warm grey of weathered wood, almost as
deeply curved as the roof of a Chinese pagoda.

In the kitchen Lucienne's mother and sisters and
aunts in all their black wept noisily, one of them
holding the crying child. And in the bedroom the
girl Lucienne was sobbing, because she realized that
the presence of her relatives in their best black meant
that her child could not be saved.

Molly looked at her for a moment—the swarthy
broad cheeks, the narrow eyes, that showed a tinge
of Indian blood.

'Would you be shy with me, Lucienne?' she asked.
'Too shy to take off your nightgown while I am
here?'

'I would never be shy with you, madame,' said
Lucienne.

Something hot came into Molly's throat as she
eased the nightgown from the girl's shoulders and
went into the kitchen for hot and cold water and a
quantity of cloths.

Tenderly she bathed the heavy breasts with alter-
nate hot and cold water, explaining that the nipples
were inverted and that this should bring them into
place. And before she left, Lucienne was holding the
baby's dark head against her breast, weeping silently,
the wailing in the kitchen had ceased, and Louis-
Paul was fixing stiff portions of whisky blanc and

home-made wine, passing the one wine-glass around and around the assembly.

Not until she was back at the red house, actually stamping the snow from her boots on the kitchen stoop, did Molly realize that it was long past the early dinner that Toddy liked. She went in quickly.

Toddy was standing in the middle of the room, his hands dangling with a peculiar slackness at his sides. He looked at her, and there was a great empty bewilderment on his face.

'You have been out?' he asked.

'Yes,' she said, elated still from her afternoon. 'I went over to Louis-Paul's with him. His wife's had her baby and—'

'He asked you?' said Toddy.

'Yes,' she said. 'He was desperate, poor lad, so I just had to offer to do what I could.'

He's afraid I'll go away, she thought. He must have come up here and found the stove cold and thought I had gone forever. The thought alternately reassured and chilled her. It was simple and ordinary for him to be anxious, but his expression was neither simple nor ordinary. Now that she had explained, he should not be staring at her still, his gaze thinned by surprise and fear.

'I'm sorry about dinner,' she said, 'but I'll hurry and fix something easy. You have a smoke and I'll tell you all about it.'

She told him, but he would not join in her enthusiasm.

'Another French-Canadian brat,' he said. 'Molly, you're a fool.'

A few weeks later she realized she now had a place even in this barren land. Louis-Paul appeared again in the kitchen, less shy, for now she was his friend.

His sister-in-law was having a baby and something was wrong. They would have taken her to Missawani, but there was every sign of a blizzard blowing up. Madame had been so good with Lucienne. Perhaps she could do something for Marie-Claire as well.

'I don't see how I could,' said Molly. 'I've helped bring little calves and pigs into the world, but never a baby—'

'She may die,' said Louis. 'They say the baby is placed wrong. They have given her blood of a newborn calf to drink, but still—'

'All right,' said Molly, 'I'll go.'

She set a cold meal for Toddy and propped a note against his plate. The thought of him nudged her mind guiltily during the dash over the snow to the little house. But that was absurd. She would be away only a few hours. Toddy would have to learn to accept an occasional absence. He was a little—well, selfish about her. He would have to learn.

With some help from an ancient grandmother, Molly delivered a child on the kitchen table of the little house. An old Cornish farm-hand had showed her once how to turn a calf that was breached. Much the same thing was involved now—deftness, daring, a strong hand timed to the bitter contractions of the girl on the table.

When she returned home late in the evening, she had not thought of Toddy for hours.

This time he was angry, mumblingly, shakingly angry.

'Molly,' he shouted, 'you must put an end to this nonsensical—'

'But it's not nonsensical,' she said, serene still from the miracle of new life she had held across her hands. 'I brought a nice little boy into the world. He might never have been born except for me.'

'These women have been popping kids for years without you.'

'I know,' said Molly, 'but sometimes they lose them. And they're so—superstitious. I can help them, Toddy. I can.'

She paused, then spoke more gently.

'What is it, Toddy? Why don't you want me to go?'

The question caught him somehow, and his face, his whole expression became loosed, as if suddenly he did not understand his own rage.

'You're my wife,' he said. 'I want you here.'

'Well, cheer up,' she said, speaking lightly because his look had chilled her so. 'I am, usually.

After that, no woman in any of the ranges ever had a baby without her husband's dogs whisking over the fields to the red house.

Molly now was famed for miles. She was good luck at a birth, and when something unexpected happened she could act with speed and ingenuity. She liked the people and felt that they liked her. Even the Curé, who hated the power-house and all it represented, bowed and passed the time of day when he and Molly met in a farm-house kitchen.

She sent away for government pamphlets and a handful of texts. Though it was true, as Toddy said, that these women had had babies without her, it pleased her that she was cutting down the percentage of early deaths.

Each of her errands meant a scene with Toddy. There was a struggle here, she felt, between her own need for life and work and what she tried to persuade herself was merely selfishness in him. In her new strength and happiness she felt that she ought to be able to draw Toddy into taking an interest in something beyond the power-house. But he would not be drawn.

Surely when the snows broke it would be possible. She would persuade him to take the old car in the barn and drive with her about the countryside. He was only a trifle bushed from the long winter. Though she had been shocked at first by the suggestion that he might be bushed, she found the hope edging into her mind more and more often now that it was nothing more.

And then one day it was Joe Blanchard's turn to come to get her. His wife was expecting her tenth child.

All day Molly was restless, going to the window to strain her eyes into the glare for a sight of Joe's sleigh and his tough yellow dogs winding out of the bush. Sunset came and she prepared dinner, and still he had not come.

Once she looked up from her plate and saw Toddy staring at her, his lips trembling in an odd small way.

'Is anything wrong?' she asked.

'No,' he said, 'nothing.'

His lips still trembled.

'Toddy,' she said, gently, and under her gentleness afraid. 'I'll probably be going out tonight. I promised Joe Blanchard I'd help Mariette.'

Toddy looked at her, and his face blazed.

'No,' he shouted, 'by God—you will stay where you belong.'

'Why?' she asked, as she had before. 'Why don't you want me to go?'

He seemed to search through his mind for words.

'Because I won't have you going out at night with that ruffian—because, damn it, it's too dangerous.'

'Then you come too,' she said. 'You come with us.'

'Don't be a fool,' he said. 'How could I leave?'

'Well, stay home tonight,' she said. 'Stay here and —and rest. We'll decide what to do when Joe comes.'

'Rest—what do you mean?'

'I think you're—tired,' she said. 'I think you should stay home just one evening.'

Toddy scraped back his chair.

'Don't be a fool, Molly. Of course I can't stay. I can't.'

He walked to the door, then turned back to her.

'I shall find you here,' he said, 'when I return.'

The evening dragged between the two anxieties— between wondering when Joe would come and watching for Toddy's return.

Midnight came, and still neither Toddy nor Joe had come. Her anxiety grew. Toddy had never stayed this late before. It had been ten-thirty first, then eleven.

The sound of the back door opening sent her flying to the kitchen. Joe stood in the doorway, his broad face beaming.

'You ready, madame?'

Molly began to put on her heavy clothes, her snow-boots. Anxiety licked still in her mind. Past twelve o'clock and Toddy had not returned.

'Joe,' she said, 'you'll wait just a minute while I go down and tell my husband?'

Her feet slipped several times on the icy steps Toddy kept cut in the hillside. She felt a sudden terrible urgency. She must reassure herself of something. She didn't quite know what.

She pulled open the door of the power-house and was struck, as she had been before, by the way the thunder of the waterfall was suddenly replaced by a low even whine.

For an instant she did not see Toddy. Louis-Paul was propped in a straight chair dozing, across the room. Then she saw Toddy, his back, leaning towards one of the turbines. As she looked, he moved, with a curious scuttling speed, to one of the indicators on the wall. She saw the side of his face then, its expression totally absorbed, gloating.

'Toddy!' she called.

He turned, and for a long moment she felt that he did not know who she was. He did not speak.

'I didn't want you to worry,' she said. 'I'm going with Joe. If I shouldn't be back for breakfast—'

She stopped, for he did not seem to be listening.

'I probably *will* be back for breakfast,' she said.

He glared at her. He moved his lips as if to speak. Then his gaze broke and slid back to the bright indicator on the wall.

At that moment she understood. The struggle she had sensed without being able to give it a name had been between herself and the power-house. In an indistinct way Toddy had realized it when he said, 'I want you here.'

'Toddy!' she shouted.

He turned his back to her in a vague automatic way, and she saw that his face was quite empty except for a strange glitter that spread from his eyes over his face. He did not answer her.

For a moment she forgot that she was not alone with him, until a sound reminded her of Louis-Paul, awake now and standing by the door. And from the expression of sick shaking terror on his face she knew what the fear had been that she had never allowed herself to name.

'Oh Louis,' she said.

'Come madame,' he said. 'We can do nothing here. In the morning I will take you to Missawani. I will bring the doctor back.'

'But is he safe?' she asked. 'Will he—damage the machines perhaps?'

'Oh no. He would never hurt these machines. For years I watch him fall in love with her. Now she has him for herself.'

The Owl and the Bens

W. O. MITCHELL (b. 1914)

I

THE Owl and the Ben and the Young Ben each got his freedom at approximately the same time—the Young Ben at four o'clock one fall afternoon, the owl that evening, and the Ben three days later. The teacher, who knew the owl, the Ben, and the Young Ben, was perhaps the only soul in the prairie town who appreciated the value that freedom had for each of the three.

He was a tall, thin, and remarkably ugly young man, the teacher, with a singularly crooked will that prompted him to think a great deal about things that could not make him money or bring him fame. But he understood children, among whom he included the Ben.

Certainly if irresponsibility was an attribute of

childhood, the Ben, surrounded always by a sour-sweet aroma of brew tanged with a gallop of manure and spiced with natural leaf tobacco, was a child. A spare, grey bird of a man, he had a flaming stare that made one wince. His eyes burned deep in rims as red as fanned coals. A grey stubble covered his creased face. Always at odds with some rule, law, or convention—shooting pheasant, antelope, or partridge out of season and without a licence; or running his still—the Ben had as much moral conscience as the wind that lifts over the edge of the prairie world to sing mortality to every living thing.

Seldom sober, the Ben knew only two stages of drunkenness; the dramatic and the unconscious. The first was loud with an obscenity expressed best in song; the second was final and left him sprawled in a drift of snow in the deep of winter, or over a downtown curb where he was at the mercy of bot-flies in summer. From these positions he was usually rescued by Jake Harris, the town constable, garbage man, and fireman, or by the Young Ben.

With the Young Ben the teacher had difficulty at first in deciding whether or not he was a child. Looking down into that solemn face with its wide, grey eyes staring up to him, and its cheeks nutmegged with freckles, he was aware of no spark of childhood there. He was forced to agree with the boy's father that the Young Ben had been 'borned growed-up'. This was a theory that the Ben had expounded many times, over beer, brew, or on one occasion, according to the school janitor, a bottle of Cobb's Blistering Remedy for Horses, which the Ben had mistaken for Lister's Household Lemon Essence.

'Thuh Old Lady comes tuh me,' the Ben would explain, 'an' she sez, "Ben, yuh better go git Doc. I

ain't feelin' none too good," she sez. "The pains is
a-comin' on real frequent now." So I went out tuh
ketch Dolly, an' her not havin' the harness ontuh
her sence thuh fall buhfore, I chased her clear down
tuh thuh other enda thuh goddam pasture witha
panna oats behind my back. After 'bout a hour I
come back tuh thuh shack tuh git my hat. There
wuz thuh Old Lady a-settin' on a apple-box a-peelin'
some puhtatuhs inta thuh slop pail.

'"Where's my goddam hat?" I sez, an' she sez,
"Yuh don't need her." "Why?" I sez, an' she sez,
"The kid's already bin borned." "Whut is it?" I sez.
"A boy," she sez, "an' han' me that there pot offa
thuh table." I asked her where wuz he at, an' she sez,
"After he finished off separatin' thuh cream, he went
out tuh chop me up some kendlin' fer thuh stove."
Thuh kid wuz borned growed-up.'

Until forced to attend school, the Young Ben
never entered the town, though he would accom-
pany his father to its edge where the prairie swelled
gently. There, overlooking the town, he would sit
watching till his father's return, his chin in his
hands, his elbows on his knees. At other times he
had been observed, as Mr. Karpack, the blacksmith
put it, 'a runnin' acrost the bald-headed prairie with
no more clo's on than tuh wad a 0.410 shotgun.' If
approached he would startle like a wild thing.

After he came to school the Young Ben had
changed little; at no time during the years that
followed did he play any games. He could run with
the speed of a ring-necked pheasant, but he could
not be bothered to take part in organized, team
games. He could not understand rules; discipline
had no meaning for him; nothing he ever did
depended on other people; he was as naked of a sense

of right and wrong as a coyote howling in the stillness of a clear fall night.

2

The teacher did his best with the Young Ben; he
whipped him regularly with the regulation length
of breeching harness given him by Mr. Thorborn,
chairman of the school board and owner of the livery
stable behind the Baptist church. And while the
Young Ben lifted one hand after the other to the
sting of the strap, the teacher sweated over the ritual,
knowing that he did it only in deference to the public opinion of the town, which felt that the Young
Ben was a bad actor like his father and should be
sent to 'an institution'.

In the course of trying to understand the Young
Ben, the teacher came to know much about the boy's
father. Some of his information was firsthand, but
the greater part of it had been picked from the mag-
pie mind of the school janitor and came to him in
bits gleaned during recesses while he smoked in the
janitor's retreat just off the boys' lavatory. The
teacher took what seemed dependable in the light
of the janitor's known weakness for exaggeration;
much of it he labelled legend that had grown up
around the Ben.

It was in the twilight of the furnace room, with
its grey dust and its spun, grey intricacies of spider
webbing, that he found out how the Ben got money
for beer and tobacco, for grain and kerosene for his
still. He learned that the Ben did no work and had
done none for several years, though formerly he con-
descended to dig an occasional grave.

One night after the Ben had drunk the remunera-
tion for the digging of a grave the day before,

several men of the town stationed themselves in the brush halfway down the dirt trail that led to Haggerty's coulee and the Ben's shack. They covered themselves with sheets from the hotel, and as the Ben came staggering and singing down the moonlit road, they presented themselves to him. They knew that Ben was superstitious, and that he only agreed to dig a grave when the most ravaging of thirsts forced him to it; but his reaction was unexpected. In drunken pugnacity he raised his nail kegs of fists and cried out hoarsely and alarmingly:

'C'mon, alla yuh—I berried yuh buhfore, an' I'm a-gonna berry yuh agin!'

The Ben's bravado was not deep-seated; he never dug another grave after that, giving rheumatism in his back as his reason. This made it harder for the teacher to believe the janitor's description of the Ben's periodic visits to Sherry's mill. At such times, he said, it was the Ben's custom to lift a fifty-pound sack of feed to his head, walk to the beer parlour of the Royal Hotel, sit down, drink his beer, stand up, and walk the quarter of a mile to his shack, all the time carrying the sack on his head as lightly as though it were a matchbox.

Denied his income from gravedigging, the Ben turned then to eggs. When Mrs. Ben was out, the Ben would sneak down to the hen-house and steal two or three eggs, never more, for he dared not let her know that eggs were disappearing. The hens as well as the ten cows—the creatures that with the Bens inhabited Haggerty's coulee—belonged to the Ben's wife. With her eggs he was able to get ten to twenty cents at the General Store. And at the Royal Hotel all that the Ben needed was to buy the first beer; his yarns bought those that followed.

Unfortunately for the Ben, egg financing came to an end. It was unfortunate because, indirectly, the shutting off of the supply by Mrs. Ben resulted some time later in the discovery of his still. The Ben was forced to accept the position of janitor in the Baptist church; this in turn led to an incident which created in the heart of the Reverend Powelly an undying, Old Testament thirst for revenge.

An unbroken chain of cause and effect led from the eggs to the Ben's conviction for running a still, though perhaps the term 'still' was too dignified for the great granite pot to which the Ben had wired on a length of copper coil. In the early days the Ben had been content to follow the usual technique of covering the still with brush at a comfortable distance from his shack; later he dug a cave for it and covered it carefully with squares of prairie sod.

Then the Ben became a member of the Baptist congregation, a prerequisite to becoming janitor. He started his one-month career inauspiciously after having made a loquacious but not too detailed account of his sins. He was then, unexpectedly, confronted by the hand of the Reverend Powelly, held out in the ritual of welcoming him into the fold. Strangely reluctant, the Ben shook hands. Many are called, but few of those chosen come to the selecting with wads of partly chewed Old Stag tobacco secreted in the palms of their right hands. The minister deposited the cud in a pot of Lilies of Jerusalem beside the pulpit. A charitable man, he forgave the Ben, judging the act to be the result of hurried thinking in an embarrassing situation.

Perhaps it was his distrust of Mrs. Ben, who threatened to tell Jake Harris about his moonshining if he took any more eggs, that caused him to hide his still in the basement of the church. It was an ideal place; no one but the Ben ever entered the coal-room where the still and its kerosene burner rested on a dark shelf of earth just inside the church building; the telltale fumes of the still were quickly absorbed by the manure pile thrown up from Mr. Thorborn's livery barn behind the church. Without fear of detection the Ben could visit his still, fill the burner with kerosene, the coil bed with ice, the pot with mash, and himself with brew.

One month after the Ben's conversion, the Sunday the Reverend Powelly had chosen for his delicately balanced sermon on the Parable of the Lost Penny, a sermon pointed at the Ben—as had also been that of the Sunday before (The Lost Sheep), and the one before that (The Prodigal's Return)—the still blew up. Ignited by the yellow, moth-wing flame of the burner, which the Ben had left turned too high, it exploded between the announcing of the Ladies' Auxiliary Chicken Dinner, to be held the following Tuesday, and the passing of the collection plate. It detonated with a thud that was felt physically, rather than heard, by every member of the congregation. In the absolute silence that settled over the congregation, there could be heard, from below, the clanging of metal objects dropping one after the other. The Ben hurried from the church.

Thinking that whatever was the matter, it would be ably attended to by the Ben, the Reverend Powelly began his sermon two pages on in his notes. The church was heated by hot-air vents along its sides, all of them leading to the basement. Out of these, soon after the explosion, there stole a yeasty breath that drifted through the congregation and blossomed unmistakably into sweet, oppressive fumes of ferment.

Below, meanwhile, the Ben feverishly collected the parts of his still from far corners and frantically shovelled out a cave in the coal in which to hide the evidence. That night he retrieved the copper coil and parts of the stove. Jake Harris, summoned tardily on Monday morning, found nothing.

3

All this time the Young Ben was finding school an intolerable incarceration made bearable by many short flights of freedom. Taking two years to a grade, he made leisurely progress; by the time he was fourteen he sat uneasily in a back seat, lifting his thin shoulders a good foot above the Grade Four pupils around him. Just once in all the Young Ben's time in school did the teacher surprise an expression on his face; it was the look that lies in the eye of a caught thing.

As well as he could, the teacher sought to ease the Young Ben's days by assigning him at intervals numerous tasks which might relieve the tension. If he wanted a window opened or closed, he let the Young Ben do it; he asked the Young Ben to fill the water jug from the school well, to post a letter for him, take a message to the janitor, ring the bell. In spite of this the Young Ben indulged in regular hooky.

It was in calling about the Young Ben's attendance that the teacher first saw the owl. It was kept in a coop of chicken netting tucked in one corner of the much interrupted fence that canted around the Ben's yard. The Ben had caught the owl; knowing that owls always alight before flying to the ground, he had set a gopher trap on the top of a dead poplar, then scattered raw meat over the ground below. He had climbed the poplar himself and had almost lost a finger and an eye in getting the owl down. He had not trapped it as a pet for his son; it was simply that he had felt like catching an owl; he had; now it was his owl to put in a chicken-wire coop.

Before he actually saw it, the teacher heard the owl. He heard first, as he climbed through the barbed strands of the fence, a sharp, snapping sound like the clear punctuation of dry, dead underbrush cracking and popping. As he straightened he heard a wild, harsh hissing, a fierce sibilance savaging deep in the owl's grey throat. He looked up and into two eyes of amazing brilliance, eyes that blinked deliberately with the coming down of their untidy grey lids, the lids of an old man. The teacher saw that the pupils of those eyes were dead black with nothing in them to tell that they lived.

Transfixed by the cold glow of the two wide eyes flaming on either side of the down-curving beak, the teacher stood for minutes, the insistent, persistent husking incessantly in his ears. And suddenly he was aware of the grey wing-shoulders weaving tirelessly from side to side. A soul-burning compulsion stirred within him, an ineffable urge to tear away the netting.

With a feeling of relief he let his gaze drop to the owl's white, feather-panted legs, to the black twig-toes that grew into talons gripping the Saskatoon sapling perch in their curved clutch. He turned away, the hissing real in his ears, the lemon eyes, like the lingering after images of extinguished lights, glowing in his mind; he felt his body, against his will, sway with a hint of empathy. He knew that the owl could never be tamed to the chicken coop and to the limp bodies of gophers and field mice brought by the Young Ben.

In the Ben shack he found Mrs. Ben uninterested in the Young Ben's attendance record, and the boy's father completely drunk over the kitchen table. As he picked his way back through the welter of mud in the yard, he avoided the chicken coop.

4

That was the year the Reverend Powelly's bitterness bore fruit. Jake Harris, the town constable, after five years of conscientious search, found the Ben's still. His perseverance had been nourished by numerous personal encounters with the minister, by impassioned exhortations to the police department at each annual ratepayers' meeting, and, as time went on without the Ben's being brought to justice, by sermons criticizing the garbage department (Community Cleanliness Next to Community Godliness), bristling with illustrative reference to the fire department (Flames of Hell Are Ready for the Unready Fireman).

In the end it was the horse, Dolly, who betrayed the Ben—Dolly and the Young Ben, who led her into the barn while Jake was paying one of his innumerable hopeful visits. Just inside the door, before Jake's startled eyes, she stumbled; her foreleg disappeared up to the hock. As Jake strained with the Bens to release her, the fruity gentleness of rising bread dough teased at his nostrils; Dolly's hoof came suddenly free, and the usual solid smell of manure within the barn became unbelievably heady and exotic. Hidden under the manure, a rotten board had given way.

The Ben came up for trial two days later. 'Judge' Mortimer held court in the town hall, a great building partitioned horizontally through its middle, like an upended crate, the lower half containing the town secretary's office and the stable of the two roan fire and garbage wagon horses. Here, seated at a fumed oak desk—amid the pervading sweetness of alfalfa, green feed, and hay, soothed with the warm smell of horses' bodies, and with just a tinct of ammonia—the 'Judge' dispensed justice.

The day of the trial, the Ben stood before the 'Judge', his hands trembling from a two-day drouth, one clear, amber bead of tobacco juice dewing the silver stubble at the corner of his mouth. He hoarsely pleaded not guilty, then kissed the Gideon Bible borrowed from the Royal Hotel for the occasion. Jake Harris told of finding the still; the Ben changed his plea to guilty; the 'Judge' pushed his metal-rimmed glasses halfway down his nose, blew out the ragged fringes of his moustache, and looked down into the well of the desk.

From below came the blurred thudding of hoofs; through the open window, the quick skipping lift of a meadow lark's song. The Ben, Jake, and the town secretary waited. The 'Judge' began pawing through the papers on his desk, looking for his Criminal Code book. He uncovered a spring mail-order catalogue and realized then that he had brought it by mistake. He opened it; he read: 'Semi-step-in Model of fine quality Rayon satin—for snug fit. $2.98.'

He blew out his moustache and with a careless flick of his hand flipped over a quarter inch of catalogue. 'Team harness—Black Steerhide. Popular and useful 5-ring-style breeching. De-Luxe. Sh. wt. 68 lbs. $92.95.'

He looked up at the Ben, leaned forward, and said: 'Ninety dollars an' costs.' He settled back.

'Er whut?' the town secretary prompted him.

'Huh? Oh—uh—er ninety days.' He drew in his chin, looked down at the catalogue, looked up again, extended his chin. He spat with a distinct plop into the spittoon beside the desk.

The Ben took the jail term: Mrs. Ben had no intention of selling any of her cows. During the three months that followed, the Young Ben cared for the owl and his father; he brought the owl gophers and field mice, and to the Ben tobacco and news or just himself. Someone had to feed the owl, and the Ben had threatened to 'thin his hide' when he got out if he didn't come regularly and stand by the barred window at the side of the town hall.

The Ben found his imprisonment hard to bear, and that was a strange thing. Never before in his life had he been so physically comfortable. His meals, brought to him each morning and noon by the Young Ben, came from the Chinaman's; they transcended anything to which the Ben had ever been accustomed. He slept between sheets and on a flounced Winnipeg couch that stood in one corner of the twelve-foot-square room that served as his cell. But these luxuries served only to sharpen the restraint that the Ben endured with difficulty for three months. Frequently people passing the town hall noticed his face close to the barred windows, his grey hair wild, his startling eyes deeper than ever in their flaming sockets.

At first there were outbursts of fury, during one of which he purpled the Young Ben's face with a flung wedge of Saskatoon pie. These ceased finally; or rather the pent energy of the man sought outlet in a continuous overflowing of movement that would not let him alone for one second of his waking hours. Harried from within himself, he moved like all caged things, his feet stitching over and over again the same pattern across the bare cement floor; from the bed to the chair, from the chair to the table with its china pitcher and red-rimmed basin, from the table to the bed again, to the chair, to the table, again and again and again.

5

It was three days before the end of the Ben's term that the pencil-sharpening incident occurred. The teacher had a standing rule that no pencils were to be sharpened during school hours. It was a rule that, while it did not take into consideration the fallibility of pencils and the break in monotony their sharpening afforded, did quench the pencil-sharpening hysterias that had frequently swept that part of the room he was not teaching.

But on this afternoon the sharpener lifted its grind of sound. It was the Young Ben, standing there by the open window, his eyes lost in the expanse of prairie stretching from the edge of the school-yard to the distant line of the sky, where the town's five grain elevators lifted their sloping shoulders.

The teacher dropped the intricacies of percentage; the low hum of the classroom faltered; the dotting sound of pencils stopped; there was absolute school-room quiet. Outside, a crow flying low over the school-yard took that moment to repeat its deliberate call, each echoing caw diluting itself with more and more prairie stillness, withdrawing, fading, fainting from sound-tint to sound-tint to silence.

'Ben!'

The boy turned, startled.

'You're sharpening your pencil!'

The teacher looked down at the chewed end of the pencil guiltily protruding. 'Take it out, Ben!'

He did, then looked at the teacher, uneasily shifting his weight from one bare foot to the other.

'Take your seat.'

When the four o'clock bell rang the teacher called the Young Ben to his desk. 'How old are you, Ben?'

'Fourteen.'

'When's your next birthday?'

'Next spring—April twenty-third.'

The teacher opened his register. He picked up his red correction pencil from his desk and he drew a red line through the Young Ben's name. He said, 'Ben—I think I'd better let you go.'

The Young Ben looked at the teacher. He looked over at the pencil sharpener. He left the room.

Outside, with the slivered warmth of the board walk dry to his bare feet, he headed for the town hall. A wind off the prairie was lapping in the leaves of the school-yard poplars that lined the walk; it brought to him the wild Indian smell of smoke from burning straw stacks, from fall leaves smouldering in back yards. Away from him the tan prairie stretched to the sky, and the sky lifted above him, where a lonely goshawk hung.

He turned off the walk to the dirt road that led to the town hall.

The papery sound of his footsteps through the dead, stalked grass stopped by the basement jail window. He waited. The Ben's head appeared, with its grey hair standing out in two tufts from his temples; then his hands with their chicken-foot knuckles and their spade nails gripped the bars. His eyes stared out at the Young Ben from raw rims red as meat, eyes that by their fixity had stopped being anything but things by themselves. The Young Ben could hear his father's breathing, harsh with a shrill edge to its rough rhythm.

He told his father that he had dropped school. He stood there in the slanting rays of the fall sun and rubbed the back of one leg with the bare instep of the other. The Ben's head and its two eyes moved slightly from side to side with impatience, as though to move the bars from his line of vision. He said nothing.

Finally the Young Ben said that he'd better be getting home; there were chores; the cows had to be brought in and milked; feed had to be thrown down; the owl had to be fed.

Low along the prairie sky the dying sunshine lingered, faintly blushing the length of one lone, grey cloud there. The Ben said:—

'Let that there goddam owl go.'

The Green Bird

P. K. PAGE (b. 1916)

I CANNOT escape the fascination of doors, the weight of unknown people who drive me into myself and pin me with their personalities. Nor can I resist the desire to be led through shutters and impaled on strange living-room chairs.

Therefore when Ernest stood very squarely on his

feet and said: 'I'm going to call on Mrs. Rowan today and I hope you will come,' I said 'Yes.' The desire to be trapped by old Mrs. Rowan was stronger than any other feeling. Her door was particularly attractive— set solid and dark in her solid, dark house. I had passed by often and seen no sign of life there—no hand at a window, no small movement of the handle of the door.

We rang the bell. A man-servant, smiling, white-coated, drew us in, took our coats, showed us into the living-room.

'So it is this,' I said to Ernest.

'Beg your pardon?' He crossed his knees carefully, jerked back his neck with the abstracted manner of the public speaker being introduced, leaned his young black head on Mrs. Rowan's air.

'It is this,' I said. 'No ash trays,' I said.

'But I don't smoke,' said Ernest.

Mrs. Rowan came then. There were dark bands holding a child's face on to a forgotten body. She sat as though she were our guest and we had embarrassed her.

Ernest handled the conversation with an Oriental formality aided by daguerreotype gestures. Mrs. Rowan responded to him—a child under grey hair, above the large, loose, shambling torso. She talked of candy and birthday cake. She said she didn't like radios.

I said 'Music,' and looked about startled as if someone else had said it, suddenly imagining the horror of music sounding in this motionless house.

She said, 'But you do miss hearing famous speakers. I once heard Hitler when I was in a taxi.' She said, 'We will only sit here a little longer and then we will

go upstairs, I have an invalid up there who likes to
pour tea.'

I felt the sick-room atmosphere in my lungs and
my longing to escape was a strong hand pushing me
towards it. I imagined the whole upstairs white and
dim, with disease crowding out the light.

Mrs. Rowan said, 'We will go now,' and we rose,
unable to protest had we wished, and followed her
up the carpeted stairs and into a front room where
a tea-table was set up. There was a large silent figure
in a chair.

'Miss Price, the invalid,' Mrs. Rowan said, 'insists
on pouring the tea. She likes it. It gives her pleasure.'
The figure in the chair moved only her eyes, staring
first at Ernest and then at me. Her face was lifeless as
a plate. Mrs. Rowan continued to talk about her.
'She's been with me a long time,' she said. 'Poor
dear.' And then, 'It's quite all right. Her nurse is
right next door.' She introduced us. Miss Price
sucked in the corners of her mouth and inclined her
head slightly with each introduction. The white-
coated, grinning man-servant brought in the tea.

'You can pour it now,' said Mrs. Rowan, and Miss
Price began, slowly, faultlessly, with the corners of
her mouth sucked in and her eyes dark and long as
seeds. She paid no attention to what we said about
sugar and cream. She finished and folded her arms,
watched us without expression.

Mrs. Rowan passed the cakestand. 'You eat these
first,' she said, pointing to the sandwiches; 'these
second,' pointing to some cookies; 'and this last,'
indicating fruit cake. My cup rattled a little.

I pretended to drink my tea, but felt a nausea—the
cup seemed dirty. Ernest leaned back in his chair,
said, 'Delicious tea.' Miss Price sat with her arms

folded; there was no indication of life except in the glimmer of her seed eyes.

'Dear,' said Mrs. Rowan suddenly but without concern, 'you haven't poured yourself a cup.'

Miss Price sucked in her mouth, looked down into her lap; her face was hurt.

'No,' I said. 'You must have a cup too.' I laughed by mistake.

Miss Price looked up at me, flicked her eyes at mine with a quick glance of conspiracy and laughed too, in complete silence. Mrs. Rowan passed her a cup and she poured her own tea solemnly and folded her arms again.

'Before you go,' Mrs. Rowan said, 'I'd like to give you a book—one of mine. Which one would you like?'

'Why,' I said, looking at the cakestand which had never been passed again and stood with all the food untouched but for the two sandwiches Ernest and I had taken, 'why—'. I wondered what I could say. I had no idea she wrote. 'Why,' I said again and desperately, 'I should like most the one you like most.'

Miss Price flicked her eyes at me again and her body heaved with dreadful silent laughter.

'I like them all,' Mrs. Rowan said. 'There are some that are written about things that happened in 300 B.C. and some written about things that happened three minutes ago. I'll get them,' she said, and went.

Ernest was carefully balancing his saucer on his knee, sitting very straight. There was no sound in the entire house.

'I hope you are feeling better, Miss Price,' Ernest said.

I saw the immense silent body heave again, this time with sobs. Dreadful silent sobs. And then it spoke for the first time. 'They cut off both my legs three years ago. I'm nothing but a stump.' And the sobbing grew deeper, longer.

I looked at Ernest. I heard my own voice saying, 'Such a lovely place to live, this—so central. You can see everything from this room. It looks right out on the street. You can see everything.'

Miss Price was still now, her face expressionless, as if it had happened years before. 'Yes,' she said.

'The parades,' I said.

'Yes, the parades. My nephew's in the war.'

'I'm sorry,' Ernest said.

'He was wounded at Ypres. My sister heard last week.' Her arms were folded. Her cup of tea was untouched before her, the cream in a thick scum on the surface.

'Now, here,' Mrs. Rowan came in, her arms full of books—like a child behind the weight of flesh—covetous of the books—of the form of the books, spreading them about her, never once opening their covers. 'Which one would you like?' she asked.

'This,' I said. 'The colour of its cover will go with my room.'

'What a pretty thought,' Mrs. Rowan said, and for some reason my eyes were drawn to Miss Price, knowing they would find her heaving with that silent laughter that turned her eyes to seeds.

'We must go,' said Ernest suddenly. He put down his cup and stood up. I tucked the book under my arm and crossed to Miss Price. 'Good-bye,' I said, and shook hands. Her seed eyes seemed underneath the earth. She held on to my hand, I felt as if I was held down in soil. Ernest said, 'Good-bye, Miss Price,' and held out his hand, but hers still clutched mine. She beckoned to Mrs. Rowan and whispered, 'The birds. I want to give her a bird,' and then to me, 'I want to give you a bird.'

Mrs. Rowan walked into the next room and returned with a paper bag. Miss Price released my hand and dug down into the bag with shelving fingers. 'No, not these,' she said angrily. 'These are green.'

'They're the only ones,' Mrs. Rowan said. 'The others have all gone.'

'I don't like them,' said Miss Price, holding one out on a beaded cord. It was stuffed green serge, dotted with red bead work, and two red cherries hung from its mouth. 'It's paddy green,' she said disgustedly, and sucked in the corners of her mouth.

'Never mind,' I said. 'It's lovely, and paddy green goes with my name. I'm Patricia, you see, and they sometimes call me Paddy.' I stood back in astonishment at my own sentences, and Miss Price gave an enormous shrug, which, for the moment, until she released it, made her fill the room. And then, 'God!' she said, 'what a name!' The scorn in her voice shrivelled us. When I looked back at her as I left she had fallen into her silent, shapeless laughter.

Mrs. Rowan showed us downstairs and called the man-servant to see us out. She stood like a child at the foot of the stairs and waved to us every few minutes as the grinning white-coated houseman helped us into our coats.

'You must come again and let Miss Price pour tea for you. It gives her such pleasure.'

Outside, on the step, I began to laugh. I had been impaled and had escaped. My laughter went on and on. It was loud, the people in the street stared at me.

Ernest looked at me with disapproval. 'What do you find so funny?' he asked.

What? What indeed? There was nothing funny at all. Nothing anywhere. But I poked about for an answer.

'Why, this,' I said, holding the bird by its beaded cord. 'This, of course.'

He looked at it a long time. 'Yes,' he said, seriously. 'Yes, I suppose it is quaint,' and he smiled.

It was as though a pearl was smiling.

The House on the Esplanade

ANNE HÉBERT[1] (b. 1916)

STEPHANIE DE BICHETTE was a curious little creature with frail limbs that seemed badly put to-gether. Only her starched collarette kept her head from falling over on her shoulder; it was too heavy for her long, slender neck. If the head of Stephanie de Bichette looked so heavy, it was because all the pomp of her aristocratic ancestors was symbolized in her coiffure, a high up-swept style, with padded curls arranged in rows on her narrow cranium, an architectural achievement in symmetrical silvery blobs.

Mademoiselle de Bichette had passed, without transition period, without adolescence, from the short frocks of her childhood to this everlasting ash-grey dress, trimmed at neck and wrists with a swirl of lilac braiding. She owned two parasols with carved ivory handles—one lilac and the other ash-grey.

[1] Translated by Morna Scott Stoddart.

When she went out driving in the carriage she chose her parasol according to the weather, and everyone in the little town could tell the weather by the colour of Mademoiselle de Bichette's parasol. The lilac one appeared on days of brilliant sunshine, the ash-grey one whenever it was slightly cloudy. In winter, and when it rained, Stephanie simply never went out at all.

I have spoken at length about her parasols because they were the outward and visible signs of a well-regulated life, a perfect edifice of regularity. Unchanging routine surrounded and supported this innocent old creature. The slightest crack in this extraordinary construction, the least change in this stern programme would have been enough to make Mademoiselle de Bichette seriously ill.

Fortunately, she had never had to change her maid. Geraldine served and cared for her mistress with every evidence of complete respect for tradition. The whole life of Stephanie de Bichette was a tradition, or rather a series of traditions, for apart from the tradition of the well-known parasols and the complicated coiffure, there was the ritual of getting up, of going to bed, of lace-making, of meal-times, and so on.

Stephanie Hortense Sophie de Bichette lived facing the Esplanade, in a grey stone house dating back to the days of the French occupation. You know the sort of house *that* implies—a tall, narrow edifice with a pointed roof and several rows of high windows, where the ones at the top look no bigger than swallows' nests, a house with two or three large attics that most old maids would have delighted in. But, believe it or not, Mademoiselle de Bichette never climbed up to her attics to sentimentalize over souvenirs, to caress treasured old belongings, or to plan meticulous orgies of housecleaning amid the smell of yellowing paper and musty air that even the best-kept attics seem to possess.

No, she occupied the very heart of the house, scarcely one room on each floor. On the fourth story, only Geraldine's room remained open, among the rooms of all the former servants. It was part of the family tradition to close off rooms that were no longer used. One after another, bedroom after bedroom had been condemned: the room where the little brothers had died of scarlet fever, when Stephanie was only ten years old; the bedroom of their mother, who had passed away soon after her two children; the room of Irénée, the elder brother who had been killed in an accident, out hunting; the room of the elder sister, Desneiges, who had entered the Ursuline convent; then the bedroom of Monsieur de Bichette, the father, who had succumbed to a long illness; to say nothing of the room belonging to Charles, the only surviving brother, which had been closed ever since his marriage.

The ritual was always the same: once the occupant of the room had departed for the cemetery, the convent, or the adventure of matrimony, Geraldine would tidy everything away, carefully leaving each piece of furniture exactly in place; then she would draw the shutters, put dust-covers on the arm-chairs, and lock the door for good. No one ever set foot in that room again. One more member of the family was finally disposed of.

Geraldine took a distinct pleasure in this solemn, unvarying rite, just as a gravedigger may take pride in a neat row of graves, with well-kept mounds and smoothly raked grass above them. Sometimes she remembered that one day she would have to close Mademoiselle Stephanie's room, too, and live on for a while, the only living creature among all the dead. She looked forward to that moment, not with horror, but with pleasant anticipation, as a rest and a reward. After so many years of housework in that great house, all its rooms would be fixed at last in order, for all eternity. Mildew and dust could take possession then; Geraldine would have no more cleaning to do then. The rooms of the dead are not 'done up'.

This was not the calculation of a lazy woman. Geraldine dreamed of the last door closed and the last key turned in the lock just as the harvester dreams of the last sheaf of corn, or the needlewoman of the last stitch in her embroidery. It would be the crowning achievement of her long life, the goal of her destiny.

It was strange that the old servant reckoned two living people among the dead: Mademoiselle Desneiges, the nun, and Monsieur Charles, a married man and the father of a family. They had both left the family roof, that was enough for Geraldine to class them as non-existent. The heavy door of the cloister had closed forever on one, while Charles, by marrying a common little seamstress from the Lower Town, had so grieved his father that the old house and all it contained had been left to Stephanie. Charles came to see his sister every evening, but Geraldine never spoke a word to him. For her, Stephanie was the whole of the de Bichette family.

On the third floor, all the bedrooms were closed, with the exception of Mademoiselle de Bichette's. On the second, only the small blue boudoir lived on, a life of dimness and disuse. On the first floor, an immense drawing-room stretched from front to back, cluttered with furniture of different periods, each piece bristling with fussy, elaborate knick-knacks. The ground-floor doors were always open, with high, carved portals to the vestibule, the parlour, the dining-room. In the basement was the old-fashioned kitchen, uncomfortable and always damp. Geraldine was the cook as well as the maid-of-all-work, but was never addressed as such.

If her mistress lived by tradition until it became a religion, Geraldine, too had her tradition, the collecting of bright-coloured buttons. Her black skirt and her white apron never changed, but she used her imagination in trimming her blouses. Red buttons sparkled on blue blouses, yellow ones on green, and so on, not to mention buttons in gold and silver and crystal. In the attic, she had discovered great chests of ancient garments which she stripped, shamelessly, of their trimmings. Apart from this innocent craze for buttons, the big woman with the ruddy complexion made no objection to touring the wine cellar every evening before going to bed, as the last of her duties, conscientiously and even devotedly performed. But where she excelled, was in the observance of tradition where her mistress was concerned.

Every morning, at seven o'clock in summer and eight in winter, she climbed the three flights of stairs and knocked at the bedroom door. . . . Two taps, two firm, decided taps, no more, no less. This was the signal for the ceremonial to begin.

Geraldine opened the bed curtains, then the window curtains, and finally the shutters. Her ageing mistress preferred to sleep in complete darkness, requiring several thicknesses of material and polished wood between herself and the wicked witchcraft of the night. She was afraid of the first rays of sunlight as well, not knowing what to do about them, since they might easily wake you long before the proper time for getting up.

Then Geraldine would return to the passage to fetch a kind of wagon equipped with everything Stephanie might need for the first few hours of the day. Two white pills in a glass of water, coffee and toast, toothbrush and toothpowder, a copper bathtub, white towels, white, starched underwear. Also a feather duster, a broom, a dust-pan . . . all that she used for tidying up the room. This wagon was as wide as a single bed, four feet wide, with three shelves. Geraldine had made it herself out of old packing cases.

When Stephanie's breakfast was finished, the maid would bathe, dress, and powder her mistress, then do her hair. Stephanie allowed her to do everything, silent, inert, trusting. After that, there was sometimes a moment of painful indecision, an anguished knot in the brain of Mademoiselle de Bichette, when Geraldine leaned over to look out of the window, examining the sky and frowning as she declared:

'I really don't know what sort of weather we're going to have today.'

Then the old lady would stare at her maid with such forlorn eyes that Geraldine would say, hurriedly:

'It's going to rain. You're not going to be able to go out this morning. I'll let the coachman know.'

Stephanie would grow calm again after that, but she would not be entirely herself until Geraldine had settled her carefully in the blue drawing-room, on her high-backed chair of finely carved wood, near the window, her half-finished lace on her knee and her crochet hook in her hand. Only then would the idea take firm root in her brain:

'It's going to rain. I can't go out. . . . All I have to do is to handle this hook and this thread as my mother taught me to do when I was seven years old. . . . If it had been a fine day, it would have been different, I would have gone out in the carriage. There are only two realities in the world . . . only two realities I can rely on . . . and close my eyes, deep inside them: the reality of going out in the carriage, the reality of making my lace. . . . How lost and strange I am when Geraldine cannot tell what the weather is going to do, and I am left in suspense with no solid ground beneath my feet. . . . It just *wracks* my brain! Oh! Not to have to think about it, to let myself be carried away by one or the other of these my only two sure and certain realities going out for a drive or sitting here, making my lace. . . .'

Even if the day turned out fine in the end, Geraldine never said so. It would have been too much of a shock for her mistress. Imagine what confusion in such a patterned existence if someone had suddenly announced a change, after she had firmly established herself for the day in the reality of lace-making, and dared to tell her she had taken the wrong road? She could never again have believed in any reality at all.

Since her childhood, Mademoiselle de Bichette had been making lace doilies of different sizes, which Geraldine used in many different ways. These doilies flowed from her fingers at the steady rate of four per week, small pieces of white lace that resembled each other like peas in a pod. They were everywhere in the house—five or six on the piano, seven or eight on all the tables, as many as ten on every arm-chair, one or two on all the smaller chairs. Every knick-knack rested on a piece of delicate openwork, so that the furniture all seemed powdered with snowflakes, enlarged as if under a microscope.

In winter, and in summer, on the days when Geraldine had decided the weather was not fit for going out, Mademoiselle de Bichette would crochet all the morning, in her blue boudoir, sitting up so straight and still that she scarcely seemed real, her feet resting on a stool covered by something that was strangely like the work the old lady held in her hands.

At five minutes to twelve, Geraldine would announce:

'Mademoiselle Stephanie's luncheon is served.'

At the mention of her name, the old lady would rise at once; the ritual phrase had touched a switch somewhere within her, so that without effort, without thinking, without even understanding, she would put herself slowly and ceremoniously in motion, descend the staircase and take her place at the table.

If Stephanie did go out, she invariably returned home at a quarter to twelve, so she had ample time to receive the announcement that luncheon was served with the necessary calm.

The outings of Mademoiselle de Bichette were governed by just as incredible a routine. She came out on the sidewalk with tiny steps, her frail little body bending under the weight of that enormous pile of scaffolded curls. Geraldine helped her mistress into the carriage, the coachman whipped up his horse, and the victoria started on its slow, quiet drive, invariably the same, through the streets of the little town. The horse knew the road by heart, so the coachman seized the opportunity for a short nap, his cap pulled down over his eyes, his legs stretched out, his hands folded on his stomach. He always waked up in time, as if by magic, when the drive came to an end, crying out and stretching himself, with a jolly air of surprise:

'Well, well, Mamzelle, here we are back again!'

Just as if the old fellow, when he went to sleep as the drive started, had not been quite sure he would come back when he awoke, or if his return would be to the country of the living!

Mademoiselle de Bichette would disappear into the house, on Geraldine's arm; the coachman would unharness the horse and put the carriage away; and it was all over. With regret, the townsfolk watched the disintegration of this strange conveyance, like a ghostly apparition cutting through the clear morning light . . . the ancient nag, pulling an antique carriage, with a sleepy coachman and a tiny figure like a mummy, swathed in ash-grey and lilac.

After luncheon, Geraldine would lead her mistress into the long drawing-room on the first floor, where, without ever laying her crochet aside, Stephanie would receive a few callers, and the maid would serve dandelion wine and madeleines.

The old lady never left her chair, forcing herself to hold her head high, though her neck felt as if it were breaking under the weight of her monumental coiffure. Sometimes, this constant, painful effort was betrayed by a twitch of the lips, the only change of expression that callers could ever distinguish upon that small, powdered face. Then Stephanie would ask: 'How is Madame your mother?' in a voice so white and colourless that it might have come from one of the closed rooms, where, according to the gossips of the town, some of the original inhabitants still lived on.

This phrase of Stephanie's had to do for greeting, for farewell, for conversation; indeed, it had to do for everything, for the wine was sour and the madeleines stale and hard as stones. The callers were all so aged and unsteady that the most utter stranger would have had the tact never to ask that preposterous question, but Mademoiselle de Bichette knew no other formula, and in any case, she attached no importance whatever to the words she was saying. If she finished a lace doily while her callers were present, she simply let it fall at her feet, like a pebble into a pool, and began another identical piece of lace. The visiting ladies never stayed very long, and Stephanie seemed to notice their departure as little as she did their presence.

At a quarter past six, Geraldine would announce that Monsieur Charles was waiting below. The programme of the day was ticking on like the mechanism of a good Swiss watch, and the invisible wheels of Mademoiselle de Bichette responded perfectly, warning the limbs of this strange little creature that they must immediately convey her to the ground floor.

Her brother would kiss her brow and smile, rubbing his stubby-fingered hands together and remarking:

'Um-phm! It feels good in the house.'

Then he would hang his overcoat up on a hall stand, while Geraldine followed his every movement with her look of triumphant disdain. With her arms crossed upon her swelling chest, she doubtless thought she looked like the statue of the Commendatore, bound on revenge. She would cast a glance of scorn on the threadbare coat, as if to say:

'Well, what did you expect? Monsieur Charles

would get married to a chit of a girl from the Lower
Town, so naturally, his father cut him off, and I
locked up his room as if he were dead. If Mademoiselle Stephanie wants him here every evening, it's
her own business, but *I'm* going to let him know that
I'm *glad* he was thrown out, if I *am* only the servant.
I know he's poor, and that's his punishment for dis-
obeying his father. He comes here because there
isn't enough to eat at home. So he gobbles up our
dinners and carries away on his nasty skin a bit of
the warmth from our fires. . . . The good-for-
nothing!'

If it were true that Charles had only one decent
meal a day, it was astonishing that he was not at all
thin. He was even fat, very fat, flabby and yellow-
complexioned, with a bald head and a shiny face,
colourless lips and almost colourless eyes. Geraldine
said he had eyes like a codfish and his clothes always
smelt of stale grease. Apart from that, she could not
forgive a de Bichette for forgetting his table manners.

'To think that his slut of a wife has made him lose
all he ever learned in decent society. . . . You
wouldn't believe it possible,' she would grumble to
herself.

As dinner-time drew near, Charles became more
and more noisily jolly. He never stopped rubbing his
hands together; he got up, sat down, got up again,
went from window to door and back a dozen times,
while Stephanie's eyes ignored him. Then the
brother and sister took their places, one at each end
of the long table in the dining-room. There was no
gas chandelier in this room, so it seemed even longer
and darker, lit only by two tall candles in silver
candlesticks. The corners of the room disappeared
into the dimness, and the shadows of the brother

and sister danced like black flames on the curiously carved oak panelling of the walls.

Every evening, the atmosphere of this dining-room seemed more impressive to Charles. Perhaps he felt unseen forms hiding in the darkness, invisible spectators of this singular repast; perhaps he feared to find the ghosts that haunted the bedrooms above, to see them take their places at the huge dining-table, where an old creature presided, small as a cat, white as the table-linen, who seemed already to be living in the uneasy world of phantoms.

As soon as Stephanie's brother had swallowed a few mouthfuls of soup, his good humour fell away, lifeless, utterly destroyed. When he entered the house, the smell of cooking would stimulate him, would intoxicate him with its marvellous promise, but now that the promise was kept, the man became gloomy again. Through his own bitter thoughts, he stared at the lace cloth, the heavy silverware, the fine china, and at this sister of his, who was still alive, in spite of her look of belonging to some other world. What mysterious thread was keeping Stephanie here on earth? To look at her, you would have thought the slightest breath might carry her away, yet there she was, still alive.

Geraldine came and went around the table and her sharp eyes seemed to plumb the very depths of the man's thoughts. The brother sat there, knowing himself watched and understood, telling himself, in his embarrassment, that his sister would have joined her ancestors long ago had it not been for this fiendish servant, who by some diabolical process had contrived to keep the dying thing alive in her father's mansion, simply in order to enjoy as long as possible the spectacle of his own failure. In what dread 'No Man's Land' of the spirit had the old witch made a pact with Monsieur de Bichette—and with Satan himself? Geraldine had inherited all the father's anger against his son, and faithful to that anger as if to a sacred promise, she was constantly reminding Charles of the curse that lay heavy upon him. At that moment he raised his head, resenting the eyes he felt fixed upon his every movement, but Geraldine was no longer there, Charles could hear the tinkle of her keys, in the passage between the staircase and the kitchen. He shuddered, for he knew very well which keys she carried at her waist. No cupboard, no inhabited room possessed a key. It chilled his heart strangely to know that the key of his room was there, along with those of the rooms of the dead. It scared him. Then he took hold of himself again and muttered:

'This damned house! . . . Enough to drive a man crazy to sit here night after night with two cracked old fools of women. . . . The wine must have gone to my head.'

But Stephanie had just got up from the table, and Charles followed her as usual.

The evening began like all the rest. Stephanie took up her lace again, while her brother walked to and fro in the long drawing-room, his hands behind his back.

And so, night after night, in complete silence, without a single word exchanged between brother and sister, the time passed until the old clock chimed ten. Then Charles, having laid up a store of warmth for the night, kissed his sister's brow, slipped on his overcoat, and with his hands in his pockets, made for Ireland Street, walking slowly along, like an idle fellow accustomed to musing as he walked.

The man followed his shadow as it flickered on the walls. The same thoughts were turning and twisting in his brain; he was used to them, as a man gets used to animals he tends every day. He knew them too well to be surprised by them; he had stopped looking at them straight in the face; they passed to and fro behind his pale eyes without ever changing his passive stare.

As he came near his own home, Charles thought of his wife. He was going back to her, in no hurry, but with a certain feeling of security, as if to a piece of property he knew belonged to him.

Suddenly, he noticed that he was nearly there. Two low houses, identical twins in misery and poverty, stood waiting for him, their tumbledown grey 'stoops' jutting out to meet the sidewalk. He rented rooms on the second floor of one of these houses.

He climbed the stairs, lit a candle and went into the bedroom. A hoarse, veiled voice, a well-known voice, that could still charm him in spite of himself, said wearily:

'That you Charles?'

He set the candle on the night table. The woman shaded her eyes with her hand. He sat down on the foot of the bed.

'How's your sister?'

'Just the same.'

This question, this reply, as on every other night, fell heavily into a dull silence. Beneath the words was stirring in the shadows the real meaning, unexpressed:

'Do you think your sister will last much longer?'

''Fraid so. . . . She's still hanging on. . . .'

At that moment, in the house on the Esplanade,

Stephanie de Bichette was crossing her tiny cold hands on her breast and abandoning to the great empty gulf of night the small emptiness that was herself, ridiculous as an old fashion plate and dry as a pressed fig.

And Geraldine lay awake, dreaming that death had closed the last door in the old house.

The Stations of the Cross

ROGER LEMELIN[1] (b. 1919)

IT all began one June evening in the main hall of the Provincial Museum.

'Monsieur le curé Ledoux! What a surprise! I did not know that modern painting interested you!'

'Perhaps, perhaps,' the old priest stammered, smiling mysteriously.

The speaker, an eminent ecclesiastic and a discriminating connoisseur of art, looked in perplexity after curé Ledoux, who, like a waggish spy, was threading his way through the groups of guests. This particular evening happened to be the first night of an exhibition of the works of a young painter, Paul Lafrance. He had just arrived back from Paris, where, for three years, he had busied himself in imitating Picasso. Paul Lafrance was almost six feet tall and did not weigh more than one hundred and thirty pounds. His long, mouse-coloured hair, his pale blue eyes, the Parisian's sceptical smile on his lips, his check suit and the short,

---

[1] Translated by Mary Finch.

fat women surrounding him, all contributed to making him appear more scrawny and more dejected. The weird designs and the violent colours of the canvases gave the walls an air of ludicrous astonishment. Some so-called connoisseurs, Provincial Government officials, were scrutinizing, criticizing, and appraising each work with pretentious gestures and glances. They had no money. The other guests, holding Martinis, were chatting about fishing and politics and glancing absent-mindedly at the paintings. These dilettantes, these business men flocking to an opening night through a taste for fashionable gatherings, behaved like gapers invading a circus famous for its five-footed giraffes. They are very extraordinary giraffes but the gapers don't buy them. Paul Lafrance had not yet sold one canvas.

'Monsieur Ledoux, you here?'

The old priest nodded, smiling artfully, his eyes almost closing. His cassock, greenish from being worn too long, was a trifle short and revealed his dusty boots, topped by thick, black, woollen socks. Now and then he rubbed a nervous hand through his tousled grey hair, and with the other crumpled a large chequered handkerchief into a ball in the opening of his roomy pocket.

Apparently unaware of the astonished murmurs that followed in his wake, he reached the first canvases and began to examine them one by one with an outstanding gravity, as if he had to condemn them to heaven or hell. Whatever was he doing at this exhibition? Those who knew him had reason to be astonished.

Monsieur Ledoux was rector-founder of St. X parish in the poorest district of Quebec. For some time there had been a great deal of talk about him all over the city. After fifteen years of untiring apostleship he was seeing his parishioners of early days (swearers, drunkards, thieves) become exemplary citizens. But it was through his new church that old curé Ledoux had become famous. This temple was costing three hundred thousand dollars. Very good. His parishioners must be workingmen of heroic calibre to have consented to such a sum. Again very good. But all that would not be enough to have Monsieur Ledoux talked about at every social gathering. Monsieur Ledoux's famous church was not like the others! That was why! Gothic in style, it was the only one in the city without pillars! The high-altar was visible from every seat. That isn't all. Monsieur Ledoux had had air-conditioning installed. It was probably the first innovation of its kind in all the churches in America! It had been said for a long time that curé Ledoux, son of peasants, was an uncouth and uncultured man. But what about this air-conditioning, this absence of pillars?

Monsieur Ledoux glided from one canvas to another with a concentrated air that one would not have expected of him. Someone offered him a Martini which he refused with a gesture of annoyance. After some twenty minutes' examination he buried his large nose in his chequered handkerchief and glanced furtively around him.

'Make up your mind, Thomas, make up your mind!'

Monsieur Ledoux was talking to himself. He often did that. Everybody called him 'Monsieur le curé', so Monsieur Ledoux often said to himself: 'Thomas! Eh! Thomas!' The priest walked towards the painter, Paul Lafrance, whose back was turned, and pulled discreetly at his sleeve.

'Monsieur l'abbé?'

'Curé Thomas Ledoux. Your work interests me. It's modern. Give me your address.'

The pale blue eyes gazed at the old priest as Paul Lafrance mechanically recited his address. Monsieur Ledoux, having moistened his pencil with saliva, wrote down the number in a little notebook. He closed it, smiling like an accomplice.

'Perhaps you will hear from me.'

He shuffled off towards the cloak-room. The painter and the guests, piqued with curiosity, gazed after him.

Monsieur Ledoux boarded a street-car. With his chin sunk in the fleshy cushion that prosperity had placed round his neck since the erection of his famous church, he appeared to doze in heavenly bliss. His head swayed from left to right with the jerks of the street-car and in rhythm with the rolling wheels on the rails. All at once the old priest sat bolt upright and opened his eyes watchfully. By an intuition peculiar to clergy, he had sensed the nearby presence of a church.

It was the Basilica of Quebec. Monsieur Ledoux stared at it intently with an affectionate expression that gave way to one of triumph. The celebrated Basilica, the Cardinal's chapel, was filled with unfortunate pillars and had no air-conditioning system. Not like Monsieur Ledoux's church! His chin disappeared once more into its cushion and Monsieur Ledoux, having made sure of Paul Lafrance's address, began to doze again.

Monsieur Ledoux got off the street-car in his parish and walked toward the presbytery. It was ten o'clock at night. Like a proud landowner he sniffed the air of his domain and glanced fondly at the humble homes of his flock. All at once he found himself in front of the unusual temple that crowned his saintly ambitions and filled him with pride. He stopped and, swaying with his hands behind his back, eyes half-closed as though in ecstasy, he gazed at it. His lips curled into a blissful smile: 'Thomas, Thomas it's really true, it is your church, your church, you old Thomas, you!'

His rapture was suddenly interrupted. Two devout women, faithful parish workers, were standing beside him and admiring the temple with him.

'What a fine church, eh, Monsieur le curé! The electric organ has been bought. All we need is the Stations of the Cross.'

Monsieur Ledoux turned round abruptly to them and said with puerile haste:

'We'll have them in a month. They'll be unique, these Stations of the Cross. The first of their kind in America, even in the whole world, perhaps, Thomas says so.'

Open-mouthed, the two housewives, delighted by this news and slightly shocked by the unexpected 'Thomas' of Monsieur Ledoux, watched him go away. Monsieur le curé, less repentant for having said too much than annoyed by this familiar use of Thomas that he had not been able to restrain before these good women, went into the presbytery furiously sniffing up a pinch of snuff. He went up to his office and on his way was addressed by the youngest of his curates, abbé Constant, the door of whose room was open. Comfortably seated in a leather arm-chair, he was busy reading James Joyce's novel, *Ulysses*. Abbé Constant, who had been ordained two years before, put himself in the category of the young clergy with advanced ideas who clamour

337

for a youthful Church, suited to the needs of the time. He often smiled at certain of Monsieur Ledoux's old-fashioned preferences but he was very fond of him all the same.

'Are you beginning to sleep away from home, Monsieur le curé?'

'I've just come back from the Museum, from the first night of an exhibition of modern painting,' Monsieur Ledoux replied, blushing.

Wide-eyed with astonishment, abbé Constant gazed at his superior without saying a word.

Monsieur Ledoux, annoyed at having blushed, added defiantly: 'Yes, I have decided that our Stations of the Cross will be modern art. The first in America. And I think I'm going to choose this artist, Paul Lafrance.'

'But . . . Monsieur le curé,' ventured abbé Constant, who was beginning to collect his wits, 'don't you think our parishioners are scarcely prepared for . . . for Stations of the Cross like that?'

Then Monsieur le curé stiffened haughtily and said with triumphant solemnity:

'And it's you, young man, who reproached me for being old-fashioned! I have eliminated pillars, have had air-conditioning installed, and now it's the turn of modern art. Well, good-night. Don't go to bed too late. You say five o'clock mass tomorrow morning.'

Abbé Constant was too astonished to go on with *Ulysses*. He went to bed.

The young curate's objection hastened the execution of the project because the curé could not tolerate anyone to doubt the worth of his ideas. Monsieur Ledoux rarely consulted his church-wardens where the financial affairs of his parish were concerned. He made his decision and, as a matter of form, called them together in order to tell them about it. As Monsieur Ledoux was cunning enough to make them believe that he had acted under their influence, these gentlemen (a fruit merchant, a grocer, and a street-car conductor) nodded their heads gravely in approval. In the matter of the Stations of the Cross, Monsieur Ledoux presented them with the accomplished fact.

The artist Paul Lafrance set the price of his work at twenty-five hundred dollars for fourteen pictures representing the different stages in the Passion of Christ, according to the rules of modern art. Moreover, the surrealist painter promised to visit all the churches in the city, in order to make sure that his Stations of the Cross would be completely different from the others. Monsieur le curé promised to pay for the cost of the canvas, the paint, the frames, and to board the artist while he was doing his work. The brightest room in the presbytery was turned into a studio by the painter and the curé. The latter was anxious to keep up a daily inspection of his Stations and to become acquainted with the mysterious caprices of Modern Art.

The sight of the long-haired artist and the fabulous price of twenty-five hundred dollars made the churchwardens open their eyes wide, but Monsieur Ledoux remarked with a knowing smile:

'Churchwardens like you are blessed by God, who allows you to buy something more rare and beautiful for a church already unique.' These gentlemen puffed out their chests, looking at one another. What a curé!

It was an extraordinary experience for Paul Lafrance. Newly arrived from Paris where, many a time in front of his artist friends, he had made fun of the French Canadian's lack of taste for painting and where, before anti-clerical dilettantes, he had slandered the Canadian clergy, he now found himself with an order for fourteen surrealist paintings from the priest of a parish of workingmen, when as yet he had not sold a single canvas during his exhibition. This was a great piece of news in all the artistic circles of Quebec and many of the painter's friends insisted on visiting his studio and meeting Monsieur le curé Ledoux. For a whole week the rumour circulated about St. X Parish that Monsieur le curé had had a celebrated artist brought by aeroplane from Paris. But Monsieur Ledoux remained impervious to questions. 'Wait until Sunday at high-mass.'

The Sunday arrived. The church was packed to the doors. The absence of pillars and the air-conditioning were never so appreciated as on that day. All the flock were craning their necks in order to get a better look at the artist, Paul Lafrance, seated among the altar-boys on a kind of throne usually reserved for visiting bishops. Lafrance, who had acquired pagan ways in Paris and given up his religion, was thinking that Art leads everywhere, even to Rome. He compared himself to Michelangelo and with some satisfaction imagined himself becoming a prince of the Church. All these glances raised towards him, the proximity of the altar and the religious propriety which surrounded him, prompted him to recall his prayers. He smiled imperceptibly at the thought that he was paid twenty-five hundred dollars to rediscover his faith. Monsieur le curé climbed into the pulpit.

'My very dear brethren:

'Heaven sends us a messenger of beauty from Europe. It is quite in keeping that Providence should direct his steps to our temple which, without doubt, is one of the dwellings on earth preferred by the Almighty. This church has been built in the most modern style and it would be illogical if the Stations of the Cross which will decorate it should be in the style of past centuries. If the art of building has been perfected to such a degree as to result in a work of art like ours, the art of painting has also evolved, and we must make it a duty to require as much of painting as of building. Thus, in honouring progress, we honour the Lord who is kind enough to bestow it upon man. My very dear brethren, you have before you, in the chancel, the celebrated painter, Paul Lafrance, who, tomorrow, will begin your Stations of the Cross, a work of which your grandchildren's children will be proud and which will make our church even more famous.'

During the days that followed, the presbytery became, in the parishioners' eyes, a mysterious laboratory where a magician armed with brushes devoted himself to all kinds of artistic alchemy. Many curious ones tried to obtain the favour of casting a glance at Lafrance's work, but Monsieur le curé kept this privilege for himself. Out of consideration, Monsieur Ledoux did not visit the studio for the first two days. Paul Lafrance took his meals at the same table as the curé and his curates and long discussions on cubism, impressionism, and surrealism took place between the abbé Constant and the artist, who seemed to get along with each other very well. In the course of these conversations, which he did not understand in the least, Monsieur Ledoux often blew his nose, pretending he had a cold in order to excuse himself for having nothing to say.

However, at the fourth meal, tired of blowing his nose, the curé became impatient and determined to find some books which would deal with these mysteries. But he dared not ask the painter in front of abbé Constant. He rose from the table briskly, during the dessert, and very politely, asked:

'Is your work progressing, Monsieur Lafrance?'

'Yes. The first picture is finished. Some last touches and it will be perfect.'

Monsieur Ledoux, warped by fifteen years of financial administration, gave himself up to a rapid calculation. One picture in two days, fourteen in twenty-eight days, ninety dollars per day. He was a little disappointed. It had seemed to him that, because of the importance he attached to this work, it should take some months to complete.

'Do you wish to see it?' asked the painter.

The two men went off to the studio and Monsieur Ledoux, on catching sight of the picture, cried out in stupefaction.

'Don't you like it?' the painter ejaculated, distressed.

Monsieur Ledoux shook his head and frowned.

'I think the feet and the arms of the Christ are unusually long. It gives an odd effect. Don't you think so?'

The painter, already inflamed by the fervour of the artist defending his work, opened his mouth to make a declaration of his principles, but a second's reflection and a brief glance at Monsieur Ledoux persuaded him to change his tactics.

'It's because it's new that it takes you by surprise. You'll become accustomed to it and then you'll like this style. Painting has changed a great deal. It's no longer photography. Moreover, you insisted that my Stations of the Cross should be an innovation.'

'I don't deny it.'

Monsieur le curé, chin in hand, was reflecting. To tell the truth, a disturbing conflict was going on inside him. Just what demon had urged him to choose this painter? Moreover, from the first glimpse on the opening night at the Museum he ought to have foreseen the dangers with which modern art threatened his Stations of the Cross! The word 'modern' and the success of his church had blinded him. Obviously, he had not acted with his customary prudence in paying a thousand dollars in advance to the painter. It was now too late to retreat. He could not dismiss the painter after the enthusiastic recommendation he had given him. Monsieur Ledoux abruptly put an end to his reflections.

'Monsieur Lafrance, I'm not disputing the beauty of your work and I think that in the long run I shall understand it. But I do not forget that I have eighteen thousand parishioners who are not so well prepared as I to appreciate your work. And they are the ones who pay for it. So please shorten those arms and feet a little. Anyhow, you know what I mean.'

The painter seemed highly shocked but the curé had already left. With clenched fists, Monsieur Ledoux went to his room muttering: 'Thomas, you're nothing but a proud old peacock. You've got yourself into a fine mess. Because you have a new church without pillars and with air-conditioning you think you're the hub of the universe. You old fool, go and pray a little while and ask God to get you out of this tight corner. Above all, thank Him for the blow to your pride.'

He met abbé Constant in the hall.

'Well, now, Monsieur le curé, what do you think of Monsieur Lafrance's work?'

'Stupendous! Stupendous!'

Monsieur Ledoux did not add anything further but went up into his room and knelt down. His prayer lasted an hour and, apparently, the Lord advised him to persevere in his project in order to punish him.

Regular torture then began for Monsieur Ledoux. He made an effort to show a great enthusiasm for the Stations of the Cross but his common sense told him: 'Thomas, you know very well that these paintings are dreadful. You're courting disaster.' In order to be convinced of the beauties of modern art he consulted a clergyman renowned for his artistic knowledge. Monsieur Ledoux even obtained some large books on the subject. All to no purpose. The frequent visits he paid to the artist's studio only succeeded in adding to his despair. Artists like Paul Lafrance are as uncompromising as the Ten Commandments. The painter went on with the work in his own way and the further it progressed the longer, it seemed to Monsieur Ledoux, the feet and arms of the Christ became. Those violently coloured paintings with monstrously grotesque figures appeared to Monsieur Ledoux like a Mardi Gras masquerade. The good curé lost his appetite and the fleshy cushion around his neck decreased considerably. He never mentioned the Stations of the Cross in the pulpit and his parishioners, who were waiting impatiently for the unveiling, were astonished. What was happening to him?

Then something most unfortunate occurred. The verger, who was a very inquisitive man, succeeded in getting into the studio while the curé was away, and glanced at the pictures. Immediately word went round the parish that the People of the Passion were all crippled and walking in paths of blood. Alarmed, the housewives called on the curé and confessed their anxiety. He smiled, closing his eyes.

'Ladies, I suspect you of inventing rumours in order to force me to satisfy your curiosity. They're all untrue. In the meantime, if it will give you any pleasure, I can tell you that the Holy Women in our Station of the Cross are the portraits of the most devout ladies in the parish.'

Delighted and flattered, the ladies left the presbytery quite content. Monsieur le curé, overwhelmed, did not know what to do. While feeling so downcast, he came face to face with abbé Constant. Forgetting his pride, he confessed hesitantly to him:

'Monsieur l'abbé, I think you were right. I have made a mistake. Our parishioners are not ready to appreciate our Stations of the Cross. What am I going to do?'

Abbé Constant, who for some days had known his curé's state of mind, behaved himself as befits a good priest. He did not laugh at him but cheered him up and offered to help him. The two priests set to work and prepared a ten-page circular in which the symbolic beauty of modern art was praised with forceful adjectives. The circular was printed and distributed to the parishioners by the altar boys. In the face of this incomprehensible action, the parishioners began to be seriously alarmed.

The work was finished one Saturday afternoon and the painter's satisfaction equalled the curé's distress. The artist received the balance of his payment, thanked the curé, and left like a great lord. To put an end to the great martyrdom he was enduring the good curé announced that the exhibition of the work would be on Sunday morning, a quarter of an hour before high-mass. Certain remarks of dissatisfied parishioners about the circular on modern art had reached the curé's ears and he fearfully visualized the moment of the ceremony. He passed a dreadful night and every time he woke up he implored Heaven to calm his anguish and to see to it that his parishioners would bow down in admiration before the Stations of the Cross.

At half-past nine, the verger, whose rising indignation was mingled with fits of laughter, hung the pictures in the empty church. Monsieur le curé, hidden behind the altar, perspired profusely while waiting for the doors to be opened.

A crowd of parishioners interested in the fate of their church stamped and jostled outside the entrances. Finally the doors opened and there was a rush into the temple. There was not a single sound from the thousand gaping mouths, so great was the stupefaction. Then there burst out fourteen rounds of horrified cries which were relayed from picture to picture in a kind of chain of explosions. The women protested the most violently.

'They're frightful. Look at the Christ! The arms are longer than the legs, the feet longer than the thighs, and the hair does not curl. Horrible! Just look at the face! The chin is pointed, the eyes are all wrong.'

Among the group of good ladies who thought themselves represented by the Holy Women of the Passion were some white with anger and others who were crying, for the Holy Women of the Stations of the Cross looked like enormous frogs. The churchwardens seemed to be in a bad humour and were whispering: 'Twenty-five hundred dollars for these daubs! A child could do them!'

Other men threw up their hands, expostulating:

'The cross is much too small and it's snowing flowers into the bargain! Just look, will you! The hands are pierced with nails and don't even bleed!'

A rebellious atmosphere reigned in the church. The parishioners were all coming to the same conclusion: Had Monsieur le curé gone crazy? Every eye searched for him.

Behind the altar, Monsieur le curé Ledoux, face white as his surplice, mopped his brow. To cap everything, the air-conditioning system had gone out of order the day before. It was July and the heat was tropical.

Ten o'clock mass began and no one paid any attention to the service. The church was full of whispers and ripples of muted laughter. How shameful! Such a shocking thing in such a beautiful church! Monsieur le curé went up into the pulpit more dead than alive. He would have preferred to be at Rome, prostrate at the Pope's feet and thinking only of the beauties of Christianity. 'Face the music, Thomas!' His voice was weak and his hands trembled.

'My very dear brethren:

'I am only an old man whose dearest wish, as you know, is to give you a church finer than all others. For a long time I have dreamed of acquiring a magnificent Stations of the Cross for you. At last, it is in front of you, but instead of the admiration that I expected, you show dissatisfaction. I do not hide the fact that I am broken-hearted by your attitude. But I pray heaven that your eyes will become accustomed to this work and recognize its beauties in the end. My very dear brethren. . . .'

Monsieur Ledoux felt himself grow faint and made no effort to resist swooning. The churchwardens, while carrying him to the vestry, remarked: 'Not surprising that you fainted! Throwing twenty-five hundred dollars to the devil like that!'

Monsieur Ledoux's fainting had sown consternation in the hearts of his flock, but not to the point of changing their opinion on his famous Stations of the Cross. These events filled the parishioners' conversation for several days and Monsieur le curé deemed it wiser to keep to his bed. As long as there was anxiety about his condition no one complained about the Stations of the Cross. But although Monsieur le curé kept out of sight he was, nevertheless, most active. From various sources of information he learned that his faithful flock were attending church less and less frequently and that those who came to the religious services spent their time laughing at the ridiculous paintings. On the other hand, the temple was invaded by a curious crowd from neighbouring parishes attracted by the peculiar Stations of the Cross.

Monsieur Ledoux's greatly celebrated church had become a kind of museum where one forgot to kneel and took the liberty of talking and laughing boisterously. Monsieur Ledoux endured many bitter moments. After having enjoyed too briefly the importance of his church, he was already suffering from its decline. Then it was that Providence deemed him to have been punished enough and inspired him with an ingenious idea. Why hadn't he thought sooner of the Mother Superior of the Convent?

She had some talent for painting and Monsieur le curé had often gone, on Sunday afternoons, to see her paint saints, ships, rivers, and roses in delicate colours with a dainty brush. He had her roused at ten o'clock at night and the good Mother Superior, all of a tremble, ran to the presbytery. When she left Monsieur Ledoux, she said these words: 'I can paint these fourteen pictures in two weeks, I promise you. But I repeat that I am not equal to the task. Pray God I may succeed.'

The Mother Superior's work was kept a great secret. Monsieur le curé went to the convent three times a day and all those who met him wondered why he wore such a cheerful expression when the church continued to be profaned by inquisitive folk who came from all over. Ten days after the Mother Superior's visit, Monsieur Ledoux telephoned to a very important person who nearly fainted after hearing the curé's words. But that is another story. Two days after his telephone call, on Saturday night, about eleven o'clock, a Government truck stopped at the side door of the church and two workmen, under Monsieur Ledoux's direction, carefully carried fourteen packages from the church to the truck.

The next morning, at ten o'clock mass, the church witnessed the finest sight imaginable. The frightful Stations of the Cross had disappeared and were replaced by fourteen beautiful paintings in delicate colours, with handsome men, beautiful women, and a Christ that resembled Clark Gable.

The flock were filled with rapture that was soon transformed into deep piety. Many good ladies shed tears of joy and all the deeply affected parishioners raised grateful glances towards the altar. The church was exorcised and restored again to the bosom of the Lord. Monsieur Ledoux went up into the pulpit in triumph.

'My very dear brethren:

'Your joy moves me to the highest degree. The magnificent Stations of the Cross that you see before you are due to the brush of the Convent Mother Superior who deserves all our gratitude. As for the other Stations of the Cross, I thought those pictures were meant, after all, for experts. So I gave them to the Provincial Museum. My very dear brethren, let us rejoice in the Lord. Our church has resumed its march toward celebrity; it is the first in the city without pillars; the only one in America to possess an air-conditioning system, and the first in the world to make a gift of the Stations of the Cross to the Museum.'

The Legacy

MAVIS GALLANT (b. 1922)

LATE in the afternoon after Mrs. Boldescu's funeral, her four children returned to the shop on St. Eulalie Street, in Montreal, where they had lived when they were growing up. Victor, the youngest, drove quickly ahead, leaving, like an unfriendly country, the trampled grass of the cemetery and the sorrowing marble angels. Several blocks behind came Marina and the two older boys, Carol and Georgie, side by side in the long black car that had been hired for the day. Emptied of flowers, it still enclosed a sickly smell of lilies and of Carol's violet horseshoe, that had borne on a taffeta ribbon the words 'Good Luck to You, Mama.'

These three sat in silence, collapsed against the prickling plush of the cushions. Marina was thankful that Victor had driven up from Bloomfield, New Jersey, in his own three-year-old Buick. It would have been too much at this moment to have shared the drive with his American wife, Peggy Ann, hearing her voice carried out on the hot city air as she exclaimed over the slummy landscape and congratulated her husband on his plucky triumph over environment. Glancing at Carol and Georgie, Marina decided they might not have cared. Their triumph had been of a different nature. They stared out of the car at brick façades, seemingly neither moved nor offended by the stunning ugliness of the streets that had held their childhood. Sometimes one of them sighed, the comfortable respiration of one who has wept.

Remembering the funeral, Marina bent her head and traced a seam of her black linen suit where the dye had taken badly. Her brothers had cried with such abandon that they had commended themselves forever to Father Patenaude and every neighbourhood woman at church. 'Those bad pennies,' Marina had heard Father Patenaude say. 'Bad pennies they were, but they loved their mother. They did all of this, you know.'

By 'all of this', he meant the first-class funeral, the giant wreaths, the large plot they had purchased *in perpetuum*, to which their father's coffin, until now at rest in a less imposing cemetery, had been removed. There was space in the new plot for them all, including Victor's wife, who would, Marina thought, be grateful to know that thanks to her brother-in-laws' foresight her bones need not be turned out, for lack of burial space, until the Day of Judgement. A smaller tract, spattered with the delicate shadow of a weeping willow, had been set aside for Victor's children. He was the only one of her brothers who had married, and his as-yet-unconceived offspring were doomed to early extinction if one considered the space reserved for their remains. Marina could only imagine the vision of small crosses, sleeping babies, and praying cherubs that had been painted for Carol and Georgie. At the same time, she wondered what Victor felt about his brothers' prescience. His expression at the funeral had been one of controlled alarm, perhaps because of his wife, whose fidgetings and whisperings had disturbed even the rolling tide of Carol's and Georgie's grief. These two had stared hard at Peggy Ann on the edge of the grave, and Georgie had remarked that nothing worthy of life or death was likely to come out of that blond, skinny drink of water—which Marina took to be a reference to the babies' plot.

The way they had been grouped at the funeral— Marina unwillingly pressed between her weeping brothers, Victor a little apart—had seemed to her prophetic. The strain of her mother's long illness had made her superstitious. Visiting her mother at the hospital towards the end, she had seen an omen in every cloud, a message in a maple leaf that, on a treeless street, unexpectedly fell at her feet. Sometimes she felt that all of them had combined to kill their mother—Victor by behaving too well, the others by behaving badly, herself through the old-maidish asperity that had lately begun to creep through her conversation like an inkstain. She had even blamed Father Patenaude, remembering, in her mother's last moments, the cold comfort her mother had brought home from the confession box. Watching the final office of death, Marina waited for him to speak the words of reassurance her mother wanted; but nothing came, and Mrs. Boldescu was permitted to die without once being told that the mores of St. Eulalie Street and not her own inade-

quacies had permitted Victor's escape into a Protestant marriage, and Georgie's and Carol's being led
away again and again by the police.

Marina had quarrelled with Father Patenaude,
right then and there in the hospital, where all the
nurses could hear. The priest's thin face had been
pink with annoyance, and the embarrassment of
Carol and Georgie caused them, later on, to press
upon him a quite unnecessary cheque. His sins of
omission—they had possibly been caused, she now
realized, through nothing sterner than lack of
imagination—were for God and not Marina to judge,
Father Patenaude said.

Mrs. Boldescu had only by courtesy been attached
to his flock. She belonged by birth and breeding to
the Greek Catholic Church, that easy resting-place
between Byzantium and Rome. The Father was
French-Canadian, with the peasant distrust of all his
race for the exotic. Perhaps, Marina thought, he had
detected her mother's contempt for the pretty, pallid
Western saints, each with his crown of electric lights.
In the soaring exaltation of her self-reproach, Father
Patenaude must have sensed the richness of past
devotions, seen the bearded priest, the masculine
saints, the gold walls glittering behind the spears of
candlelight, the hanging ruby lamp swaying in the
thick incense-laden air. Victor's marriage had probably offended him most. Even Georgie and Carol,
for all their cosmic indifference to the affairs of their
sister and brother, had been offended.

However Mrs. Boldescu might deplore the devia-
tion of her youngest son, she trusted his good business sense. It was to Victor that the shop had been
left. Now, driving back to it for the final conference,
Marina could not have said if Carol and Georgie

minded. Their feelings towards each other as children had been so perfunctory that jealousy, then, would have struck any one of them as much too familiar to be comfortable. Of course, Carol and Georgie might have changed; meeting over their mother's bed, after a separation of years, they had had no time to sift their memories, even had they chosen to do anything so out of character. Their greeting had been in the matter-of-fact tones of consanguinity, and Marina had retired at once to a flower-banked corner of the hospital room, so that her brothers might have scope and space for their emotions.

The two had scarcely glanced at her again. Pale and tired, graced with only the ghost of a racial bloom they had long disavowed and now failed to recognize, Marina appeared to satisfy their image of a sister. To her, however, the first few moments had been webbed in strangeness, and she had watched her brothers as if they came from an alien land. They knelt by the bed, barred with the shadow of the hospital shade, their glossy, brilliantined heads bowed on clasped hands. Disliking their rings, their neckties, their easy tears, she remembered what had formed them, and saw behind her brothers a tunnel of mouldering corridors, the grey and stifling walls of reformatories named for saints. Summoning this image, like a repeated apology, she was able to pardon the violet horseshoe, the scene of distracted remorse on the brink of the grave. Their strangeness vanished; boredom took its place. She remembered at last what her brothers were like—not the sombre criminal of sociological texts, denied roller skates at a crucial age; still less the hero-villain of films; but simply men whose moments of megalomaniacal audacity were less depressing than their lack of common sense and taste. It was for their pleasure, she thought, that people manufactured ash trays shaped like little outhouses, that curly-haired little girls in sailor suits were taught to tap-dance, and night-club singers gave voice to 'Mother Machree' and 'Eli, Eli'.

Still, she thought, neither of them would have married into apostasy like Victor, nor flustered poor Father Patenaude by listening to his sermons as if analysing them for truth and intellectual content, as she herself did every week. The Father was horrified that the shop had been left to Victor instead of to them. 'It might have been their redemption', Marina had heard him say after the funeral, as she threaded her way out between the elaborate graves. 'And they were so good to her; they loved their mother.'

Certainly, their periodic descents on St. Eulalie Street had been more impressive than Victor's monthly cheque and letter, or Marina's faithful presence at Sunday dinner. Carol and Georgie, awash in the warm sea of Mother's Day, had left in their wake a refrigerator for the shop that could hold fifteen cases of beer, a radio inlaid with wood in a waterfall pattern, a silver brush and mirror with Old English initials, a shrine containing a Madonna with blue glass eyes, a pearl-and-diamond pin shaped like a daisy, a Persian lamb coat with summer storage prepaid for ten years, two porcelain lamps of shepherd and shepherdess persuasion, and finally the gift that for some reason appealed most strongly to Carol and Georgie—a sherry decanter and ten tiny glasses, each of which sounded a note of gratifying purity when struck with a knife.

The coat, the pin, the shrine, and the brush and

mirror had been left to Marina, who, luckily, bore the same initials. Carol and Georgie, awarded similar tokens, had been warm in their assurances that neither of them wanted the shop. No one, they said, was more suited to shopkeeping than Victor—a remark that offended Victor's wife into speechlessness for half an hour.

She and Victor were standing on the sidewalk in front of the shop when the hired car drew up to the curb. Peggy Ann, when she saw them, made exaggerated gestures of melting away in the sun, and then incomprehensible ones of laying her head on a pillow, which drew an unflattering remark from Georgie.

'Home,' Carol said, evidently without sarcasm, looking up and down the shadeless chasm of brick, here and there enlivened by Pepsi-Cola signs. A few children, sticky with popsicles, examined the New Jersey licence of Victor's Buick and then the shining splendour of the rented limousine. Not recognizing it, they turned back to the Buick and then suddenly scattered into the street, where Georgie had thrown a handful of quarters. Some of the children, Marina's pupils at a parochial school named for Saint Valerie the Martyr, glanced at her shyly.

'They look scared of you,' Georgie said. 'What do you do, beat them?'

'I'd like to,' Marina said.

'I'm sure she doesn't mean that,' Peggy Ann said, smiling.

A wide ribbon of crepe hung on the shop door, and green shades were pulled at door and window, bearing in shadow the semicircle of words on the glass, 'Rumania Fancy Groceries', and then in smaller letters, 'Mrs. Maria Boldescu.'

'How many times did I get up on a ladder and wash that window!' Georgie said, as if the memory were enchanting.

'Victor, too?' said Peggy Ann. 'I'll bet he was an old lazy.'

No one replied, and Victor fitted the key into the padlock while Carol, restless, hummed and executed a little dance step. The smell of the shut-up store moved out to meet them. Carol, with a look of concern, went at once to the cash register, but Marina had forestalled him. 'I took it all out when Mama took sick,' she said.

'Good idea,' said Georgie, approving.

'You were awfully clever to think of everything,' Peggy Ann said. 'Although it seems to me that, with crepe on the door and everything, no one would break in.' She stopped, as if she had uttered an indelicate thought, and went on rapidly, 'Oh, Victor, do look! What a sweet little store. Look at all the salami and my goodness, all the beer! Cases and cases!'

'We bought Mama the beer licence,' Carol said. He walked around, rattling change in his pocket.

'She must have been pleased,' said Peggy Ann. 'Victor, look at all the things—all the tins of soup, and the spaghetti.'

Marina, parting the blue chintz curtains at the end of the counter, moved into the kitchen behind the shop. She lifted her hand and, without glancing up, caught the string of an overhead light. Two doors, varnished to simulate oak, led off to the bedrooms—the one she had shared with her mother, until, at twenty-three, she had overcome her mother's objections to her having a place of her own, and the other room in which had slept, singly or together, the three boys. The kitchen window looked out on a fenced-in yard where Mrs. Boldescu had tried to grow vegetables and a few flowers, finally managing a tough and spiky grass. Marina opened the window and pushed back the shutters, admitting a shifting layer of soot. Weeds grew as high as the sill, and wild rhubarb, uncontrolled in this summer of illness, flourished along the fence. A breath of city air entered the room, and an old calendar bearing a picture of the shrine at St. Anne de Beaupré suddenly flapped on its pin. She straightened it, and then, from some remembered prudence, turned out the light.

Carol, who had come in behind her, glanced at the calendar and then at her. Then he said, 'Now that we're alone, tell me just one thing. Was that a nice funeral or wasn't it?'

'It was charming,' she said. 'It was nice that you and Georgie were both free for it at once.'

Carol laughed; evidently he expected this sour, womanly reprimand, and now that their mother was dead he would expect it still more from Marina. 'You ought to get married,' he said.

'Thanks. The boys I grew up with were all so charming.' She sat down, tipping her chair against the wall in a way her mother had disliked. She and Carol were alone as they had seldom been in childhood, able now to take stock of each other. Twenty, fifteen years before they had avoided each other like uncongenial castaways, each pursuing some elusive path that led away from St. Eulalie Street. Considering the way they had lived, crowded as peas in a pod, their privacy, she now thought, must have been a powerful act of will. In the darkening room, she saw herself ironing her middy blouse, the only one she owned, a book propped insecurely on the ironing board. Georgie and Carol came and went like cats, and Victor shouted outside in a game of kick-the-can. Again, she did her homework under the over-head light while Georgie and Carol, shut in their room for punishment, climbed out the window and were fetched home by the police. At last, her memory alighted on one shining summer with both the older boys 'away' (this was the only word Mrs. Boldescu had ever used) and Marina, afloat with happiness, saying to every customer in the shop, 'I'm going to France; have you heard? I'm going to France.'

'I'm *talking* to you,' said Carol. 'Don't judge all the boys you knew by me. Look at old Victor.'

'The pride of the street,' said Marina, remembering that summer.

'*Was* he?' said Peggy Ann. She stood in the doorway, holding back the curtains with either hand. 'I never get a thing out of him, about the store, or his childhood, or anything. Victor, do look at this room! It's just like a farm-house kitchen! And the adorable shrine. . . . Did your mother bring it from Rumania?'

'I bought that,' said Carol. He looked at it, troubled. 'Does it look foreign or something?' he said to Marina. 'It came from Boston.'

'I would have said Rumania,' said Peggy Ann. She sat down and smiled at the coal-and-wood stove.

'Well,' Victor said, smiling at them all. 'Well, the old place.' He dropped his cigarette on the floor and stepped on it.

'It's all yours now,' Georgie said. He sat down at the round table under the light, Carol beside him. Victor, after glancing about uncertainly, sat opposite, so that they appeared to face him like inquisitors. 'Yours,' Georgie repeated with finality.

'I wouldn't say that,' Victor said, unnecessarily straightening his necktie. 'I mean to say, I think Mama meant me to have it in trust, for the rest of you. My idea was—'

'We ought to have a drink,' Georgie said. He looked at Marina, who was sitting a little apart, as if to confound the prophecy of the graveyard that they would some day all lie together. 'Would it be all right, today I mean?'

'You're old enough to know if you want a drink,' Marina said. She had no intention of becoming the new matriarch of the family; but the others still waited, uncertain, and she finally found in a cupboard a bottle and the glasses that were her brother's special pride. 'Mama's brandy,' she said. 'Let's drink to Victor, the heir.'

'No,' said Victor, 'honestly, now, I keep trying to tell you. I'm not exactly the heir in the way you mean.' He was still talking as the others picked up their glasses and drank. Marina filled the glasses again and then sat away from the table, tipping her chair against the wall. The kitchen was cool after the flat glare of the cemetery and the stuffiness of the drive home. Sounds filtered through the shop from the street; a cat dropped from the fence and sniffed the wild rhubarb plants. The calendar, its shrine surrounded by a painted garland of leaves, stared at her from the opposite wall.

Her brothers talked on, Victor with some sustained and baffling delicacy retreating from the idea of his inheritance. Opening her eyes, Marina saw the calendar again and remembered the summer—the calendar bore its date—when she had looked at the room and thought, Soon I'll never have to see any of this again unless I want to.

'. . . would care to live here again,' Peggy Ann's high voice cut into a silence. Carol refilled the glasses, and the conversation rose. Peggy Ann leaned toward Marina and repeated, 'I was saying, we think we should keep the store and all, but I don't think Victor would care to live here again.'

'I can't imagine why not,' Marina said, looking thoughtfully at the torn linoleum. 'Mama thought it was Heaven. Where she grew up, they all lived in one room, along with a goat.'

'I know,' Peggy Ann said, distracted. 'It would make a difference in your point of view, wouldn't it? But you know, Victor left so young.'

'You might say that all of my brothers left young, one way or another,' said Marina. 'You might even say I was the patsy.' She handed her glass to Carol, who filled it, frowning a little; he did not like women to drink. 'You might even say,' Marina went on, 'that it was Victor's fault.'

'I don't see how it could be *Victor's* fault,' Peggy Ann said. 'He was so different from the rest, don't you think?' She folded her hands and regarded them primly. 'I mean to say, he's a C.P.A. now, and awfully well thought of. And we own our own home.'

'A triumph of education,' said Marina. 'The boy who went to college.' She finished her brandy and extended the glass, this time to Georgie.

'*You're* educated,' said Peggy Ann graciously. 'Victor's awfully proud of you. He tells everyone how you teach in the very same school you went to! It must be wonderful for those children, having someone from the same—who understands the sort of home background. I mean it must help you a lot, too, to have come from the same—' She sighed and looked about the room for succour. 'You must have liked your school,' she said at last. 'Victor hated his. Somebody beat him with a snow shovel or something.'

'I loved mine,' Marina said. She looked into the depths of her glass. '*Loved* it. I had a medal every week that said on it "Perfection". Just the same, I was ungrateful. I used to say to myself, Well, all told, I don't give a goddam if I never see these dark green walls again. . . . But then, as you say, the home background helps a lot. I look at my pupils, and I see nine little Carols for every little Victor. I don't see myself anywhere, though, so I guess there's nothing much between the Victors and the Carols.'

'Yes, I see what you mean,' said Peggy Ann. She slid back her white organdie cuff and glanced at her watch. 'The boys do talk on, don't they? Of course, they haven't seen each other for so long. . . . There's something we wanted to talk to you about, but I guess Victor's just never going to get around to it.' She smiled at Marina, wide-eyed, and went on. 'We wondered if you wouldn't want to have this little apartment for your own.'

'My own?'

'To live in,' Peggy Ann said. 'We thought it was such a good idea. You'd be right near your school, and you wouldn't have to pay any rent—only the heat and gas. If there *is* heat or gas,' she said uncertainly, glancing around. 'It was Victor's idea. He thinks the store belongs to the family and you should all get something out of it. Victor says you really deserve something, because you always took such good care of your mother, and you made so many sacrifices and everything.'

'Live here?' said Marina. She straightened her chair suddenly and put down her glass. 'Courtesy of Victor?' She looked across the table at her brother, and then, rising, unhooked the calendar from its pin. 'Victor—' she said, cutting through a remark of Carol's—'dear, sweet little Victor. Now that you're proprietor of Rumania Fancy Groceries, there's a keepsake I want you to take home. You might like to frame it.' She placed the calendar carefully before him on the table.

'I was just coming to that,' said Carol. 'I was just going to say—'

'Well, I said it,' said Marina, 'so shut up.'

'What a memory,' Georgie said. 'God—women and elephants!' He pulled the calendar towards him and read aloud, 'Nineteen thirty-seven.'

'The year I did not go to France,' said Marina. 'The year I had the scholarship to Grenoble.'

'I remember,' Victor said, smiling a little but glancing uneasily at his wife.

'You should,' his sister said. 'You damn well should remember.'

'Victor, what *is* it?' said Peggy Ann. 'You know, we should start back before dark.' She looked appealingly at Marina standing over the table.

Turning the calendar over, Georgie read, 'Sergeant-detectives Callahan and Vronsky, and two phone numbers. You ought to know them by heart, Vic.'

'Not exactly,' Victor said. He shook his head, amused and rueful. 'I'd rather just forget it.'

'We haven't,' Carol said. He pushed the calendar back towards his brother, staring at him.

'It's a long time ago now,' Victor said, relaxing in his chair as if the effort of leaving were hopeless. 'You sort of started it all, as I remember.'

'*I* started it,' said Marina. She moved around the table to stand between Carol and Georgie, the better to face Victor. 'I had the scholarship in France and Mama had the money to send me.'

'What has that—' Carol began, annoyed, glancing up at her.

'Women,' Georgie said. 'They always have to be first in the act. It was Carol started it.'

'Your brother-in-law, Carol,' said Marina to Peggy Ann, 'was arrested for some schoolboy prank one Sunday morning as the Boldescu family returned from church. Brother Georgie was "away", and after Carol's departure, amid the tears of his sister and mother—'

'Peggy Ann doesn't want to hear this,' Victor said.

'—a gun was discovered on a shelf in the shop, between two tins of chocolate empire biscuits,' said Marina. 'Which our mother took and with a rich Rumanian curse—'

'That part's a lie,' said Georgie, shouting.

'—flung as far as she could out the kitchen window. I guess her arm wasn't too good, because it fell in the snow by the fence.'

'She never swore in her life,' said Georgie. 'That's a lousy thing to say the day of her funeral.' His voice went hoarse, brandy having failed to restore the ravages of weeping.

'Since when do you drink so much, too?' Carol asked her. 'I'd like Mama to see you.' Virtuously, he pushed her empty glass out of her reach.

'In the spring,' said Marina, 'after the snow melted some, little brother Victor wandered out in the yard—'

'I was a kid,' Victor told his wife, who wore a faint, puzzled smile, as if the end of this could only be a wonderful joke.

'A stripling,' Marina said. 'Full of admiration for the pranks of his older brothers.'

'Tell the story or shut up,' said Carol.

'Found the little gun,' said Marina, 'all wet and rusty. Was it, Vic? I've forgotten that part. Anyway he took it to school and after making sure that every boy in class had admired it—'

'The dumb little bastard,' said Carol, looking moodily at the floor.

'—took it to a pawnshop that can be seen from the front door here, and, instead of pawning it, poked it into the stomach of a Mr. Levinson. It was noon—'

'Twelve o'clock noon,' said Carol. 'Jesus.'

'I don't believe this,' said Peggy Ann. Her eyebrows drew together, fumbling in her handbag, she found a handkerchief with a rolled tiny black border. 'I don't believe it.'

'As I said, it was noon,' said Marina. She clutched the back of Carol's chair, looking straight at Victor. 'Little children were passing by. Mr. Levinson called out to them—small girls in convent dresses, I think they were. Victor must have been nervous, because he took one look at the little girls and cut for home, running down the street waving the gun like a flag.'

'It isn't true,' said Peggy Ann, mopping her eyes. 'Anyway, if he ever did do anything wrong, he had plenty of example. I name no names.'

'Don't cry,' Victor told her. 'Marina's acting crazy. You heard what Carol said; she's an old maid. She always took sides against me, even though I never gave Mama half the trouble—'

'We know,' Georgie said, smiling. 'Mama knew it. That's why she left you the store. See?' He tapped Victor affectionately on the arm, and Victor jumped.

'I never took sides,' Marina said. 'I never knew any

of you were even alive.' She brushed lint from her dyed suit and glanced across at Peggy Ann's fragile and costly black summer frock. 'Do I finish this story, or not?'

'Tell it, tell it,' said Georgie. 'You don't have to make it a speech. Callahan and Vronsky came and told Mama for six hundred there'd be no charge. So Mama paid it, so that's the end.'

'They looked at Mama's bank-book,' Marina said. 'Vronsky had a girl my age at home, he said, just eighteen, so that meant he had to pat my behind. Mama had just the six, so they said that would do.'

'Six,' Georgie said. The injustice of the sum appeared to overwhelm him anew. 'For a first offence. They would have settled for one-fifty each in those days.'

'You weren't around to advise us,' Marina said. 'The nice thing was that we had it to give. As I said before, that was the year I didn't go any place.'

'For Christ's sake stop harping on that,' Victor said. 'Sure, Mama did it for me. Why wouldn't she want to keep me out of trouble? Any mother would've done it.'

'Any,' said Peggy Ann, looking around the table. 'Any mother.'

'You keep your snotty face out of this,' Carol said. He stood up, shouting. 'Do you know what she had to do to get six hundred, how many bottles of milk and pounds of butter and cans of soup she had to sell?' He leaned over the table, tipping a glass of brandy. It dripped on Peggy Ann's dress, and she began once more to cry.

Marina sat down, exhausted. 'It was Victor's insurance policy,' she said. 'We looked at it that way. They wrote their names on the back of the calendar.

They told Mama if he ever got in trouble again she should call them.'

'It was the only thing I ever did,' Victor told his wife, who pushed away his consoling hand. 'The only thing in my whole life.'

'Then we paid the money for nothing,' said Marina. 'It was your immunity. You should have kept on doing things, just for the hell of it. That's why Mama kept the calendar: insurance for Heaven on the front and on the back for this earth. She told Father Patenaude about it afterward, but he never saw the joke.'

'Never mind all that,' said Carol, impatient. 'Let's get this the hell over with. You got the store, Vic; now we want to know what you're going to do about this,' and he pointed again to the calendar.

'What can I do?' Victor said. 'What do you want me to do, turn myself in?' Gaining confidence, he pushed back his chair. 'It's crazy to even talk about it. We came back here to talk about the store. I thought that was settled.'

'Well, it isn't,' said Georgie. 'Mama left it to you, but there's a couple of guys who owe you six. You ought to collect it.'

'Collect it?' Victor said. He looked at Marina. 'Are you in this, too? You want me to go out and beat up a couple of middle-aged cops, old men? Make a lot of trouble? And for what? You know we'd never get that money back.'

'For Mama,' Carol said, sitting down.

'I never heard anything so crazy,' Peggy Ann said. 'Why should Victor get mixed up in all these old things?'

'If Mama had wanted it, she'd have said so in her life-time,' Victor said.

'She left you the shop,' Georgie said, 'and the calendar along with it.'

'How about it?' Victor asked Marina once more. 'Did you plan this together, to show me up in front of my wife? Or are you so jealous because Mama left it to me? Do you think I ought to make a lot of trouble for Mama's sake?'

'For mine,' Marina said, twisting her fingers. She did not look up.

'She's crazy,' Georgie said. 'Listen,' he told her, 'you'd better get married or something. Or something.'

'Honestly, Victor,' said Peggy Ann. 'It's too awful.'

'I know.' He stood up. 'Look,' he said, 'this damn place is no good to me. I only wanted it to keep it in the family for Mama's sake. But I give up. Wherever she is, she sees me now, and she knows I'm acting for the best.'

'You'd better not talk about where she is,' Carol said, glancing at the ceiling. 'Unless you do something before you die,' and he glanced at Peggy Ann.

'The hell with this,' Victor said. He drew the key to the shop from his pocket and placed it quietly on the table. 'We can't work anything out. You're all so jealous and—'

'And awful,' said Peggy Ann. 'Just awful.'

'Melodramatic,' Victor said firmly. 'As for Marina, she gets crazier every time I see her, crazier by the year. If she was so damn crazy to study in France, she could have taken a job and saved some money. She blames me because I got out and she never had the guts. You could have gone next year, or the next,' he told her.

'There was the war,' she said, still looking away.

'So I started the war,' Victor said. 'I sent Mama

money every month. I never gave her trouble, only
that once. The hell with it; I'm going. Come on,' he
told his wife, who stumbled after him between the
curtains, adjusting her hat.

'I'm sorry I met you under such circumstances,'
she paused to say to Marina. 'I imagine at heart
you're a very fine person.'

'Come on,' Victor said, and in a moment the front
door slammed behind them.

Peggy Ann had left her handkerchief on the table.
Carol looked at it and grunted. 'He deserves her,' he
remarked.

Marina looked around the room, now nearly dark.
Carol pulled the light cord, and the sickly ring of
yellow swayed back and forth on the walls. Marina
clutched the edge of her chair, in a sudden impulse
to run after Victor and away; but Carol, who had
picked up the key, now held it out to her.

'It's yours now,' he said. 'Yours, and in the family.'
He was smiling, and Georgie, a little behind him,
smiling, too.

'What for?' Marina said. She put her hands behind her. 'What am I supposed to do with it?'

'Keep it,' Carol said. 'Run the business. With the
beer licence it's a nice little business now. If you
want to fix up this place behind it, we'll kick in.'

'We figured it out,' Georgie said. 'Mama would
have wanted it. Victor's a rat. He doesn't deserve it.
Look at what he wouldn't do for Mama. He's only
a rat. But what about you? You can't teach forever,
and it doesn't look like you're going to get married.
So we set the thing up for you.'

'For *me*?' Marina said. 'For *me*?' Carol took her
hand and pressed the key into it.

'If you're still so crazy to go to France,' he said,

indulgent at the thought of her feminine whim, 'you could make enough in a year to close it up for a month next summer, maybe. Anyway, it's a hell of a lot more than you'll make as a teacher.'

He started to say something else, but Marina flung out her arm, almost striking him as she threw the key away. 'For me?' she cried again. 'I'm to live here?' She looked around as if to find, once more, the path away from St. Eulalie Street, the shifting and treacherous path that described a circle, and if her brothers, after the first movement, had not held her fast, she would have wrecked the room, thrown her chair out of the window, pulled the shrine from the wall, the plates from their shelves, wrenched the curtains from the nails that held them, and smashed every one of the ten tiny glasses that were her brothers' pride.

The Bully

JAMES REANEY (b. 1926)

As a child I lived on a farm not far from a small town called Partridge. In the countryside about Partridge, thin roads of gravel and dust slide in and out among the hollows and hills. As roads go, they certainly aren't very brave, for quite often they go round a hill instead of up it and even in the flattest places they will jog and hesitate absurdly. But then this latter tendency often comes from some blunder a surveying engineer made a hundred years ago. And although his mind has long ago dissolved, its forgetfulness still pushes the country people crooked where they might have gone straight.

Some of the farm-houses on these ill-planned roads are made of red brick and have large barns and great cement silos and soft large strawstacks behind them. And other farm-houses are not made of brick, but of frame and clap-board that gleam with the silver film unpainted wood attains after years of wild rain and shrill wind beating upon it. The house where I was born was such a place, and I remember that whenever it rained, from top to bottom the whole outside of the house would turn jet-black as if it were blushing in shame or anger.

Perhaps it blushed because of my father who was not a very good farmer. He was what is known as an afternoon farmer. He could never get out into the fields till about half-past eleven in the morning and he never seemed to be able to grow much of anything except buckwheat which as everyone knows is the lazy farmer's crop. If you could make a living out of playing checkers and talking, then my father would have made enough to send us all to college, but as it was he did make enough to keep us alive, to buy tea and coffee, cake and pie, boots and stockings, and a basket of peaches once every summer. So it's really hard to begrudge him a few games of checkers or a preference for talking instead of a preference for ploughing.

When I was six, my mother died of T.B. and I was brought up by my Aunt Coraline and by my two older sisters, Noreen and Kate. Noreen, the oldest of us, was a very husky, lively girl. She was really one of the liveliest girls I have ever seen. She rode every horse we had bare-back, sometimes not with a bridle at all but just by holding on to their manes. When she was fifteen, in a single day she wall-papered both our kitchen and our living-room. And when she was sixteen she helped my father draw in hay just like a hired man. When she was twelve she used to tease me an awful lot. Sometimes when she had teased me too much, I would store away scraps of food for days, and then go off down the side-road with the strong idea in my head that I was not going to come back. But then Noreen and Kate would run after me with tears in their eyes and, having persuaded me to throw away my large collection of breakfast toast crusts and agree to come back, they would both promise never to tease me again. Although Kate, goodness knows, had no need to promise that for she was always kind, would never have thought of teasing me. Kate was rather like me in being shy and in being rather weak. Noreen's strength and boldness made her despise Kate and me, but she was like us in some ways. For instance Noreen had a strange way of feeding the hens. Each night she would sprinkle the grain out on the ground in the shape of a letter or some other pattern, so that when the hens ate the grain, they were forced to spell out Noreen's initials or to form a cross and a circle. There were just enough hens to make this rather an interesting game. Sometimes, I know, Noreen spelt out whole sentences in this way, a letter or two each night, and I often wondered to whom she was writing up in the sky.

Aunt Coraline, who brought me up, was most of the time sick in bed and as a result was rather pettish and ill-tempered. In the summer time, she would spend most of the day in her room making bouquets out of any flowers we could bring her; even dandelions, Shepherd's 'Purse, or Queen Anne's Lace. She was very skilful at putting letters of the alphabet into a bouquet, with two kinds of flowers, you know, one for the letters and one for the background. Aunt Coraline's room was filled with all sorts of jars and bottles containing bouquets, some of them very ancient so that her room smelt up a bit, especially in the hot weather. She was the only one of us who had a room to herself. My father slept in the kitchen. Aunt Coraline's days were devoted to the medicine-bottle and the pill-box, making designs in bouquets, telling us stories, and bringing us up; her nights were spent in trying to get to sleep and crying softly to herself.

When we were children we never were worked to death, but still we didn't play or read books all of the time. In the summer we picked strawberries, currants, and raspberries. Sometimes we picked wild berries into milkpails for money, but after we had picked our pails full, before we could get the berries to the woman who had commissioned them, the berries would settle down in the pails and of course the woman would refuse then to pay what she had promised because we hadn't brought her full pails. Sometimes our father made us pick potato beetles off the potato plants. We would tap the plants on one side with a shingle and hold out a tin can on the other side to catch the potato bugs as they fell. And we went for cows and caught plough-horses for our father.

Every Saturday night we children all took turns bathing in the dish-pan and on Sundays, after Sunday-school, we would all sit out on the lawn and drink the lemonade that my father would make in a big glass pitcher. The lemonade was always slightly green and sour like the moon when it's high up in a summer sky. While we were drinking the lemonade, we would listen to our victrola gramophone which

Noreen would carry out of the house along with a collection of records. These were all very old, very thick records and their names were: *I Know Where the Flies Go*, *The Big Rock Candy Mountain*, *Hand Me Down My Walking Cane*, and a dialogue about some people in a boarding-house that went like this:

'Why can't you eat this soup?'

Various praising replies about the soup and its fine, fine qualities by all the fifteen members of the boarding-house. Then:

'So WHY can't you eat this soup?'

And the non-appreciative boarder replies:

'Because I ain't got a spoon.'

Even if no one laughed, and of course we always did, the Record Company had thoughtfully put in some laughter just to fill up the centre. Those Sunday afternoons are all gone now and if I had known I was never to spend any more like them, I would have spent them more slowly.

We began to grow up. Noreen did so gladly but Kate and I secretly hated to. We were much too weak to face things as they were. We were weak enough to prefer what we had been as children rather than what we saw people often grew up to be, people who worked all day at dull, senseless things and slept all night and worked all day and slept all night and so on until they died. I think Aunt Coraline must have felt the same when she was young and decided to solve the problem by being ill. Unfortunately for us, neither Kate nor I could quite bring ourselves to take this line. I don't know what Kate decided, but at the age of eleven I decided that school-teaching looked neither too boring nor too hard so a school-teacher I would be. It was my one chance to escape what my father had fallen into. To become a teacher one had to go to high school five years and go one year to Normal School. Two miles away in the town of Partridge there actually stood a high school.

It was not until the summer after I had passed my Entrance Examination that I began to feel rather frightened of the new life ahead of me. That spring, Noreen had gone into town to work for a lady as a housemaid. At my request, she went to look at the high school. It was situated right next the jail, and Noreen wrote home that of the two places she'd much rather go to the jail, even although they had just made the gates of the jail three feet higher. Of that summer I particularly remember one sultry Sunday afternoon in August when I walked listlessly out to the mail-box and, leaning against it, looked down the road in the general direction of town. The road went on past our house and then up a hill and then not over the top of the hill for it went crooked a bit, wavered and disappeared, somehow, on the other side. Somewhere on that road stood a huge building which would swallow me up for five years. Why I had ever wanted to leave all the familiar things around me, I could hardly understand. Why people had to grow up and leave home I could not understand either. I looked first at the road and then into the dull sky as I wondered at this. I tried to imagine what the high school would really be like, but all I could see or feel was a strong tide emerging from it to sweep me into something that would give me a good shaking up.

Early every morning, I walked into high school with my lunch-box and my school-books under my arm. And I walked home again at night. I have none of the textbooks now that were used at that school, for I sold them when I left. And I can't remember

very much about them except that the French book
was fat and blue. One took fifteen subjects in all:
Business Practice (in this you learned how to write
out cheques and pay electric light bills, a knowledge
that so far has been of no use to me); there was
English, Geography, Mathematics, French, Spelling,
History, Physical Training, Music, Art, Science (here
one was taught how to light a Bunsen Burner) and
there must have been other subjects for I'm sure
there were fifteen of them. I never got used to high
school. There were so many rooms, so many people,
so many teachers. The teachers were watchful as
heathen deities and it was painful to displease them.
Almost immediately I became the object of everyone's disgust and rage. The Geography teacher
growled at me, the English teacher stood me up in
corners. The History teacher denounced me as an
idiot. The French teacher cursed my accent. In
Physical Training I fell off innumerable parallel-
bars showing, as the instructor remarked, that I
could not and never would co-ordinate my mind with
my body. My platoon of the cadet corps discovered
that the only way to make progress possible in drill
was to place me deep in the centre of the ranks away
from all key positions. In Manual Training I broke
all sorts of precious saws and was soundly strapped
for something I did to the iron-lathe. For no reason
that I could see, the Art teacher went purple in the
face at me, took me out into the hall and struck my
defenceless hands with a leather thong. The French
teacher once put me out into the hall, a far worse
fate than that of being put in a corner, for the halls
were hourly stalked by the principal in search of
game; anyone found in the halls he took off with him
to his office where he administered a little something

calculated to keep the receiver out of the halls thereafter.

Frankly, I must have been, and I was, a simpleton, but I did the silly things I did mainly because everyone expected me to do them. Very slowly I began to be able to control myself and give at least some sort of right answer when questioned. Each night when I came home at first, Kate would ask me how I liked high school. I would reply as stoutly as I could that I was getting on all right. But gradually I did begin to get along not too badly and might have been a little happy if something not connected with my studies had not thrown me back into a deeper misery.

This new unhappiness had something to do with the place where those students who came from the country ate their lunch. This place was called a cafeteria and was divided into a girls' cafeteria and a boys' one. After about a month of coming to the boys' cafeteria to eat my lunch, I noticed that a certain young man (he couldn't be called a boy) always sat near me with his back to me at the next long table. The cafeteria was a basement room filled with three long tables and rows of wire-mended chairs. Now my lunch always included a small bottle of milk. The bottle had originally been a vinegar bottle and was very difficult to drink from unless you put your head away back and gulped it fast. One day when I had finished my sandwiches and was drinking my milk, he turned around and said quietly: 'Does baby like his bottle?'

I blushed and immediately stopped drinking. Then I waited until he would finish his lunch and go away. While I waited with downcast eyes and a face red with shame, I felt a furious rush of anger against

Kate and Aunt Coraline for sending milk for my lunch in a vinegar bottle. Finaly, I began to see that he had finished his lunch and was not going to leave until I did. I put the vinegar bottle back in my lunch-box and walked as quickly as I could out of the boys' cafeteria, upstairs into the classroom left open during the noon-hour so that the country people could study there. He followed me there and sat in the seat opposite me with what I managed to discover in the two times I looked at him, a derisive smile upon his face. He had a North American Indian face and complexion, with heavy lips, and he wore a dark green shirt. With him sitting beside me, I had no chance of ever getting the products of New Zealand and Australia off by heart and so I failed the Geography test we had that afternoon. Day after day he tormented me. He never hit me. He would always just stay close to me, commenting on how I ate my food or didn't drink my vinegar and once he pulled a chair from beneath me. Since our first meeting I never drank anything while he was near me. Between him and my friends the teachers, my life in first form at high school was a sort of Hell with too many tormenting fiends and not enough of me to go round so they could all get satisfaction. If I'd had the slightest spark of courage I'd have burnt the high school down at least.

At last, in the middle of November, I hit upon the plan of going over to the public library after I had eaten my lunch. Lots of other country students went there too. Most of them either giggled at magazines or hunted up art prints and photographs of classical sculpture on which they made obscene additions, or if more than usually clever, obscene comments. For over one happy week the Bully seemed to have lost me, for he did not appear at the library. Then I looked up from a dull book I was reading and there he was. He had my cap in his hand and would not give it back to me. How he had got hold of it I couldn't imagine. How I was to get it back from him, I couldn't imagine either. He must have given it back to me, I can't remember just how. Of course it wasn't the sort of hat anyone else wore, as you might expect. It was a toque, a red-and-white woollen one that Noreen used to wear. Every other boy at school wore a fedora or at least a helmet.

During the library period of my bullying he sat as close up against me as he could and whispered obscenities in my ear. After two weeks of this, being rather desperate, I did not go to the boys' cafeteria to eat my lunch but took my books and my lunch and went out into the streets. This was in early December and there was deep snow everywhere. I ran past the jail, down into the civic gardens, across the river, under a bridge, and down the other side of the river as fast as I could go. I had no idea where I was going to eat my lunch until I saw the town cemetery just ahead of me. It seemed fairly safe. I could eat my sandwiches under a tree and then keep warm by reading the inscriptions on gravestones and walking about.

The second day or the third, I discovered that the doors of the cemetery's mausoleum were open and that there were two benches inside where you can be buried in a marble pigeon-hole instead of the cold ground. To this place I came day after day, and I revelled in the morbid quiet of the place. I sat on one of the walnut benches and whispered irregular French verbs to myself or memorized the mineral resources of Turkey or the history of the Upper

Canada Rebellion. All around and all above me dead citizens lay in their coffins, their rings flashing in the darkness, their finger-nails grown long like white thin carrots, and the hair of the dead men grown out long and wild to their shoulders. No one ever disturbed me. People's finger-nails and hair do keep on growing after they're dead, you know. Aunt Coraline read it in a book.

No one ever disturbed me at the mausoleum. The wind howled about that dismal place but no other voice howled. Only once I had some trouble in getting the heavy doors open when the factory whistles blew and it was time to start walking back to school. I usually arrived back at school at twenty minutes after one. But one day the wind weakened the sound of the whistles and I arrived at school just at half-past one. If it had been allowed, I might have run in the girls' door and not been late. But it was not allowed and since the boys' door was at the other end of the building, by the time I had run to it, I was quite late and had to stay after four.

Just before Christmas they had an At Home at the school. The emphasis in pronouncing At Home is usually put on the AT. Everyone goes to the AT Home. The tickets are usually old tickets that weren't sold for last year's operetta, cut in half. Noreen forced me to take her because she wanted to see what an AT Home was like. She did not mind that I could not dance. She only wanted to sip at second-hand what she supposed to be the delightful joys of higher education. We first went into the rooms where school-work was exhibited. Noreen kept expecting some of my work to be up and kept being disappointed. I was very nervous with a paint-brush so none of my drawings were up in the art display. At the writing exhibit none of my writing was up. I had failed to master the free-hand stroke, although away from the writing teacher I could draw beautiful writing that looked as if it had been done by the freest hand imaginable. At the Geography exhibit not one of my charts of national resources had been pinned up. Noreen was heart-broken. I had learned not to care. For instance, almost everyone's window-stick got into the Manual Training show. Mine didn't because I had planed it down until it was about a quarter of an inch thick, and as the Manual Training teacher pointed out, it couldn't have held up a feather. But I didn't care.

Noreen and I went into the girls' gymnasium where we saw a short, brown-coloured movie that showed Dutch gardeners clipping hedges into the shapes of geese and chickens, ducks and peacocks. The Dutch gardeners cut away with their shears so fast that the ducks and peacocks seemed fairly to leap out of the hedges at you. Noreen and I wondered how these gardeners were going to keep employed if they carved up things that fast. Then we went into the boys' gym where young men stripped almost naked and covered with gold paint pretended to be statues. After watching them for a while Noreen and I went up to the Assembly Hall where dancing was in progress and young girls hovered shyly at the edge of the floor. Some of these shy young girls were dressed in handmade evening gowns that seemed to be made out of very thin mosquito netting coated with icing sugar. Noreen had one of her employer's old dresses on. It was certainly an old dress, made about 1932 I guess, for it had a hunch-back sack of cloth flying out of the middle of the back. Noreen, I know, thought she looked extremely distinctive. I only thought she looked extremely extraordinary.

And she did so want to dance. So we went up to the third floor and there Noreen tried to teach me how to dance in one lesson, but it was no use. She asked me to introduce her to some of my friends who danced. I had no friends but there was one boy who borrowed everything I owned almost daily. Here was a chance for him to repay me if he could dance. We soon captured him, but although Noreen clung tightly to him for a good deal of the evening and although we led him to the mouth of the Assembly Hall, all the time proclaiming quite loudly how nice it must be to dance, he didn't ask Noreen for a dance. So we went down into the basement to the Domestic Science Room where punch was being served and thin cookies with silver beads in the middle of them. There was a great crowd of people in the Domestic Science Room and before we knew it, he had given us the slip. Then Noreen said, 'Where do you eat your lunch? Kate was telling me how she makes it every night for you.'

I replied that I ate it in the boys' cafeteria.

'Oh, what's that? Come on. Show me.'

'It's not very interesting,' I said.

'But show me it. Show me it,' Noreen insisted stubbornly.

'It's down here,' I said.

We went past the furnace room.

'That's the furnace room, Noreen. There's the girls' cafeteria. Here's the—'

It was dark inside the boys' cafeteria and I felt along the wall just beside the door for a light button. I could hear someone climbing in one of the windows. Someone who didn't want to buy a ticket, I supposed. Probably someone who came here regularly at noon and thought of leaving a window open for himself. Before I could tell her not to, Noreen had found the light switch ahead of me and turned it on. The person climbing in the window turned out to be my friend the Bully. Like a wild animal he stared for a second at us and then jumped back through the window.

'Well, who on earth was that? asked Noreen.

'I don't know,' I said, trembling all over.

'Don't tremble like a leaf!' said Noreen scornfully. 'Why you look and act exactly like you'd seen a ghost. What was so frightening about him?'

'Nothing,' I said, leaning against the wall and putting my hand to my forehead. 'Nothing.'

The Christmas holidays were haunted for me by my fear of what would happen at school when I went back there after New Year's. But I never complained to my father or Aunt Coraline. They would have been only too glad to hear me say that I didn't want to go back. I must somehow stick it until the spring and the end of first form at least. But I knew that before the spring came the Bully would track me down, and if I met him once again I knew it would be the end of me. I remember in those Christmas holidays that I went walking a lot with Kate over the fields that were dead white with snow. I wished then that we might always do that. I told Kate about my unhappiness at high school and it drew us closer together. If I had told Noreen she would only have called me a silly fool and made me hate her. But Kate was always more sympathetic towards me.

The first morning when I was back at school I found a note in my desk. All it said was this: *I want to see you eating where you should eat today, baby.*

At noon I hid myself in the swarm of city students who were going home for lunch and arrived at the mausoleum by a round-about way. I couldn't get over the notion that someone was following me or watching me, which could easily have been true, since he had many friends.

I was just in the middle of eating my lunch. I was sitting on a bench in front of the Hon. Arthur P. Hingham's tomb. I saw the Bully trying to open the great doors to the mausoleum. But he couldn't seem to get them open. At last he did. All I can remember is seeing the advancing edge of the door for I toppled off the bench in a dead faint. By the time I came to it was half-past one so I started to walk home. My head ached violently as if someone had kicked it, which turned out to be the case, there being a red dent just below my left eye that turned blue after a few hours. On the way home that afternoon I had just reached a place in the road where you can see our house when I decided that I could not bear to go to high school any longer. So I went home and I told them that I had been expelled for walking in through the girls' door instead of the boys' door. They never doubted that this was true, so little did they know of high schools and their rules. Noreen doubted me, but by the time she heard about my being expelled it was too late to send me back. Aunt Coraline cried a bit over it all; my father told me the whole thing showed that I really belonged on the farm. Only Kate realized how much school had meant to me and how desperately I had tried to adapt myself to it.

That night as I lay in bed, while outside a cold strong river of wind roared about the house shaking everything and rattling the dishes in the cupboard downstairs, that night I dreamt three dreams. I have never been able to discover what they meant.

First I dreamt that Noreen was the Bully and that I caught her washing off her disguise in the water-trough in the yard. Then I dreamt I saw the Bully make love to Kate and she hugging and kissing him. The last dream I had was the longest of all. I dreamt that just before dawn I crept out of the house and went through the yard. And all the letters Noreen had ever made out of grain there while she was feeding the chickens had all sprouted up into green letters of grass and wheat. Someone touched me on the shoulder and said sadly, *I haven't got a spoon*, but I ran away without answering across the fields into the bush. There was a round pond there surrounded by a grove of young chokecherry trees. I pushed through these and came to the edge of the pond. There lay the Bully looking almost pitiful, his arms and legs bound with green ropes made out of nettles. He was drowned dead, half in the water and half out of it, but face up. And in the dim light of the dawn I knelt down and kissed him gently on the forehead.

The Haying

DOUGLAS SPETTIGUE (b. 1930)

MY father said sometimes a man comes to change his way of thinking. He said that just this morning when haying was still the same and he couldn't have known how it was going to be. Because this morning haying meant circles of haycocks in a sunny field, clover smells and dust motes in the barn. But Van came back at the end of the morning, wanting a job

*again, and haying is different now. Now it means
staring out hard at the rain and getting straight in
your mind how it used to be but not wanting to think
how it is.*

We had started as soon as the dew was off the hay
and had already got two loads in before Van came.
I drove and my father walked along beside and
pitched on. I could tell how long to stop each time
without even looking because my father always took
three forkfuls to a haycock. When it was piled too
high on the wagon my father would climb up and
take the reins and I would lie out flat in the hay
while he drove the team up to the barn. I would
keep my eyes closed and guess where we were by the
sounds. First there would be the soft puffy noise of
their hoofs on the sand coming out of the lane and
then the hard pounding when we came through the
gate by the barn; then the load would tip up at the
front until I would think I was going to fall right off
and then just in time there would be the really loud
booming on the barn floor when the team would
level in and stop fast with their noses to the boards
at the end. I would slide down between the load and
the loft to unhitch them and bring them around one
at a time past the wagon and hitch them to the
pulley rope at the big door before my father was
ready with the unloading fork. When he had the
fork clamped in the load I would drive out the team
to pull up the pile of hay to the mow. I could do
that without looking, too, because that was the
way we always did it. My father said it was the best
way.

We were starting the third load when I said,
'There's Van,' since I saw him first, and I stopped
the team.

'Go on,' my father said, 'He's got a hundred yards to come yet.'

We went on working for fear of rain and my father talked out loud which meant he was surprised and trying to get straightened around. He said:

'Van couldn't have done so well in town or we wouldn't be seeing him again. I figured he'd find they didn't need an upholsterer in Orangeville but I'm surprised he held out so long. Well, we'll see if he's learned anything. Sometimes a man comes to change his way of thinking.'

I remember how he said it and what else he said before Van came near. And I agreed because I didn't care for Van either but I figured we ought to keep him for the haying. I said so to my father and he said yes, that was what we would do. Because we wouldn't want him around in winter, he said, with a temper like his. Sooner or later he would burn the barn down, my father said.

If only he had. If he had just burned down the barn so that now I couldn't be sitting at the big door and looking out at the rain. So I couldn't see my mother running out to the road and so there wouldn't be anything behind me in the loft.

Van was thin. When he came up to us he leaned against the wagon rack, staring at the horses, the field, and the sky and not saying a word, maybe figuring everything looked the way it was.

'We weren't counting on you for today, Van,' my father told him, and that was all he said. Then he sent me to the barn for a fork and to the house to let my mother know for dinner.

My mother didn't say much. She didn't want Van back but she knew my father needed help with the haying.

'I can set another place as easy as not,' she said, 'so it makes no difference to me. But I favour leaving well enough alone as your father knows, and you can tell him he won't get all his hay in today anyhow because it's going to storm.'

Now she is at the end of the lane, just going out the gate, and not caring about the storm, I guess, or about anything except the change.

With Van helping us we could take a bigger load but I didn't like it with Van. My father built while Van pitched on and then after a while they changed because Van wasn't so strong as my father even though my father was sick at his heart. Van pitched up fast, with the sweat sticking the hair to his forehead until he had to lean against the wagon and my father said:

'Here, you and me'll trade places, Van,' not thinking about his heart. That was how my father was.

But they couldn't trade places. Now maybe they could; now it doesn't matter any. But I mean working, they couldn't ever trade places. My father worked steady and in the easy way he showed me what to do. Van was jerky and excited. He would dig into a haycock as if to take it all up at once but then he couldn't and he would lose half. If he had gone at it the way my father told him he would have liked it more.

'Take it easy,' my father would say, but Van never seemed to hear. He understood all right, but he pretended not to hear.

He was that way from the start. When my father turned out to be sick last year we wrote and asked them for a man. At first we didn't want a foreigner until we figured out the saving. But we had more work than enough for my father and me and it couldn't have made any difference to my mother so we took him.

I don't know much about him. He came from different places and I think he had been a German soldier in the war and after that a furniture man. He didn't know much English so we seldom talked to him but my father said he knew a lot of other languages. All but the right one, my father said. We called him Van because you couldn't pronounce his real name.

I guess Van talked some while I was up at the house because washing up before dinner my father told me where he'd been. Van couldn't find the sort of work he had wanted in Orangeville so he had taken odd jobs. But he kept looking around, my father said, trying all winter to get into a furniture place, when he couldn't even hold the jobs he got. He would start and stop and make the foremen mad, thinking he was better than they were for all his languages. But not talking to them in a language they could understand. Saving it all up inside him like holding your foot against a stream and then letting it go all at once.

My mother isn't in sight. There is a clump of elms half way to Andersons' and she must be there. I can't see her from the barn but I know she is there, running in the wet and telling herself out loud what to say. She will go to Andersons' because they are the closest neighbours. But they warned us about Van so there won't be much to explain. We just couldn't tell beforehand and he was cheaper.

The rain falls and falls and falls and the sky is no lighter. The rain smell mixes in with the fresh hay, filling up the whole barn until the drumming and the trickling and the smell are all the same.

In good weather I jump off the rafters into the hay. The sun comes through the cracks where the boards don't fit together and where the dust motes get in the way they make beams across the barn thick enough to walk on. And where they land on the hay they make bright lines and bright white circles from the knot-holes even though the hay is greeny brown. When you jump on them they move and splash across you but you can't blot them out. Only if the sky clouds over, then they blot out.

Van came half-way up the ladder before I saw him. I was jumping in the hay after dinner because the horses were already fed and my father hadn't come out yet. I had jumped and when I rolled over and sat up there was Van on the ladder looking at me through the rungs.

I didn't want him because he didn't belong in our loft and because he looked at me the way he did. It was the same look he had when my mother asked him one time if he had a wife and you could see him running it over in his mind before he made a zoom with his hand like a bomber-plane and never said yes or no. But their letter said he was a widower which means he did have and he could just as easy have said. This time the look was the same only more of it, somehow, like when rain comes harder on the roof and you wait for the thunder to follow.

'Come and jump, Van,' I invited him, knowing he would say no.

He just shook his head and stayed on the ladder, which spoiled the jumping because it's no good when somebody is watching. I didn't know if he wanted to jump and couldn't or if he wanted to talk and couldn't do that, either.

So I asked him, 'What did you come back for, Van?'

He took time the way an old man does before he let it come and then it would have been funny to hear him trying to say it all and making circles with his hands, except for the look.

'I don't get a job,' he said. 'I go this place and that place. Nobody wants upholster. They don't want me in the city; you don't want me here. I got no place to go, no place to stay. What should I do?'

'I am here already two years. When I come to this country, they say I don't need the English, don't need the money. They say I need only the head and the hands. But they don't let me be upholster. Nobody wants upholster.

'You don't want me. You don't want to know I am alive. You keep me for the haying, I know. Then I am done. Then you forget. Is the sun maybe not so bright when I am alive? Is your hay maybe too tough when I am alive? No. It don't hurt you to take me in. But you got to live alone. O.K., you live alone. You do what you like. Cut your hay like you always did. Stay by yourself if you can. You and nobody else.'

'My father is coming,' I said. I was afraid of Van.

The horses were ready and we went right off to the field. I drove and Van walked beside the wagon where I could look down at him sometimes because I couldn't tell the timing so well with him and my father pushing us now, looking anxious at the sky. We worked hard. All you could hear were the harness creaking and the rustling sounds of the hay.

Van seemed relieved when the clouds came, as though he'd been waiting for them, and it not being his hay to spoil. He wanted to get the wagon in quick and not wait till it was full.

'It'll go around us,' my father said and went right on building the load.

There's something about racing a storm in a hay field that you feel but can't talk about. There's something about a storm any time but it's stronger when you're haying. You want to do tremendous things and the driving and the pitching and the building all fit together and even the horses get eager and harder to hold. Van swung the hay up faster, too. But when the wagon went ahead you could see him stop to look back across the field where the new clover was already showing silver in the wind and the big yellow-winged grasshoppers were buzzing around and the smell of drying hay was piling up until you choked with it and wanted to cry. Maybe Van wanted to cry; maybe he was all filled up with it, too. Or maybe he just thought it would blow the haycocks down and then there wouldn't be any haying anymore and that was all he cared.

I've heard my father say that some men can't imagine rain when there's sunshine or sun when the sky is grey. Van was that kind. Maybe it all happened because it's raining today and he couldn't see that tomorrow it wouldn't be raining because the sun always shines again after. It was the same down at the crick last summer when I wanted him to make me a boat.

'Boat,' I said, showing him with my hands.

Van said, 'Too small,' meaning that the crick was dried up to a trickle and to mud cakes on the white stones. I told him how that was just for August and how in the fall it would fill up again and be lots big for a boat.

'It's the same every year,' I told him but Van couldn't understand things going on the same like

we could. Before today. Everything before today.

*It's hard to think away from it, from Van and my
father and mother when they keep crowding in. It's
being in the barn with him that does it, and looking
toward the house.*

Nobody is coming from Andersons' yet.

Going up the lane Van walked and my father and
I were on the load where we always ride. Van used
to ride on the tail-board which is the bumpiest place
but today we were going too fast. The really black
part of the storm, the part that had the thunder and
the lightning streaks in it, went on past us to the
north and we got the side part that spreads out over
you in plain grey and looks hazy at the edges when
you see it against the blue. Lying on the load is the
best place to watch.

It spread over us maybe faster than my father
thought, though mostly he could tell about clouds,
because he never usually drives the team so hard.
Before we got to the gate going into the barn-yard
the sky was all grey and in the swirls of dust the
wind picked up you could feel those first big drops
that catch you off guard no matter how long you've
seen them coming and don't seem to be really rain
at all. We thumped on to the threshing floor with
the team sounding like a whole army of horses in the
nearly empty barn and by the time I had them out
to the door and hitched on to the pulley rope you
could hear it drumming on the roof. I guess that was
the first time I ever noticed my father to be wrong.

'We can take off half a load,' he said, 'and the rest
will stand over night.' He drew down the big hay-
fork where it hung from the track beam and drove
it into the load and clamped it there. Then we waited,

my father up on the load where it was half dark and heavy and me at the threshing door with the team, holding their heads and watching Van come into the yard and over to the ramp.

He wasn't minding the rain. He was taking his time, head-down so the rain showed shiny on his hair, scuffing up the dry dirt from underneath and whistling towards his boots. I had never heard Van whistle before; I don't see how he could have wanted to then. Even so it wasn't my father's kind of whistle, clear and high and glad. It was low and soft and lonely. It was funny—I don't know how. He came whistling right past me without looking and the horses cocked their ears. It wasn't so much a rainy day whistle as a fall one, like when you go off to the bush alone, and wander about not knowing what to do with yourself, wanting something awfully bad and not being able to find it. It isn't hickory nuts you're after and it isn't old puff-balls, but it's something, you don't know what.

My father told him to go up into the mow and roll back the loads that were there. Then he hollered for me to go and I clucked to the team and then we were out in the rain. The fork took it up all right. You can tell by the way the pulley rope comes out easily at first and then it suddenly comes tight and lifts off the ground and the horses bend their necks a bit to take the weight. Then right away it goes slack again and you know the fork is on the ridge track and racing across over the mow. You turn the team and come back on the run, taking up the rope behind you.

One run and the rope was greasy with mud and rain-soaked hayseeds. Maybe that was what took the fun out of it or maybe it was just the sound of rain drumming on the roof and spilling off the eaves. Because rain is nice in a way and most times you would take it as all right but still it makes you quiet and readier to sit and think than to run around. And today it hurts to think.

There is Andersons' Ford coming past the elm trees, coming fast, and noisy enough to hear as far as me. 'We told you', they'll say. And they did, but they didn't really see, not any more than we did. And besides, we thought when he went he was gone for good.

My mother had got him to put a cover on her parlour chair. He came into the parlour while we looked at it and Mrs. Anderson was there. He wouldn't touch the cover with his hands though they weren't nearly so brown under the nails as mine. He stood close by the chair so everybody would know who did it but Mrs. Anderson said,

'That's a real fine cover, Vera,' to my mother. And then to Van she said,

'Are you an upholsterer?'

So my mother had to explain, 'No, he's our hired man.'

That was when Van left. I still remember his face when he went out and they all noticed it too because Mrs. Anderson warned us he looked like a bad one. But he didn't need to go, we said then. He was our hired man and we only let him do the chair to please him.

The Ford is in the yard now. They are all in the house and the car door is open in the rain. It comes down steady and straight in lines across the threshing door and the drumming never slackens on the roof.

After the first forkful I had turned the team

around and pulled the rope back through the pulley, watching the little rivers on the ramp and waiting for my father to holler. But before he hollered I heard him say:

'You'll never get it rolled back that way. You and me'll trade places, Van.'

So I fed handfuls of hay to the horses to give my father time to get into the loft and Van time to fix the hay-fork into the load. When Van hollered I clucked to the team and we went down the ramp.

It pulled, but it didn't pull heavy and the horses noticed the difference. I had to speak sharp to them and right away I knew something was wrong. I whoaed the team and heard my father whoa once and the way he did made me run back up the ramp.

My father came by me and the look on his face was the queerest you ever saw. It was saggy, his cheeks and his jaw all loose and his whole face an awful grey. Not the grey colour of rain or of the sky but the stone grey of old foundations where the filling has rotted loose and crumpled away.

He went right past me toward the house and soon my mother came out and went down the lane. And here in the barn I took a peek up in the shadows toward the mow where the dark and the drumming and the smell of hay all mixed together and when my eyes could see what was there I went back and brought the team in out of the rain and took off their bridles. Then I sat down and waited, trying hard to see it all straight at last, the way it was and the way it will have to be.

My mother and Mr. Anderson and Harold Anderson are coming out, the men slouched over in their coats and my mother not caring about the rain. They come up the ramp and the men don't look at me.

They stare at the loft a while, not talking, and then Harold climbs up on the wagon and now I turn and watch. He pulls the trip-rope but it doesn't trip because there is no hay on the fork. He pulls hard and the long thing that hangs below the fork sways and moves with the rope because the rope is knotted about its neck. It swings high up there in the nearly dark, where the hay smell is sweetest and the rain is closest on the roof. Then they lower him down to our wagon.

My mother doesn't go over to where they are pulling on the rope. She stops at the door and she is all muddy and splashed.

'You better come up to your father,' she says, but she says it sharp and dry like old hay that has been too long in the barn and has no more green in it.

I don't move any, sitting on the threshing floor and looking out at the rain.

'How is he?' I asked her and my voice doesn't sound right either.

'You better come to the house,' she says and then all at once she is down on her knees in front of me on the floor.

'Don't do anything bad,' she is saying, taking hold of my shoulders and shaking back and forth. She says:

'Don't do anything bad.'

But I won't do anything bad. There isn't anything bad to do, or anything good. There is just seeing we were wrong, that's all, and wanting not to be here any more. Because we didn't like him in the good weather and we drove him away. But Van came back to us with the rain and haying looks different, now.

The Time of Death

ALICE MUNRO (b. 1931)

AFTERWARDS Leona Parry lay on the couch, with a quilt around her, and the women kept stoking the fire although the kitchen was very hot, and no one turned the light on. Leona drank some tea and refused to eat and talked, beginning like this, in a voice that was querulous and insistent but not yet hysterical: I tell you, I wasn't out of this house twenty minutes—

(Three-quarters of an hour, Mrs. McGee thought, but she did not say so, not at this time. But she remembered, because there were three radio serials she was trying to listen to, she listened to every day, and she couldn't listen, Leona was there in her kitchen going on and on about Patricia. Leona was sewing this cowgirl outfit for Patricia on Mrs. McGee's sewing-machine; she raced the machine and she pulled the thread straight out to break it instead of pulling it back although Mrs. McGee had told her don't do that it's liable to break the needle. Patricia was going to be dressed like a cowgirl that night when she sang at a concert up in Priorsville, she was singing three western pieces. She sang with the Maitland Valley Entertainers, who went all around the countryside giving concerts and playing for dances; Patricia was introduced as the Little Sweetheart of Maitland Valley, the Baby Blonde, the Pint-size Kiddie with the Great Big Voice. Leona had started her singing, in public that is, when she was three years old.

Never was ascared once, Leona said, leaning forward with a jerky pressure on the pedal, her kimono fallen open to show her lean brown-freckled chest, her slack breasts in the pinky-grey night-gown. It just comes natural to her to perform. She don't care, it could be the King of England listening, she'd get up and sing her piece, and when she's through singing she'd sit down, that's the way she is. . . . She's even got a good name for a singer, Patricia Parry, doesn't that sound like you just hear it announced over the air? Another thing is natural blonde hair. I have to do it up in rags every night of her life but that real natural blonde is a lot scarcer than natural curly. It don't get dark, there's that strain of natural blondes in my family don't get dark—My cousin I told you about, won the Miss St. Catharine's 1936, she was one, my aunt that died.)

Mrs. McGee did not say, and Leona said firmly: Twenty minutes. And the last thing I said as I went out the door of this house was you keep an eye on the kids! She's nine years old isn't she? I'm just going to run over to Mrs. McGee's sew up this outfit, keep an eye on the kids! And I went out the door and down the steps and down to the end of the garden and just as I took the hook off the gate something stopped me, I thought, *something's wrong!* What's wrong? I said to myself. I stood there and I looked back at the garden, and all I could see was the cornstalks standing and the cabbages there frozen, we never got them in this year, and I looked up and down the road and all I could see there was Mundy's old hound laying out in front of their place, no cars comin' one way or the other and the yards all empty it was cold I guess and no kids playin' out—And I thought, My Lord, maybe I got my days mixed up and this isn't Saturday morning it's some special day I forgot about—Then I thought all it was was the snow coming I could feel in the air, and you know how cold it was, the puddles in the road was all turned to ice and splintered up—but it didn't snow, did it, it hasn't snowed yet—And I run across the road then over to Mrs. McGee's and up her front steps and she says, Leona, What's the matter, you look so white, she says—

Mrs. McGee heard this too, and said nothing, because it was not a time for any sort of accuracy. Leona's voice had gone higher and higher as she talked and any time now she might break off and begin to scream: Don't let that kid come near me, don't let me see her, I don't trust myself! Every curl I put in her head myself I'd pull it out by the roots I could get my hands on her—And the women in the kitchen would crowd around the couch, their big bodies indistinct in the half-dark, their faces looming pale and heavy, hung with the ritual-masks of mourning and compassion. Now lay down, they would say, in the stately tones of ritual-soothing, lay down, Leona, she ain't here, it's all right—

And the girl from the Salvation Army would say, in her chill gentle voice, You must forgive her, Mrs. Parry, she is only a child—Softly the Salvation Army girl would say, It is God's will, we do not understand. The older Salvation Army woman, with the oily sallow face and the deep, almost masculine voice, said, In the garden of Heaven the children bloom like flowers. God needed another flower for his garden and he took your child. Sister, you should thank Him and be glad—

The women from Mrs. McGee's church were uneasy when the Salvation Army women spoke, because they could not dispute what they said and they could not say Religious Things themselves. They went on making tea and buttering muffins, which sat on the table untasted because Leona would not take them and the others felt it would not be right to eat unless she did. All the women except the two from the Army wept from time to time; Mrs. McGee, a woman heavy-breasted and childless, wept almost continuously. Leona drew up her knees and rocked herself back and forth as she wept, and threw her head down and then back (some of them noticed, with a slightly guilty feeling, that there were lines of dirt on her neck) and grew quiet again for a while and said something like: That one I nursed till he was ten months old, nobody can say I didn't take good care of him, I always said he was the best one of them all—

In the dark overheated kitchen there was a feeling of solemn tenderness, of humility before this scrawny, unwashed, unliked and desolate Leona. The women there together felt the dignity of this sorrow in their maternal flesh, they kept it jealously among them like a tribal mystery. When the men came in— the father, a cousin, a neighbour, bringing a load of wood asking shamefacedly for something to eat— they were at once aware of this exalted and alien sisterhood among their women, and they were disturbed; they went out and said to the other men: Yeah, they're still at it. The father, a little drunk, and belligerent, because he felt that something was expected of him and he was not equal to it, it was not fair, said, Yeah, that don't do Benny any good, bawl their eyes out—

George and Irene had been playing their cutout

game, cutting things out of the catalogue. They had this family they had cut out of the catalogue, and they were cutting out clothes for them, and things for the house they lived in, and for their farm, because they lived on a big farm. Patricia watched them cutting and she said, Look at the way you kids cut! Lookit all the white around the edges! How are you going to put those clothes on, she said, you didn't even cut any fold-over things. She took the scissors and cut very neatly, not leaving any white around the edges; her pale shrewd little face was bent to one side, her lips bitten together. She did things the way a grownup does—carefully, seriously, and matter-of-factly. She did not pretend things. She did not even play at being a singer, though she was going to be a singer when she grew up, she was going to sing on the radio or go in the movies. She liked to look at movie magazines and magazines with pictures of clothes and rooms in them; she liked to look in the windows of nice houses up-town and to watch the ladies who lived in them and listen to the way they talked.

Benny was trying to climb up on the couch. He grabbed at the catalogue and Irene slapped his hand; he began to whimper. Patricia picked him up competently and carried him to the chair by the window, saying absent-mindedly, Bow-wow, Benny see bow-wow, bow-wow—

Bow-wow? said Benny interrogatively as she put him on the chair. Benny was eighteen months old and the only words he could say were Bow-wow and Bram. Bram was for the scissor-sharpening man who came along the road about once a month; Benny remembered him when he came, and ran out to meet him on the road. Other little kids only thirteen, fourteen months old, knew more words than Benny, and could do things like waving bye-bye and clapping their hands, and most of them were cuter to look at. Benny was long and bony and his face was like his father's—pale, mute, and unexpectant, so that you could see it already underneath a soiled peaked cap. But he was good; he would stand for hours just looking out of the window, saying, Bowwow, bow-wow, now in a low questioning tone, and now crooningly, stroking his hands down the windowpane. He liked you to pick him up and hold him like a little baby; he would lie looking up and smiling, with a little timidity and misgiving. Patricia knew he was stupid; she hated stupid things. He was the only stupid thing she did not hate; once in a while she looked at him and felt tired and sad, she did not know why. She would go and wipe his nose, expertly and impersonally; sometimes she talked to him, trying to get him to repeat words, saying anxiously, Hi, Benny, *Hi*, and he would look at her and smile in his slow dubious way. That gave her this feeling; it was an uncomfortable feeling and she would go away and leave him, she would go and look at a movie magazine.

She had had a cup of tea and part of a sugar-bun for breakfast; now she was hungry. She rummaged among the dirty dishes and the bread wrappings and puddles of milk and porridge on the kitchen table; she picked up a bun, but it was sopping with milk and she threw it down again.

This place stinks, she said. She kicked at a crust of porridge that had dried on the linoleum. Lookit that, she said. Lookit *that*! What's it always a mess around here for? She walked around kicking at things dispiritedly, with a pinched sullen face. Then she got the scrub-pail from under the sink, and a dipper, and she began to dip water from the reservoir of the stove.

I'm going to clean this place up, she said loudly. It never gets cleaned up like other places. The first thing I'm going to do I'm going to scrub the floor and you kids have to help me—

She put the pail on the stove.

That water is hot to start with, Irene said.

It's not hot enough. It's got to be good and boiling hot. I seen Mrs. McGee scrub *her* floor.

They stayed at Mrs. McGee's all night. They had been over there since before the ambulance came. They saw Leona and Mrs. McGee and the other neighbours start to pull off Benny's clothes and parts of his skin seemed to be actually coming off too, and Benny was making a noise not like crying, a noise like a dog made after its hind parts were run over by a car, but worse and louder—And Mrs. McGee cried to them, Go away, go away from here! Go over to my place! After the ambulance had come and taken Benny away she came over and told them that Benny was going to the hospital for a while, and they were going to stay at her place. She gave them bread and peanut butter and bread and strawberry jam.

The bed they slept in had a feather tick and smooth ironed sheets; the blankets were pale and fluffy and smelled faintly of mothballs. On top of everything else was a Star-of-Bethlehem quilt; they knew it was called that because when they were getting ready for bed Patricia said, My, what a beautiful quilt! and Mrs. McGee, looking surprised and distracted, said, Oh, yes, that is a Star-of-Bethlehem—

Patricia was very polite in Mrs. McGee's house. It

was not as nice as some of the houses up-town but it was a brick bungalow with an imitation-marble fireplace and wine brocade curtains and large ferns in baskets; it was not like the other houses out along the highway. Mr. McGee did not just work in the mill like the other men; he had a store.

George and Irene were so shy and alarmed in this house that they could not answer when they were spoken to.

They all woke very early; they lay on their backs, uneasy between the fresh sheets, and watched the room getting light. This room had mauve silk curtains and venetian blinds and mauve and yellow roses on the wall-paper; it was the guest-room. Patricia said, We slept in the guest-room.

I have to go, George said.

Well you can't, said Patricia. You have to wait till we hear them get up.

Why?

You'd make too much noise. You have to go past their door to get to the bath-room and you'd wake them up, it's not polite.

Irene said, See if there is a pot under the bed.

They got a bath-room here they don't have any old pots, Patricia whispered angrily. What would they have a stinking old pot for?

George said stolidly, Well if you don't let me go 'm going to pee the bed.

Patricia got up and tip-toed to the dresser and got a big china vase. When George had gone she opened the window very slowly with hardly any creaking and emptied the vase and dried it out with Irene's underpants.

Now, she said, you kids shut up and lay still. Don't talk out loud just whisper.

George whispered, Is Benny still in the hospital?

Yes he is, said Patricia shortly.

Is he going to die?

I told you a hundred times, no.

Is he?

No! Just his skin got burnt, he didn't get burnt inside. He isn't going to die of a little bit of burnt skin is he? Don't talk so loud—

Irene began to twist her head into the pillow.

What's the matter with you? Patricia said.

He cried awful, Irene said, her face in the pillow.

Well it hurt, that's why he cried. When they got him to the hospital they gave him some stuff that made it stop hurting.

How do you know? said George.

I know.

They were quiet for a while, and then Patricia said, I never in my life heard of anybody that died of a burnt skin. Your whole skin could be burnt off it wouldn't matter you would just grow another. Irene stop crying, shut up—

Patricia lay quite still, looking straight up at the ceiling, her sharp little profile white against the mauve silk curtains of Mrs. McGee's guest-room.

For breakfast they had grapefruit, which they had not tasted before, and cornflakes and toast and jam. Patricia watched George and Irene and snapped at them: Say please! Say thank-you! She said to Mr. and Mrs. McGee, I wouldn't be surprised if it snowed today, would you?

But they did not answer. Mrs. McGee's face was swollen. After breakfast she said, Don't get up, children, listen to me—Your little brother—

Irene began to cry and that started George crying too; he said sobbingly, triumphantly to Patricia, He did so die, he did *so*! Patricia did not answer. *It's her fault*, George sobbed, and Mrs. McGee said, Oh, no, oh, no! But Patricia sat still, with her face wary and polite. She did not say anything until the crying had died down a little and Mrs. McGee got up sighing and began to clear the table. Then she offered to help with the dishes.

The women of Mrs. McGee's church had decided to buy the children new shoes for the funeral. Patricia was not going to the funeral because Leona still said she did not want to see her again as long as she lived; but she was to get new shoes too; the women felt it would be unkind to leave her out. Mrs. McGee took the three of them down to the shoe-store and explained to the man who owned it; they stood together nodding and whispering gravely. The man told them to sit down and take off their shoes and socks. George and Irene took theirs off and stuck out their feet, with the black dirt-caked toe-nails. Patricia whispered to Mrs. McGee that she had to go to the bath-room and Mrs. McGee told her where it was, at the back of the store. She went back there and took off her shoes and socks and got her feet as clean as she could with cold water and paper towels. When she came back, Mrs. McGee was saying softly to the store-man, And if you'd've seen the bedsheets I had them on. . . . Patricia walked past them not letting on she heard.

Irene and George got Oxfords and Patricia got a pair she chose herself; they had a strap across. She looked at them in the low mirror; she walked back and forth looking at them until Mrs. McGee said, Patricia, never mind shoes now! Would you believe it? Mrs. McGee said softly aside to the store-man as they passed out of the store—

When the funeral was over they went home. The women had cleaned up the house and put Benny's things away. Their father was sick from too much beer in the back shed before the funeral; he stayed out in the woodshed. Their mother had been put to bed. She stayed there for three days, and their father's sister looked after the house.

Leona said they were not to let Patricia come near her room. Don't let her come up here, she cried, I don't want to see her, I haven't forgot my baby boy! But Patricia did not try to go upstairs at all; she paid no attention to any of this. She looked at movie magazines and did her hair up in rags. If someone cried she did not notice; with her it was as if nothing had happened.

The man who was the manager of the Maitland Valley Entertainers came to see Leona. He told her that they were doing the programme for a big concert and barn-dance over at Rockland and he would like to have Patricia sing at it, if it wasn't too soon after what happened and all—Leona said she would have to think about it. She got out of bed and went downstairs. Patricia was sitting on the couch reading a movie magazine; she kept her head down.

That's a fine head of hair you got there, Leona said. I see you been doing it up your ownself. Get me the brush and comb!

To her sister-in-law she said, What's life? You got to go on.

She went down-town and bought some sheet music, two songs: May the Circle be Unbroken, and It Is No Secret What God Can Do. She had Patricia learn them; Patricia sang those two songs at the concert in Rockland. People in the audience began whispering, because some of them had read about

Benny in the paper. They pointed out Leona, who was sitting up beside the platform, and near the end of It Is No Secret Leona put her head down, she was crying. Some of the people in the audience cried too. Patricia did not cry.

In the first week of November (and the snow had not come, the snow had not come yet) the scissors-man with his cart came along the highway. The children were playing in the yards and they heard him coming. When he was still far down the road they heard his unintelligible chant, mournful and shrill, and so strange that you would think, if you did not know it was the scissors-man, that there was a madman loose in the world. He wore the same stained brown overcoat, with the hem hanging ragged, and the same crownless felt hat; he came up the road, calling like this, and the children ran into the houses to get knives and scissors, or they ran out into the road calling excitedly, Old Brandon, old Brandon . . . (for that was his name . . .).

Then in the Parries' yard Patricia began to scream: I hate that old scissors-man! I hate him! she screamed I hate that old scissors-man! I hate him! she screamed, standing stock-still in the yard with her face looking so wizened and white. The shrill shaking cries brought Leona running out, and the neighbours; they pulled her into the house, still screaming. They could not get her to say what was the matter; they thought she must be having some kind of fit. Her eyes were screwed up tight and her mouth wide open; her tiny pointed teeth were almost transparent, and faintly rotten at the edges; they made her look like a ferret, like some wretched little animal insane with rage or fear. They tried shaking her, slapping her, throwing cold water on her face;

at last they forced her to swallow a big dose of soothing-syrup, with a lot of whisky in it, and they got her to bed.

That is a prize kid of Leona's, the neighbours said to each other as they went home. That *singer*, they said, because now things were back to normal and they disliked Leona as much as before. They laughed and said, Yeah, that future movie-star. Out in the yard yelling you'd think she'd gone off her head.

There was this house, and the other wooden houses that had never been painted, with their steep patched roofs and their narrow slanting porches, the wood-smoke coming out of their chimneys and dim children's faces pressed against their windows. Behind them there was the strip of earth, ploughed in some places, run to grass in others, full of stones, and behind this the pine trees, not very tall. In front were the yards, the dead gardens, the grey highway running out from town. The snow came, falling slowly, evenly between the highway and the houses and the pine trees, falling in big flakes at first and then in smaller and smaller and thicker flakes that did not melt on the hard furrows, the rock of the earth.

Benny, the War in Europe, and Myerson's Daughter Bella

MORDECAI RICHLER (b. 1931)

WHEN Benny was sent overseas in the autumn of 1941 his father, Mr. Garber, thought that if he had to give up one son to the army, it might as well be

Benny who was a quiet boy, and who wouldn't push where he shouldn't; and Mrs. Garber thought: 'my Benny, he'll take care, he'll watch out;' and Benny's brother Abe thought 'when he comes back, I'll have a garage of my own, you bet, and I'll be able to give him a job.' Benny wrote every week, and every week the Garbers sent him parcels full of good things that a Jewish boy should always have, like salami and pickled herring and *shtrudel.* The food parcels were always the same, and the letters—coming from Camp Borden and Aldershot and Normandy and Holland —were always the same too. They began—'I hope you are all well and good'—and ended—'don't worry, all the best to everybody, thank you for the parcel.'

When Benny came home from the war in Europe, the Garbers didn't make much of a fuss. They met him at the station, of course, and they had a small dinner for him.

Abe was thrilled to see Benny again. 'Atta boy,' was what he kept saying all evening, 'Atta boy, Benny.'

'You shouldn't go back to the factory,' Mr. Garber said. 'You don't need the old job. You can be a help to your brother Abe in his garage.'

'Yes,' Benny said.

'Let him be, let him rest,' Mrs. Garber said, 'What'll happen if he doesn't work for two weeks?'

'Hey, when Artie Segal came back,' Abe said, 'he said that in Italy there was nothing that a guy couldn't get for a couple of Sweet Caps. Was he shooting me the bull, or what?'

Benny had been discharged and sent home, not because the war was over, but because of the shrapnel in his leg, but he didn't limp too badly and he didn't talk about his wound or the war, so at first nobody noticed that he had changed. Nobody, that is, except Myerson's daughter Bella.

Myerson was the proprietor of Pop's Cigar & Soda, on Laurier Street, and any day of the week, you could find him there seated on a worn, peeling kitchen chair playing poker with the men of the neighbourhood. He had a glass-eye and when a player hesitated on a bet, he would take it out and polish it, a gesture that never failed to intimidate. His daughter, Bella, worked behind the counter. She had a club foot and mousy hair and some more hair on her face, and although she was only twenty-six, it was generally supposed that she would end up an old maid. Anyway she was the one—the first one—who noticed that the war in Europe had changed Benny. And, as a matter of fact, the very first time he came into the store after his homecoming she said to him: 'What's wrong, Benny? Are you afraid?'

'I'm all right,' he said.

Benny was a quiet boy. He was short and skinny with a long narrow face, a pulpy mouth that was somewhat crooked, and soft black eyes. He had big, conspicuous hands, which he preferred to keep out of sight in his pockets. In fact, he seemed to want to keep out of sight altogether and whenever possible, he stood behind a chair or in a dim light so that people wouldn't notice him—and, noticing him, chase him away. When he had failed the ninth grade at Baron Byng High School, his class-master, a Mr. Perkins, had sent him home with a note saying: 'Benjamin is not a student, but he has all the makings of a good citizen. He is honest and attentive in class and a hard worker. I recommend that he learn a trade.'

And when Mr. Garber had read what his son's teacher had written, he had shaken his head and crumpled up the bit of paper and said—'A trade?'— he had looked at his boy and shaken his head and said—'A trade?'

Mrs. Garber had said stoutly, 'Haven't you got a trade?'

'Shapiro's boy will be a doctor,' Mr. Garber had said.

'Shapiro's boy,' Mrs. Garber had said.

And afterwards, Benny had retrieved the note and smoothed out the creases and put it in his pocket, where it had remained. For Benny was sure that one day a policeman, or perhaps even a Mountie, would try to arrest him, and then the paper that Mr. Perkins had written so long ago might prove helpful.

Benny figured that he had been lucky, truly lucky, to get away with living for so long. Oh, he had his dreams. He would have liked to have been an aeroplane pilot, or still better, to have been born rich or intelligent. Those kind of people, he had heard, slept in mornings until as late as nine o'clock. But he had been born stupid, people could tell that, just looking at him, and one day they would come to take him away. They would, sure as hell they would.

The day after his return to Montreal, Benny showed up at Abe's garage having decided that he didn't want two weeks off. That pleased Abe a lot. 'I can see that you've matured since you've been away,' Abe said. 'That's good. That counts for you in this world.'

Abe worked very hard, he worked night and day, and he believed that having Benny with him would give his business an added kick. 'That's my kid brother Benny,' Abe used to tell the cabbies. 'Four

years in the infantry, two of them up front. A tough
hombre, let me tell you.'

For the first few weeks Abe was very pleased with
Benny. 'He's slow,' he thought, 'no genius of a
mechanic, but the customers like him and he'll
learn.' Then Abe began to notice things. When
business was slow, Benny—instead of taking advantage of the lull to clean up the shop—used to sit
shivering in a dim corner, with his hands folded
tight on his lap. The first time Abe noticed his
brother behaving like that, he said: 'What's wrong?
You got a chill?'

'No. I'm all right.'

'You want to go home, or something?'

'No.'

Then, when Abe began to notice him sitting like
that more and more, he pretended not to see. 'He
needs time,' he thought. But whenever it rained, and
it rained often that spring, Benny was not to be found
around the garage, and that put Abe in a bad temper. Until one day during a thunder shower, Abe
tried the toilet door and found that it was locked.
'Benny,' he yelled, 'come on out, I know you're in
there.'

Benny didn't answer, so Abe got the key. He
found Benny huddled up in a corner with his head
buried in his knees, trembling, with sweat running
down his face in spite of the cold.

'It's raining,' Benny said.

'Benny, get up. What's wrong?'

'Go away,' Benny said. 'It's raining.'

'I'll get a doctor, Benny. I'll. . . .'

'Don't—you mustn't. Go away. Please, Abe.'

'But Benny. . . .'

A terrible chill must have overcome Benny just

then for he began to shake violently, just as if an inner whip had been cracked. Then, after it had passed, he looked up at Abe dumbly, his mouth hanging open. 'It's raining,' he said.

His discovery that afternoon gave Abe a good scare, and the next morning he went to see his father. 'It was awful spooky, Paw,' Abe said. 'I don't know what to do with him.'

'The war left him with a bad taste,' Mrs. Garber said. 'It made him something bad.'

'Other boys went to the war,' Abe said.

'Shapiro's boy,' Mr. Garber said, 'was an officer.'

'Shapiro's boy,' Mrs. Garber said. 'You give him a vacation, Abe. You insist. He's a good boy. From the best. He'll be all right.'

Benny did not know what to do with his vacation, so he tried sleeping in late like the rich and the intelligent, but in the late morning hours he dreamed bad dreams and that made him very frightened so he gave up that kind of thing. He did not dare go walking because he was sure that people could tell, just looking at him, that he was not working, and he did not want others to think that he was a bum. So he began to do odd jobs for people in the neighbourhood. He repaired bicycles and toasters and lamps. But he did not take any money for his work and that made people a little afraid. 'Isn't our money good enough for him? All right, he was wounded, so maybe *I* was the one who shot him?'

Benny began to hang around Pop's Cigar & Soda.

'I don't like it, Bella,' Mr. Myerson said, admiring the polish of his glass eye against the light. 'I need him here like I need a cancer.'

'Something's wrong with him psychologically,' one of the card players said.

But obviously Bella liked having Benny around, and after a while Mr. Myerson stopped complaining. 'Maybe the boy is serious,' he thought, 'and what with her club-foot and all that stuff on her face, I can't start picking and choosing. Beside, it's not as if he was a crook!'

Bella and Benny did not talk much when they were together, afraid, perhaps, that whatever it was that was 'starting' up between them, was rich in delicacy, and would be soiled by ordinary words. She used to knit, he used to smoke. He would watch silently as she limped about the store, silently, with longing, and burning hope and consternation. The letter from Mr. Perkins was in his pocket. He wanted to tell her about the war—about things.

'I was walking with the sergeant. He reached into his pocket to show me a letter from his wife when. . . .'

There he would stop. A twitching would start around his eyes and he would swallow hard and stop.

Bella would look up from her knitting, waiting for him the way a mother waits for a child to be reasonable, knowing that it is only a question of time. But Benny would begin to shiver, and, looking down at the floor, grip his hands together until the knuckles went white. Around five in the afternoon he would get up and leave without saying a word. Bella would give him a stack of magazines to take home and at night he would read them all from cover to cover and the next morning he would bring them back as clean as new. Then he would sit with her in the store again, looking down at the floor or at his hands, as though he were in great pain. Time passed, and one day instead of going home around five in the afternoon he went upstairs with her. Mr. Myerson, who was watching, smiled happily. He turned to Mr.

Shub and said: 'If I had a boy of my own, I couldn't wish for a better one than Benny.'

'Look who's counting his chickens already,' Mr. Shub said.

Benny's vacation continued for several weeks and every morning he sat down in the store and stared at his hands, as if he expected them to have changed overnight, and every evening he went upstairs with Bella pretending not to have heard the remarks, the good-natured observations that had been made by the card-players as they passed.

Until, one afternoon, she said to him: 'I'm going to have a baby.'

'All right,' Benny said.

'Aren't you even going to say luck or something?'

Benny got up and bit his lower lip and gripped his hands together hard. 'If you only knew what I have seen,' he said.

They had a very simple wedding without speeches in a small synagogue and after the ceremony was over Abe slapped his younger brother's back and said: 'Atta boy, Benny. Atta boy.'

'Can I come back to work?'

'Sure, of course you can. You're the old Benny again,' Abe said. 'I can see that.'

And when Mr. Garber got home, without much more to expect but getting older, and more tired earlier in the day, he turned to his wife and said: 'Shapiro's boy married into the Segals.'

'Shapiro's boy,' Mrs. Garber said.

Benny went back to the garage but this time he settled down to work hard and that pleased Abe a good deal. 'That's my kid brother, Benny,' Abe used to tell the cabbies, 'married six weeks and he's already got one in the oven. A quick worker, I'll tell you.'

Benny settled down to work hard and when the baby was born he even laughed a little and began to save money and plan things, but every now and then, usually when there was a slack period at the garage, Benny would shut up tight and sit in a chair in a dark corner and stare at his hands. Bella was good with him. She never raised her voice to say an ugly thing, and when he woke up screaming from a dream about the war in Europe she would stroke his neck and say tender things. He, on the other hand, began to speak to her confidentially.

'Bella?'

'Yes.'

'I killed a man.'

'What? You what? When did you. . . .'

'In the war.'

'Oh, in the war. For a moment I—A German you mean. . . .'

'Yes, a German.'

'If you ask me it's too bad you didn't kill a dozen. Those Germans I. . . .'

'I killed him with my hands.'

'Go to sleep.'

'Bella?'

'Yes.'

'Are you ashamed that I. . . .'

'Go to sleep.'

'I saw babies killed,' he said. 'What if. . . .'

'There won't be another war. Don't worry about our baby.'

'But. . . .'

'Sleep. Go to sleep.'

The baby grew into a fine, husky boy, and whenever there was a parade Benny used to hoist him on his shoulders so that he could see better. He was amazed, truly amazed, that he could have had such a beautiful child. He hardly had nightmares at all any more and he became talkative and somewhat shrewd. One night he came home and said: 'Abe is going to open a branch on Mount Royal Street. I'm going to manage it. I'm going to be a partner in it.'

So Benny finally threw away the paper that Mr. Perkins had written for him so long ago. They bought a car and planned, the following year, to have enough money saved so that Bella could go to a clinic in the United States to have an operation on her club foot. 'I can assure you that I'm not going to spend such a fortune to make myself beautiful,' Bella said, 'and plainly speaking I'm not doing it for you. But I don't want that when the boy is old enough to go to school that he should be teased because his mother is a cripple.'

Then, a month before Bella was to go to the clinic, they went to see their first cinemascope film. Now, previous to that evening, Bella had made a point never to take Benny along to see a war film, no matter who was playing in it. So as soon as the newsreel came on—it was that special one about the hydrogen bomb tests—she knew that she had made a mistake in bringing Benny with her, cinemascope or no cinemascope. She turned to him quickly. 'Don't look,' she said.

But Benny was enthralled. He watched the explosion, and he watched as the newsreel showed by means of diagrams what a hydrogen bomb could do to a city the size of New York—never mind Montreal.

Then he got up and left.

When Bella got home that night she found Benny huddled up in a dark corner with his head buried in his knees, trembling, with sweat running down his face. She tried to stroke is neck but he moved away from her.

'Should I send for a doctor?'

'Bella,' he said. 'Bella, Bella.'

'Try to relax,' she said. 'Try to think about something pretty. Flowers, or something. Try for the boy's sake.'

'Bella,' he said. 'Bella, Bella.'

When she woke up the next morning he was still crouching there in that dark corner gripping his hands together tight, and he wouldn't eat or speak—not even to the boy.

The living-room was in a mess, papers spilled everywhere, as if he had been searching for something.

Finally—it must have been around noon—he put on his hat and walked out of the house. She knew right then that she should have stopped him. That she shouldn't have let him go. She knew.

Her father came around at five o'clock and she could tell from the expression on his face that she had guessed right. Mr. and Mrs. Garber were with him.

'He's dead?' Bella asked.

'Shapiro's boy, the doctor,' Mr. Garber said, 'said it was quick.'

'Shapiro's boy,' Mrs. Garber said.

'It wasn't the driver's fault,' Mr. Myerson said.

'I know,' Bella said.